RESCUE
STORIES OF SURVIVAL
FROM LAND AND SEA

RESCUE

STORIES OF SURVIVAL
FROM LAND AND SEA

EDITED BY DORCAS S. MILLER
ADRENALINE SERIES EDITOR CLINT WILLIS

Thunder's Mouth Press and
Balliett & Fitzgerald Inc.

New York

An Adrenaline Book™

Published by
Thunder's Mouth Press
841 Broadway, 4th Floor
New York, NY 10003

and

Balliett & Fitzgerald Inc.
66 West Broadway, Suite 602
New York, NY 10007

Distributed by Publishers Group West

Book design: Sue Canavan

frontispiece photo: © Corbis/Galen Rowell

Manufactured in the United States of America

ISBN: 1-56025-258-8

Library of Congress Cataloging-in-Publication Data

Rescue: stories of survival from land and sea / edited by Dorcas S.
Miller.
        p. cm.
    ISBN 1-56025-258-8
        1. Survival after airplane accidents, shipwrecks, etc.   2. Rescue
work. I. Miller, Dorcas S., 1949-

    G525.R4.2000
    904—dc21

                                                            00-021412

To Kris and Al

contents

photographs

introduction

The assigned reading when I was an Outward Bound student in 1970 included *Endurance*, Alfred Lansing's classic account of Sir Ernest Shackleton's epic Antarctic journey. When pack ice crushed his ship, Shackleton led his 27 hungry men across disintegrating ice, then he and a small crew sailed 800 miles in an open boat to find help. Amazingly, Shackleton lost not a single man.

Our instructors hoped the book would suggest to us what humans can endure and achieve. The Outward Bound program is based upon the premise that individuals can learn to transcend their self-imposed limits. Kurt Hahn, the program's founder, had noticed during World War II that veteran seamen often survived difficult conditions—such as exposure to cold water when their ships went down in the Atlantic—while younger seamen died. He theorized that the older men lived in part because they had faced and surmounted previous challenges. Hahn figured that training could stand in for such experience.

The questions that Kurt Hahn asked—who survives and why?—surface in the selections presented in *Rescue*. Some of the people in these stories save themselves because no one else will save them. If Antoine de Saint-Exupéry (*Wind, Sand and Stars*) had remained with his plane, he would have died of thirst.

If Doug Scott, with two broken legs, and Chris Bonington, with broken ribs, had waited on the flanks of the Ogre, they would still be there (*The Everest Years*). John Colter (whose epic escape and journey are described in *Three Years Among the Indians and Mexicans*) could have hung around to bargain with the Blackfeet, but they would have killed him outright.

These men were well prepared for their ordeals. Saint-Exupéry and his friends pioneered mail routes to Africa and South America, sharing an esprit de corps that took for granted risk and self-reliance. Bonington and Scott were veterans of previous Himalayan ordeals; they knew what they were up against. Colter was a seasoned mountain man with the strength and intelligence to outrun and outwit his opponents. Grenfell had learned survival skills from the people who knew them best—the fishermen and Native people who lived along the Labrador coast.

Rescuers have their own stories to tell. Pete Sinclair (*We Aspired*) describes the physical and mental demands of a complicated technical rescue on the North Face of the Grand Teton. When he accidentally saves a fellow man's life (*The Breath of Angels*), sailor John Beattie's reactions run from bewilderment to awe. In "Consequences, Part I," Alan Kesselheim recounts his emotions when trying to save his brother and another paddler who have capsized on a remote Canadian lake.

Rescuers can also find themselves in danger. Sebastian Junger's chilling narration of a helicopter going down in a hurricane (*The Perfect Storm*) explores the issues that arise when conditions are so bad that the rescuers need to be saved.

It's easy to get into trouble. Staying safe means taking care of yourself, which often requires a maturity that comes only with experience and self-examination. Peter Freuchen's brief account of hunger on the Greenland ice cap (*Arctic Adventure*) offers insight into how character develops in the most difficult situations. Mark Jenkins' vignette from his past (*To Timbuktu*) examines the fine line between going out on a lark and becoming lost at sea.

All of these stories help answer Kurt Hahn's original questions about survival. Most of the people who get into trouble here expect to make it through their difficulties; they draw deeply from an inner well of strength and confidence. Some find comfort and strength in their belief in a higher being. Many of the individuals have been in difficult situations before and trust their training and experience to pull them through. Still others are simply fortunate that they can rely on the skill, courage, and good will of the people who save them.

After a rescue, there is a tendency to look back over the events and analyze what went right and what went wrong. Although this is a useful process, it is far too easy to make judgments based on hindsight, with all the information at hand. It's much harder to step into the actual situation and understand what it takes to make decisions in the crush of the moment.

Twenty years later, I can see how people might say my companions and I made mistakes when one boat swamped on a windy day. In hindsight, I would have done things differently. With the information I had then, in the water, I would do the same.

I've faced similar choices as a rescuer, making decisions that are easy to second guess. An associate and I once had the responsibility of evacuating a man with a broken femur from a wilderness river. The easiest and cleanest way to get him to a road head was to take him down the river—through whitewater. We delivered him safely, but should we have looked for another way?

At some point, anyone who goes out must deal with dangers such as storms, bad rock, avalanches, equipment failure and human error. Whether we survive depends largely on training, calmness, clarity, strength of character, and luck (and there are those who say that we make our own luck). Sometimes, the outcome also depends on whether our companions or rescuers have those qualities as well.

—Dorcas S. Miller

from We Aspired:
The Last Innocent Americans
by Pete Sinclair

Pete Sinclair (born 1935) dropped out of college to climb, and with three friends pioneered a dangerous route up Mount McKinley's southwest rib in 1959. He later became a climbing ranger at Grand Teton National Park; he also married and earned a degree. Sinclair knew that one day there would be a call for a rescue on the Grand Teton's North Face, and that it would be the most difficult rescue of his career.

L ate in the 1967 season, J.J. Cook, "Cookie," invited us on a moonlight float trip down the Snake River. We were a diverse group that had been drawn to the valley under the Tetons. Cookie was a fly fisherman and river guide, whose daughter married the maharaja of Sikkim. There was my wife, Connie, a native of Jackson, whose mother kept the stage station on Teton Pass; her Father had driven the freight wagons from the train, over the pass, into the valley. Professor Crabtree of the Stevens Institute in Hoboken, who was originally from Kansas, provided commentary. Zaidee, Jim Huidekoper's almost grown-up daughter, was there too. Her dad was a rancher who had been a peer of one of the Kennedys at Harvard.

Also traveling with us was a bottle of Hudson's Bay rum.

Down river, Cookie got too close to the bank. "Man the scuppers, we're going ashore!" yelled Crabtree. I chuckled about that. Then I thought of it again and chuckled and giggled some more. Everybody else had stopped chuckling some time earlier. Everybody else had stopped nipping on the rum some time earlier too.

Then I got maudlin.

Teewinot, Owen, and the Grand, called the Cathedral Group, viewed from the northeast, were faintly backlit from the sun down over the horizon. I was in the grip of a complicated mood. I knew the mountains and didn't, loved them and feared them, felt gratitude and fulfillment and loss and regret. I started talking to the mountains loudly with a drunk's postured seriousness. The vision of how it was going to be between me and the world was beginning to cloud over, leaving me with an unfocused sense of grievance, so I did the natural thing. I said something mean to my wife. I told her that I loved the mountains as much as I loved her, and if it weren't for the fact that she were so beautiful, I'd leave her in a minute and go off into the mountains. I'd had the mood to just up and head for the hills twice before: while standing on the deck of the USS *Albany* off the Azores as a midshipman in the navy and when looking at some hills while on an artillery maneuver at Fort Sill, Oklahoma. The mood seemed to be compounded of mountains, water, and a sense of doing the wrong thing.

Connie wasn't fooled by the beautiful part. I was being a bastard and there wasn't much she could do. What can you say to a drunk in a rubber raft?

I noticed that my companions regarded me as a drunk who bordered on being unfunny. I determined to show them that I was serious about staying in the mountains. We stopped on a sandbar, and I announced that I was going to spend the night there, my last night alone with the mountains or something such. To prove to my companions that I could take care of myself, I gathered wood for a fire. I wasn't particular about what I gathered; damp seemed as good as dry, and damp was handier since to get dry wood I'd have to swim for it. I carefully laid the fire and struck match after match after match. When the matches were gone, I allowed myself to be talked into getting back into the raft, feeling shrewd because I knew that I wasn't nearly as drunk as they thought I was. When we arrived at the landing, I proved how sober I was by refusing to abandon ship. I did finally agree to get out long enough so they could load the raft on top of the car and me into the raft.

It was after 1:00 when we got back to the cabin. Ralph Tingey was there, and I explained to him about how I wouldn't abandon the raft, and he explained to me about how there was a party calling for help on the North Face of the Grand, and suddenly I wasn't so drunk any more.

I've often wondered what my mates were thinking at that moment. I don't mean about going on a rescue with a drunk; I mean about going up on the North Face for a rescue. To the degree I was able to think, my thoughts wandered between disbelief and relief. Ever since I had been a ranger, the image of a North Face rescue had been there. It obviously had to happen someday, we said. Once a climb only the most experienced were audacious enough to undertake, the North Face was by the mid-sixties being done by aspiring young climbers in the third year of their apprenticeship in mountaineering. It had become the test which established mastery over the old mountaineering skills. Inevitably, we felt someone would take the test before they were fully prepared—out of eagerness to move into the current realms of glory, blank wall climbing, gymnastic climbing, and, already on the horizon, vertical ice climbing.

Yvon Chouinard, among others, warned ambitious young climbers that the relative absence of technically difficult pitches is itself one of the dangers of the North Face. Bad weather or a minor injury would create a horror show survivable only by those with seasoning that cannot be acquired in three years. It would have been presumptuous for a youngster, no matter bow technically gifted, to have accused Chouinard of being a nervous Nellie, so his admonitions helped. Nevertheless, warnings inspire as well as caution: we had the North Face in mind as one place where an injury or death would certainly happen. After eight years, we had lost all confidence in our ability to predict who would not get into trouble, but we had lots of faith in the force of numbers. Nothing good resulted from more people. Given the number of people coming to the mountains, sooner or later everything imaginable would happen.

In the years since I had moved into the ranger station, and especially since Dunbar Susong had become the assistant district ranger, we had improved our equipment. We had acquired, for example, an Austrian cable-rescue rig like those used on Eiger North Face rescues. More important, we had the team. Never before could we have mustered a team like that of 1967. In the years of working out techniques, gathering material, and building up manpower, our argument had been What if there is a North Face rescue? The seven of us who would go up on the rescue had all climbed the North Face. It was as if the mountain had kindly waited.

It would have to wait a bit longer. There was nothing I could do at the moment, and fortunately for the good name of the Park Service, and of my children, not much anybody could do. I had to get some sleep and sober up. I gave just a fleeting mental grin at myself for the recent sentimentality about my beloved mountains. In eight years on the rescue team, I had never let my guard so far down. That wasn't by any means the first night I had partied, but it was the only time I ever allowed myself to forget that within the hour I might be on my way up on a rescue. Again, it was as if the mountain had been waiting.

I told Ralph that we'd check it out with the spotting scope in the morning and went to bed. Whether that decision was made because instinctively I knew it was the right one or merely because I was so hopelessly befuddled that it was the only thing I could do is one of the things I'm fated never to know. Had I been sober, I might have reasoned that we could commit ourselves to a full-scale operation or send out a two-man scouting party. The only standard procedure in competent rescue work is in where you store your gear, but usually a report of a party in trouble that is based on indirect evidence such as a report of a shout heard from a cliff or a party overdue, merits only the sending out of a scouting party. As it happened, had we done that, there would not have been any net loss of time, but we might have burned out two of our strongest climbers, Rick Reese and either Ted Wilson or Ralph. But no one argued that we send out scouts first. The mood of this one was different.

Ralph had given me, in the most objective terms, the information he had acquired and sorted during the previous three hours, including lights he had spotted at the place the party was reported to be, and he was careful to point out that there was nothing conclusive. Yet, it was obvious that he was convinced. The spotting scope could confirm his assessment, but it could not deny it. There would be no risking losing a day while we accustomed ourselves to the sensation that this was it, as had happened on the Appie rescue. We would go whether we picked them out in the spotting scope or not. We'd go together, and we'd ask for a helicopter—as soon as I sobered up.

Ralph, still shaking from two hours of sitting in the mist-chilled meadow, woke me up with the news that he'd seen the party. We started organizing. He took me out to the scope. The moment I looked into the scope, I realized what a difficult task I had given him. It had taken him thirty minutes to locate them. The scope was at the limit of its capability. The slightest movement, a passing breeze or car, distorted the field of vision. His precise memory of the route had allowed him to method-ically search it, not merely pitch by pitch, but almost move by move. To sweep that scope fifty feet at a time would have been precise work. Ralph had had to move its field of vision no more than fifteen feet at a time. After he spotted them, he watched for an hour. There was no doubt: only one of the figures was moving. They'd be on that ledge until we moved them off it. We assumed that it was the girl who was hurt. She weighed 120 pounds as against the man's weight of 170.

Did we have enough evidence to justify chartering a helicopter? There was a note of pleading in my voice as I asked Doug for one. I'm afraid of helicopters. When in one, I cannot shake the impression that I am being wafted into the air thousands of feet over very unyielding metamorphic rock by a dragonfly with a thyroid problem. But given a choice between a few minutes of fear and five thousand feet of heavy carrying, I'd take the fear. If I hadn't, I would have been overruled by the rest of the team anyway.

I like a helicopter pilot who doesn't waste time trying to reassure his nervous passengers. With the exchange of a few brief sentences, ours saw that we understood the problem. Even a helicopter is not indepen-

dent of the winds and what the various shapes of the mountains can do
to them. Once he understood that we didn't expect him to take off and
make a beeline for the ledge upon which were our clients, our pilot was
interested in hearing what we knew of the terrain and air currents in the
vicinity of the Cathedral Group. The Grand and Owen are on a north-
south line, with the Grand to the south. Owen and Teewinot are on an
east-west line, with Teewinot to the east. In the middle of this triangle
of summits is a glacier, Teton Glacier. The North Face falls directly to
this glacier. Outside this triangle is a series of canyons. To the east, of
course, is Jackson's Hole. Our cabins were on the east side of the meadow
at the base of Teewinot. North of Teewinot and Owen is Cascade
Canyon. West of Owen and the Grand, behind them from our perspective at our cabins, is the South Fork of Cascade Canyon, with a basin
called Dartmouth Basin at the head of it. South of the Grand is Garnet
Canyon. The col between Garnet Canyon and Dartmouth Basin is called
the Lower Saddle. The most popular routes up the Grand start from this
twelve-thousand-foot saddle that is big enough so that a hundred people could all find level places to bivouac. The Exum Guide Service hut
is on this saddle, as is a roughed-out heliport.

To fly directly up the glacier would be equivalent to paddling a
canoe up a rapid. Our pilot chose to approach from the back. He
picked his way up Cascade Canyon and then turned south up the
South Fork, feeling out the terrain and looking for updrafts which
would lift us to our maximum safe altitude of thirteen thousand feet.
It was like putting in a kayak upstream of a rapids. Mt. Owen and the
Grand are almost joined by a huge buttress with the descriptive title the
Grandstand. The Grandstand is the back wall of the Teton Glacier as
viewed from the valley. It was a possible route, not a preferred one. We
merely glanced at it, intent on finding and really seeing what still was
no more substantial than a report of shouts in the mountains and two
watery shadows wavering in the lens of the spotting scope.

The same imagination which for years had me falling failing off the
North Face of the Grand in my dreams had me, in the few seconds
between the time we thought we should spot them and when we did

spot them, hoping that we hadn't really seen anything, that nobody had fallen off the Grand, and that I was just having a hangover. I was having a hangover all right, but there were also two people on a ledge.

The first thing that we noticed was that it was the man who was down. The girl was trying to jump up and down for joy but was considerably inhibited by the two thousand feet of exposure to the glacier below the ledge on which she was leaping about.

With me in the helicopter was Rick Reese, tacitly acknowledged by all of us as the strongest climber on the rescue team. I was to assess the condition of the party and try to talk to them through a battery-powered bullhorn (part of our riot control equipment). Rick was to look over the route. The implacable steepness of the North Face is relieved by four prominent ledges called the First, Second, Third, and Fourth ledges, as you ascend the face. Also, as you ascend, the ledges become shorter and narrower and slope fairly steeply eastward toward the valley and also northward toward the glacier. So, while these ledges are a break in the steepness of the face, they're not the sort of place where you'd want to let your attention wander.

Our two victims were at the lower end of the Second Ledge (altitude 12,800). This meant that they would be relatively easy to get to. The Second Ledge connects to another ledge that crosses the West Face and ends at the Upper Saddle (altitude 13,000). The Upper Saddle is on the Owen-Spalding Route, the regular route between the summit and the Lower Saddle. Over the years we had carried maybe a ton of wounded humanity off the mountain via this route. It was tedious, not without problems, but reasonable and familiar. What I mostly thought about that way off was that it involved murderously backbreaking work because it was seldom steep enough or on the fall line enough to permit a straightforward lowering. If we took that route, we'd be bearing the weight of the victim mainly on our arms and backs. Our other options were on very unfamiliar terrain. We had long ago formulated a plan to be used in the event of a North Face rescue. If the party were on the First Ledge or below, we would lower. If they were above the Second Ledge, depending upon how high they were, we would either raise the litter toward the summit until we could go down the regular route or lower it to the top of the Second Ledge and traverse around the connecting ledge to the regular route. We had covered all the eventualities except the one which we now faced. Their position on the lower third of the Second Ledge was equally remote from the connecting ledge and the First Ledge. In terms of our planning the route of evacuation, our victims were in no-man's-land.

Raising and traversing techniques are rarely used in rescue work. When they are, as on an Eiger rescue, it's apt to be world news. Raising requires some device for gaining mechanical advantage and is practically impossible except on vertical or near vertical rock where the litter can be held away from the face by one or two men. An overhang is ideal. Traversing, especially an ascending traverse, requires an almost unbelievable amount of physical energy. The angle doesn't have to ease from the vertical much before the litter bearers begin to feel that they both are lifting against gravity and are in a tug-of-war against the raising device, which feels as if it is trying to pitch them forward on their faces, and are at the same time keeping their balance sideways. It's like trying to both lift and drag a heavy rock while standing sideways on a steep slope.

Although raising and traversing are not to be considered in usual circumstances, we were hoping that one or the other of these would be possible. Our sensible reason for so hoping was that we didn't want to enter ourselves and the litter into the hail of rocks whistling, spinning, and cascading more or less constantly down the face. Gravity was normally our ally, in lowering we cashed in on the potential energy the victim had stored in climbing to the site of the accident. But on this face, gravity would be firing rocks at us.

I think there was also a less sensible reason for hoping we could raise or traverse: we hadn't done much of it. Maybe it was an opportunity to outwit nature, to cheat a little. Maybe we wouldn't have to be competent, disciplined, hardworking, and brave—just clever.

Rick was not encouraged. It was a long way from where they were to the top of the Second Ledge. It was also a very long way down to the glacier.

I had no more reason for cheer based on what I could perceive. I could not make them hear me above the roar of the helicopter and so was unable to determine the exact nature and extent of his injuries. I hoped the victim could be loaded into a one-man carrying seat and be carried off at least the worst of it on the back of a rescuer, Rick, to be precise. The man merely raised one arm, slower and more weakly than I wished, and let it drop. His back didn't appear to be injured, so we would take along the carrying seat. If he could stand the jostling, the rescue would be greatly simplified. I wished that his wave had been more enthusiastic.

As soon as we realized that we weren't going to find out anything more, perched there in midair, we told the pilot that it would be fine with us if he got the hell out of there. He had not been having an easy time with the down, up, and cross drafts. I had been trying not to picture the consequences of a falling rock taking a bad bounce off the face and nicking a rotor blade, a possibility which the pilot most likely did not suspect. I did not distract him by mentioning it.

As we soared past the North Ridge and down across the West Face, Rick and I turned our attention to the questions of logistics. What quantity of what type of gear would we have to get to the ledge by what means? Later, the problems would become, cumulatively, technical, physiological, and—after a certain point in time, technical difficulty, or terror—psychological. The point of logistics is to anticipate these problems. Get it right technically and the physiological and psychological problems are less likely to accumulate. It would be nice to have to take only the carrying seat. It would be a disaster if we took only the carrying seat and had to have the litter. This sort of uncertainty fixed the terms under which the mountain would meet us for the next two and a half days. We'd never see clearly beyond the immediate step.

Since we couldn't decide whether to take him up and out or down and out, we had to have gear brought to the Upper Saddle that would allow us to go either way. That was simple enough, in theory. The catch was that we could have no more gear than five of us could transport on our backs from the Upper Saddle to the Second Ledge. We could not be completely equipped for either eventuality nor could we carry as much food as we wanted to. The idea was to get to the site as quickly as possible without expending all our energy. Ted, Mike Ermath, Rick, and I would move what we had with us from the Lower Saddle to the Upper Saddle and across the West Face to the accident site.

Ralph stayed at the Lower Saddle to lead the less experienced support team up to the ledge with equipment we would radio for on the basis of further knowledge. Bob Irvine was already on the mountain someplace, climbing with Leigh Ortenburger. This meant that by the time we got to the accident site, we would have men and equipment in the valley, at the Lower Saddle, at the Upper Saddle, and strung out along the trails and route in between.

I couldn't see that my years of experience and preparation made any difference than if this had been my first rescue—the reverse, in fact. I had already made a mistake in vetoing the suggestion that the bolt kit be brought because I thought I knew the mountain well enough to be sure that we could find blocks enough to put rope slings around or piton cracks enough for anchors and thereby avoid the time-consuming job of drilling holes in the granite for bolts. Eight years earlier, I wouldn't have dared make such a judgment. From the helicopter, we had seen that we would need the bolt kit.

I made no mistakes on personnel. The choice of Ralph to lead the less-experienced support team was perfect. Ralph was a sleeper. Slightly built, a devout Mormon, and a doctoral student in Arabic at Johns Hopkins, he was less intimidating than the grouchy old salts like Bob Irvine and me or than the dashingly impressive Rick Reese and Ted Wilson. Yet he was a better technical rock climber than any of us. The combination of his reassuring bearing plus his obvious competence was just what the younger climbers would need to feel confident and perform at their best. Because they were bigger than Ralph, they would want to carry their weight; because Ralph was less known to them than us, they wouldn't do something stupid trying to impress him. Most important of all, what they didn't know, Ralph would tell them, and they'd know he was right because he would be. I did not know that the support team needed such sophisticated leadership because I did not know the support team. With Ralph there, it didn't matter that I didn't know them. Maybe I had learned some things.

The trip from the Lower Saddle to the Upper Saddle we'd all made uncounted times before. When we left the Lower Saddle with a heavy load, we turned our minds off and turned them back on when we got to the Upper Saddle. Had we become so indifferent to the scenery? No, it's just that if we'd turned our minds on while carrying those loads, what would have come through was not the scenery but the pain. We had been told by climbers at the Lower Saddle that Leigh and Bob had not come down from the summit. I was not surprised when, at the Upper Saddle, some climbers told us that Bob and Leigh had heard the cries for help, had judged them to be on the Second Ledge, and had already set out on the same route we had judged to be the best one. I smiled as I pictured those two mathematicians sitting on top of the Grand systematically sorting out the possibilities while the frantic cries for help rang through the peaks.

I had trusted that we would find Bob and Leigh, all five of us had, although we had two technically competent but young climbers with us, Hugh and Larry Scott, in case we didn't. The Scotts reacted well to warming the bench; their day would come if they stuck around long enough. They understood why we wanted only the most tested of us there, and they were as happy to find that Bob and Leigh were where we hoped they'd be as were the rest of its.

We went around the mountain to join Lorraine Hough and Gaylord Campbell on their ledge. Gay had suffered much and was suffering still. He had a double compound fracture of the lower leg, splinted between an ice axe and an ice hammer. There were loose pieces of bone floating in the flesh.

So much for the carrying seat. The seat would have to be taken back and the litter brought around the mountain. The two heavy and awkward reels of steel cable would have to come up from the Lower Saddle to the Upper Saddle and over. We would lower.

The traverse we had just come over was longer and more difficult than we had expected. I had been on it before but always from the perspective of a difficult climb behind me. It had all altogether different character when contemplated as a route for transporting heavy and awkward equipment. Ted went back for ropes—alone. We had used all ours as fixed handlines, including a chewed remnant of Gay's climbing rope. Ted had volunteered. It was a compromise of safety for speed, but as he pointed out, the ropes were needed and he could do it. As he left, my glance fixed on a white powder mark nearby. There had been many of them on the ledges along the traverse. I had kept them in the periphery of my consciousness. These powdery scars were caused by falling rock. There were hundreds of scars. Any of the rocks that produced them would have been big enough to knock Ted off the mountain.

While Ted was on the traverse, we expended an hour and a half of time and a great deal of Gay's remaining energy and tolerance for pain replacing his makeshift splint with an inflatable splint.

Ted returned, weighted down and unbalanced by three ropes. Nearly everyone in America has seen a picture of the Grand Teton, whether they know what it is they're looking at or not. The Grand Teton and the Matterhorn are our visual definitions of mountain; pictures of both are everywhere. The right side of the usual view of the Grand is the North Face. The West Face is behind. These are the steepest, darkest, and coldest parts of the mountain. From the West Face there is no visible evidence that there are humans on earth. You can't even see the potato fields in Idaho, just mountains and desert. When Ted returned from traversing these two faces alone, he remarked, "Now I know what Hermann Buhl meant by solitude." Ted had gotten about as far away from the hearth as humankind can venture and stay with us.

We murmured our appreciation to Ted and spent another half hour of daylight taking stock. Lori had to be escorted off the mountain. Leigh was the logical one to do this, and Bob said as much. "I don't see how we can possibly ask Leigh to help us. We're getting paid." The $2.40 an hour plus overtime wasn't the issue. We had contracted to do this. Gay thought that a large rock had come off the mountain, shattered on the ledge beside him, and cartwheeled him down to Lori's ledge twenty feet below. There were certain facts that made it appear to us that that might not be exactly what happened, that Gay may have fallen while improperly protected, but it could have. In any case, there was no denying the fact that rocks would be coming off the mountain. This operation was going to have a high element of objective danger. Leigh's skills could do very little about that. He was on vacation—out on a pleasure climb. He had done all that duty, friendship, and reason bound him to do. I recalled my first rescue, the evacuation of Tim's body. Leigh had volunteered for that one. He'd been with me earlier in the summer when we'd run on to a rescue situation while out on a climb. I recalled a couple of times we'd been on this side of the mountain together, putting up new routes. I looked across to the summit of Mt. Owen and tried to pick out the ledge below the summit on which he and I once bivouacked, delayed by one of Emerson's notoriously modestly rated 5.7s. I either had to ask him or insist that he leave. I couldn't leave it up to him to volunteer. Cashing in all the chits I had and taking out a mortgage for the shortfall, I looked straight at him and asked him to stay with us. It was much easier than the time I begged for a hamburger in Texas.

How were we to get that mass of gear across from the Upper Saddle? Would Ralph, Hugh, and Larry bring it over on our fixed lines? They had the technical skills, but would they know where to look for invisible ice on rock? Could they tell gravel that would hold one's weight from that which would not, or which loose blocks are usable and which are not? Would they instinctively make the right move in a bombardment of rock? The fact that I had these questions did not reflect on the abilities of the Scotts. All these things are things you learn without knowing how you learned them. One day you dodge a rock and realize you knew to dodge right instead of left. The rock had hit and gone by before you had a conscious thought. It happens a couple more times and you begin to believe that you know. But you can't explain what it is you know or how you came to know it. You feel unable to help someone who doesn't know. We decided to play it safe this time; we'd pushed luck enough with Ted's solo traverse. Rick, Mike, and I would take Lori across and return with Ralph and the gear. The team at the Upper Saddle would escort her on down to the Lower Saddle, from where she could be flown out in the morning. Bob, Leigh, and Ted had been worked hardest that day, so they'd stay with Gay. We would either return by moonlight or bivouac somewhere on the way. One more thing, a radio call for morphine. With such pain, there was a possibility of shock.

As we discussed his fate, Gay joined in. I tried to be polite. From my point of view, very little of what we had to discuss was any of his concern. His job was to deal with his pain as best he could and to avoid dying of shock, if possible. We'd take care of the business of getting him off the mountain. But I knew he'd not be able to accept that point of view, if for no other reason than the boredom of thinking about one's own pain and nothing else. So I tried to appear attentive to his remarks and avoided contradicting him when he made suggestions that couldn't or shouldn't be acted upon. I'd learned another thing in eight years; argue only if you have to. If the decision is yours to make, the event and not argument will determine who's right.

At 10:00 p.m., Mike, Ralph, and the two Scotts were bivouacked on the West Face with the gear we came for. Lori was on the way down, and Rick and I were making the last radio contact from the Upper Saddle. A new helicopter had been procured, operational to twenty thousand feet. Doug would try to drop the medicine, morphine, and antibiotics to the site. That failing, he'd lower medicine and the bolt kit to us by rope from the helicopter. Rick and I were staying at the Upper Saddle. We were sure a drop was possible there. Doug, who by this time had been directing rescue operations for a decade and a half, had thoughtfully driven up to our cabin for the radio contact so that Connie could listen in.

The transmission over, I had nothing to do until dawn except try to sleep. The operation thus far had been far from perfect, but had there been any fundamental mistakes? The bolt kit had been a mistake, but not one that caused any delay. We couldn't get a prescription for medicine until we could radio down the victim's condition, and I knew that we could get the bolt kit by whatever means we got the medicine. Not committing ourselves to the litter and cable rig from the beginning was another matter. I was badly hungover, I had little sleep, and I was scared, any one of which undoubtedly affected my judgment. But I also lacked an adequate philosophy for coping with technology. I was never able to rely on the helicopter wholeheartedly. As had happened many times before, I wondered if it might not be better to not use it at all. I knew what muscles could do, and I was, after eight years of practice, confident of my ability to judge skill. Suppose I'd just sent an advance team of two or three and . . . the possibilities began to multiply. I was tired of tactics and second-guessing myself. Here we were. It was a beautiful evening, cold and clear. The setting was spectacular. We were just seven hundred feet below the summit. The bivouac site was fairly comfortable as bivouac sites go. It was wonderful to be able to sleep. Who would have thought you'd be allowed to sleep on a North Face rescue?

I slept from 11 to 3. By 3 a.m., the heat stored in the mountain granite had gone. That is a very bad time for humans. I awoke wide-eyed and shivering into my North Face nightmare. The stars had begun to dim without the sky becoming perceptibly lighter. The Anglo-Saxons had a word specifically for this time of day, *uht*. Their word *uhtceare* translates "care before dawn" or "star-dying fear." The buried awareness that another party was climbing the face below us surfaced in my thoughts. I wondered dimly whether we would kill one of them with the rocks we would be knocking off and dozed off for a few minutes. I awoke again feeling that I had not completed a thought—oh yes, the other party. I recalled out of childhood a gravel bank and a strange boy, rock in hand, arm cocked. The image was vague, but not the panic. The sky was perceptibly lighter. The sun would rise at least once more.

The sky was already pink when we heard the helicopter. We scrambled out of our bivouac garb, embarrassed to be caught unready and uneager. The party on the face didn't have a radio and so did not know that a medicine drop was to be made. They were less prepared than we were. Leigh woke up, out of what Bob and Ted insist was a snoring sleep, to the roar of the helicopter. Before he could assimilate the clamor into his consciousness there was an object flying through the air at him. Leigh flinched and made a basket catch. They had morphine at last. Doug had brought enough extra to make a drop to us if the drop on the face had failed, but it hadn't, so we had only equipment to transport.

Getting back to the site took two valuable hours of sunlight. Taking the Scotts part way along the traverse with us enabled us to retrieve two 150-foot ropes. As Larry Scott untied the upper end of the second rope and cast it off to me, the logistics phase of the rescue ended. We were cut off from our supply line. We had a lowering block and two 300-foot reels of steel cable, two 150-foot nylon ropes, three 120-foot ropes, sundry hardware, and a lot less than the recommended minimum daily requirement of food. (It was two years before Ted confessed that he had turned down a stack of sandwiches, prepared for us by the park wives, because he could not bring himself to add another ounce to his pack.)

Fortunately, we could get started before having to commit ourselves to a line of descent. Whatever we did ultimately, we first had to negotiate the four hundred feet to the First Ledge. An indication of how we had to change our concept of scale is the fact that this first, easy, and obvious step in what we had to do was the longest technical rock lowering in the history of the team. We eased ourselves into it by lowering the first one hundred feet using rope, which we had done hundreds of times, instead of the cable, which we'd done only in rescue practice. Ted was litterman for that one hundred feet, and it exhausted him. Ted had been our morphine substitute. He'd stayed up all night talking to Gay, nursing him.

By unspoken agreement, we parceled out the worry. No one can deal with all the fears; each has to pick a big worry and let that mute the others. Mike was our safety inspector. He questioned and double-checked all knots and anchors.

The cable presented some interesting problems—interesting to Bob, who gravitated to the problem. It turned out that the slightest slack, such as one strand rolling off another on the drum, resulted in a bone-shaking and terrifying jolt to Gay and his litterman, Mike on our first use of the cable. Nylon rope is forgiving. It is soft and strong and will stretch half its length again before failing. None of us knew how much a steel cable would take. It was stronger than our ropes—we knew that—but it looked very tiny; and it appeared to have no resiliency. Resiliency is a quality a climber is conditioned to regard as essential. To us, the steel cable felt like it would be stubbornly unyielding to a certain point and then pop. The cable slipping off an overhang, the litter dragging slightly on a rock, or a slight change in angle or weight left a little slack in the cable, which would be taken up all at once in a drop at the litter. It seemed like a foot of drop each time, but it was only an inch or two. The litterman seldom knew when a jolt was coming. Imagine if your chair dropped an inch to the floor sometime soon. The causes of the jolts were deduced by Bob, and we had the choice of believing him or worrying about it ourselves.

We belayed the litter with rope, to back up the lowering cable. Our belay technique seemed marginal. We would have preferred to have had the rope run through a friction device, but we didn't. That meant that if the cable failed, the belayer would suddenly have three hundred pounds of weight to support, more if his rope wasn't taut. His rope couldn't be taut, because that caused the cable to bounce. It was in the best interests of the litterman to have the belay rope slack, as long as he was a litterman and not a falling object. It was in the best interests of the belayer, whose job was to never forget that litter and litterman could become falling objects without notice, to keep the rope taut. It was a regrettable conflict of interests.

Rocks started booming down. The litterman tried to secure or knock off, as many rocks as he could before he got below them. Inevitably he missed some, and the running cable sent them after him. We were lowering the Stokes litter in a horizontal position, both because of the nature of Gay's injury, and because that way he could only look up. When you're helpless, there's something to the warning not to look down. That meant that he lay face up to the rocks. The litterman tried to shelter him with his body, which was more reassuring than effective.

It's amazing that he did not take a serious hit. Still, the lowering to the First Ledge wasn't too bad.

Leigh, knowing well why I had asked him to stay on, had proceeded directly to the First Ledge to search out a way off the mountain. Every climber knows that Leigh Ortenburger was the author of *A Climber's Guide to the Teton Range* and assumes correctly that he was a very experienced climber. Many climbers know also that his guide established a new standard of accuracy and thoroughness. What perhaps only I knew was how reassuring such a historical perspective can be in a situation like the one we were in. There were possibly a hundred climbers in the country who were technically better than Leigh but not one I would have rather had there. We didn't know yet what we had to do on that mountain, but we had with us the one man in the world who knew exactly everything that had been done on that mountain.

I regarded Rick as my personal reservoir of strength. From him came the energy to overcome inertia. His mind, his muscles, and his wit were constantly at work.

Ralph was the spirit of sacrifice, quietly doing the unwanted work as if feeling privileged to be there.

I puttered about, muttering to myself or to anyone who would listen to me.

Once on the First Ledge, forward motion mired down in indecision. Even the morphine couldn't keep Gay happy as we talked first this way and then that. Leigh had scouted out the possibility of reaching the Grandstand with 600 feet of cable. That is, we could drop straight off the Ledge to the north. I could estimate a 120-foot rappel within a margin of 10 percent. I had no confidence in judging twice that distance, and I could not contemplate looking down five times that and having any notion at all about what I was looking at. Usually I knew how far up I was because I knew how many leads had been made. I had a lot of practice judging distance looking up. Even on a tall building where the surface is uniform, looking up feels very different from looking down. On a mountain, the two perspectives are totally foreign to each other. A 10 percent error in 600 feet is a five-story building. I was prepared to believe that Leigh's estimate was very close, but we couldn't see any ledges below us on the alleged 600-foot wall. The litter would be down there, and we wouldn't be able to rappel down to it. Even if Leigh was right, the advantages of a single 600-foot lowering appeared to be outweighed by the disadvantages.

The advantages were three. One, we'd only have to set up one really solid anchor. With the time that would save, we could set up an anchor that could hold the entire rescue team and gear if need be. Two, the wall was vertical to overhanging, meaning there would be little bumping, dragging, grunting, and sweating and fewer rocks pulled down. Three, it was an elegant solution. Just cast off and drift down the mountain in the invisible gravitational current, like a spider descending from the ceiling.

The principle disadvantages were that after lowering the litter, the six remaining at the top would have to descend the North Face route, following the First Ledge down to its lower end and then descending fairly straightforward but rotten rock a thousand feet or so to the glacier. Then they would have to climb back up the Grandstand a thousand feet to the litter and take it back down. Second, the litter would have to be lowered unbelayed. The rockfall would be less, but the ones that came would be coming from a long way up. However strong the cable, stretched taut over the lip of an overhang and taking a direct hit? or if it didn't reach and they had to dangle there for six or eight hours? I remarked to Leigh, "The man who went down that six hundred feet wondering if it would reach, listening to rocks sail by him, might never get entirely back to us." He agreed that this was a possibility. We dropped rocks off and counted the seconds. Some said six seconds, some said eight, an uncertainty of two hundred feet. We were also uncertain about what would happen when we came to the end of the first reel and had to join the second three hundred feet of cable to it. Most of all, I, at least, did not want to split the party. The regular route it was to be.

We stuck to that plan for one hundred feet down the First Ledge. Then Leigh made the first move in what has become one of the legendary feats of American mountaineering. He had gone down the ledge, looked over the edge, and announced in a tone of undeniable authority that, one, we could get to the Grandstand in two 300-foot lowerings and, two, the rest of us could follow the litter because there was, in addition to the ledge 300 feet below us, a smaller intermediate ledge exactly halfway down the first 300-foot pitch. It was inadequate for the litter, but adequate for the rest of us. This meant that we could tie our 150-foot ropes together, hang them double down to the intermediate ledge, rappel 150 feet to that ledge, retrieve our rope by pulling on one strand, and repeat the process to join the litter at the 300-foot level. If there was no comparable ledge in the lower 300-foot segment, we could use the two 150-foot lengths as one fixed and irretrievable 300-foot strand. We would have to abandon them and somehow get on the Grandstand with two 120-foot ropes (we'd had to cut the third one for slings), but the problems on the Grandstand were more manageable. Suddenly, Leigh's view seemed reasonable.

The debate this time was shorter. These discussions, I now realize, were as much acclimatization time as they were times of rational deliberation. We needed to accustom ourselves to the scope of the thing. A kind of pressure had been building in me since dawn. It took a long time to get across the traverse, and the traverse had to be counted as not even part of the problem but blessedly easy access to the accident site. I began the day with a feeling akin to being late for an appointment. The constant reviewing of the options had made me uncertain about decisions already made. No decision had been self-evident. Furthermore, the whole world seemed to be tuned in. Radio communication in the park had been shut down so that the channels were free for our use. We knew that everyone we knew who could get near a radio, including our families, was keeping track of us. We were asked many times for estimates of our progress, information needed in order to coordinate our support below, should we ever reach lower slopes, and my estimates had been consistently too optimistic. I even found time to worry about my upcoming doctoral examinations. I hadn't covered half the material I had planned to that summer. The Climber's Camp had been closed, and an era was ending for climbers in America and for me in the Tetons. Relations with my superiors were not good. Things weren't so good in the country in 1967 either. My big tests were coming all at once; the values and efforts of a lifetime were being tested, and I felt unprepared.

Certain worries I could, and did, enumerate to anyone who would listen. It seemed to help them to have me complain. Emerson discovered on the Everest expedition that if A expresses doubt, B expresses confidence. I didn't want to face the fact that we were going to have another bivouac. I didn't like being out of food or worrying about the other party, which had climbed up to us and had started the descent back down the regular route. I found their shouts of joy, when they arrived safely on the glacier, obnoxious. Irvine and I had enjoyed grumbling to each other for years. Now he was being excessively chipper. Sleeping bags had been flown up to the base of the glacier on the strength of one of my optimistic predictions. A team had assembled there ready to bring them up to us, but we weren't going to get anywhere within reach. Most of all, I didn't like the sound rocks made as they came by with a slicing whir or hit with a crack. I didn't like where I was, what I had done, or what I had yet to do. But Leigh's solution was a thing of beauty, and we'd do it.

Now we truly were racing against the descending sun, trying to get down before it did. Leigh tested his claim that the unknown distances were known to him, by rappeling into the unknown in search of the two ledges. He went on and on. We were fishing for a ledge with him as bait. He radioed back, "I've got one!" The first three-hundred-foot lowering would work. As we got the litter down to the three-hundred-foot ledge, it appeared that we were holding our own against time, if the rest of us were fast enough in getting down as well.

I was one of the last down to the intermediate ledge. I was shocked to find that the ledge was a large detached flake with a flat top. The last man off a rappel has to go without a belay. I assigned myself that duty as a sort of punishment for having made so many bad guesses that day. I studied the flake I was on, and my curiosity was rewarded with the discovery that the flake was not part of the mountain! My hands became moist. The flake was delicately balanced, a piton driven behind it would pry it away from, and possibly off, the wall. I was not at all delicately balanced. Every time I moved, the cable reel in my pack tried to pitch me off the wall. I was sure that soon my legs would begin trembling uncontrollably, sewing machine legs, as we called it. It happens sometimes when you overload on oxygen and adrenalin. I had to stand balanced on that flake because when I leaned against the wall, I thought I could feel the flake move outward. I had to lean against the wall because soon my legs wouldn't support me and I would fall off the mountain.

My eyes wouldn't focus on one thing. The knot at my waist. It's untied! The carabineer. It's open! The piton. It's pulling! The gap behind the flake. It's wider! I wanted to check everything at once. I jerked my eyes from one to the other so fast I didn't check any of them. I started the rounds again, knot, carabineer, piton, piton crack, rope. I felt as if I was standing on grease. I couldn't see anything wrong, which made it worse. Where is it? What's going to do it?

I felt as if I were floating in my boots. My boots. They're untied! They weren't. Boots untied! Jesus Christ, what am I going to do, cut the rope and jump off? I won't have to. I'll be shaking so hard I'll shake myself off. But I'm not shaking, idiot. I wasn't. While all this was happening, nothing was happening: I'd glanced around twice and shifted my weight once. I laughed and that was it. For years, I had awaited the moment when I would not be able to will myself to do what I was afraid to do. All that while, something had happened. Over the years I had learned the right habits. Rock was rock, mass and gravity were mass and gravity, balance was balance, a knot was a knot, routine was routine. I didn't have to understand anything. All I had to do was what I'd done hundreds of times before. I had no extraordinary mental resources, just discipline born of experience and mindless habit. Aristotle said virtue is habit. It had taken me twenty-three years to learn how to rescue my brother properly.

Not that everything became suddenly peachy. I got down to the big ledge and found that the anchor that had been laboriously placed wouldn't do. It was thirty feet too far to the east. Thirty feet horizontally along the ledge here meant a vertical difference of sixty feet down on the Grandstand. The cable might reach, but the rope wouldn't, because some rope had to be used in knots and in belaying. Someone suggested that the litterman rappel off the end of his belay rope and hang from the litter for the last few feet. It was too late and we were too tired for anything as fancy as that, but I found the idea attractive. Bob quietly and firmly objected. He was right. That did not change the fact that I had never wanted anything in the world more than I wanted to get down to that Grandstand before dark. The drill bits were dull; we would lose an hour drilling new holes. I got two solid whacks on my hard hat from falling rocks just for aggravation. The new holes would have to be drilled thirty feet to the west, on what we hoped was the other side of all intervening rockfall area. I decided to be the hero. I should have been thinking, and I knew it, but I wanted to pound on the mountain for a while. I didn't pound long enough and ruined the first hole by driving in the bolt before the drill hole was deep enough. My friends were standing over on the ledge, with the valley becoming dark behind them, waiting for me to do my job, and I was just flailing away at it. Finally, I called on the reserves and asked Rick to drill the holes properly. The mountain may have gotten me on the run, but I knew it couldn't get him off balance.

Then things started to work. Rick got the anchor in. Leigh tested his theory that it was three hundred feet and not more to the Grandstand, as he had tested the upper half. He went over the edge. If he was wrong, he would have to climb back up three hundred feet. The friction of a single rope with the weight of three hundred feet creates a tremendous amount of heat. Because two ropes had to be tied together, no mechanical device, like a rappel bar, which would absorb and dissipate the heat, could be used. Leigh had permanent burn scars from that rappel. But when he stood finally on the Grandstand, the end of the rope dangled chest high. The distance was within three feet of being exactly three hundred feet, a margin of error of one percent, half that for the whole six hundred feet. As they say, not bad for government work.

Mike joined Leigh; he too was burned. The sun was well down. I offered to let someone else take the litter, but they declined. Since I'd been babbling about little else for the past two hours, they'd guessed that I badly wanted off. With that rappel to think about all night and falling rocks to keep them awake, they couldn't have expected to get much rest, but my need was greater.

I caught a glimpse of the last red as Gay in the litter and I, attached to a sling outside, went over the edge of an overhang and rotated freely four feet from the wall. The head lamp I had borrowed from Gay was almost out. Leigh's penlight, two hundred feet below, looked like a single ray of light pointed at the heavens. My sling seat cut into my legs, and I thought about circulation and retaining consciousness. I had eaten only four bites of cheese, two bites of candy, and half a C-ration can of beans that day. I was, nevertheless, happy. I was on a grand piece of rock, massive, uncluttered, and overhanging for the last 260 feet.

I was proud of my skills with the litter and would like to have shown Gay how smoothly I could get him down. There was more important work to do. The litter could not be allowed to swing too far to the east, or it wouldn't reach. I had to concentrate on that. For the first time, I began to warm to Gay. Up to this point, he had contributed far too much to the discussions about the tactics of the rescue for my taste. His interest in the matter was understandable, but I'd rather that victims be spectators. There's something to be said for my position, too. The victim's judgment is not unbiased.

Dangling from the end of that tiny cable, smaller in diameter than a pencil, we were similarly in a largely passive situation. We chatted about what was happening to us and got so we could anticipate the jolts in the cable. Gay felt that he could distinguish between a jolt caused by a strand rolling off another strand on the reel and a jolt caused by the friction of the cable over the terrain, which created varying tensions in different segments of the length of the cable. He'd had a lot of time to ponder about what caused the jolts. We sounded like two sidewalk superintendents at a construction site.

We approached a bulge not far above Leigh. By hanging from my slings underneath the litter, I could reach the rock with both hands and feet. Scratching and crawling, I pulled the litter a few precious feet westward along the wall. Gay, though he was being badly bumped, reported my gains and spoke words of encouragement. Suddenly there was nothing for me to grasp, and we pendulumed sickeningly eastward, but then stopped and swung back. "It caught! Right there!" cried Gay. I struggled back into a vertical position and saw that the last three inches of a projecting rock held the cable in exactly the right position. Now we could talk to Leigh in normal voices, and I was almost ebullient. Leigh said, "M'God, Sinclair, is that dim glow your head lamp? I thought you were smoking your pipe." I had actually started to smoke my pipe during the lowering but the stem was too long. By neglecting to bring a short-stemmed pipe, I had missed my chance to become a legend. Leigh had cleared out a place for the litter under an overhang. With the radios to carry our instructions, we swung Gay into position a few inches at a time as neatly as would a dragline operator. We propped a couple of rocks under the foot end, and with the cable for a belay, he was safe for the night, with his head and torso protected, though his legs were exposed. Thoughts of the full length of cable exposed all night to unknown and unseen quantities of rockfall gave me a second's pause. I had an image of the cable being severed near the top, its full length whipping down the face to jerk the litter out of its bed, but fretting about things like that was no longer as entertaining as it had been on the detached flake. I jammed another rock in beside the litter and let it go at that. There couldn't be any such thing as absolute safety.

Objectively speaking, we weren't in all that terrific a position. Four men were perched on a sloping, wet ledge, at the wrong end of a three-hundred-foot, overhanging, flesh-burning rappel, with the singing of falling rocks to lull them to sleep. I derived a small amount of comfort from the thought that all four, Rick, Ralph, Bob, and Ted, were Salt Lake City climbers, if not the fathers, at least the uncles of the new generation of hard men coming out of that area. They weren't all Mormons, but they were all clean-cut and uncynical. Their virtues would protect them. Mike was alone, one hundred feet below us, where he had gone to explore the route. We had been slow, but not because we didn't keep pressing. Mike had gone down alone while we were fiddling with the litter. We'd made use of every second of daylight.

I too had lowered my weary bones into better bowers. Leigh and I were on a little platform scratched into the debris in the moat between the face and a snow patch. I was at the edge of the platform. (I'm certain Leigh planned that while I was busy with the litter.) When I dozed off, my hand slipped from my lap and hung in space. I didn't like that sensation. My legs were cramped, and when I dozed, my feet slid into the snow. When they tingled with cold, I woke up and wiggled my toes to restore circulation. Rocks dropped in occasionally. One hit the snow between Leigh's foot and mine and filled the neck of my down jacket with snow.

"What's that?" I said, as if I didn't know.

"I dunno," muttered Leigh, as if he didn't either, and went immediately back to sleep. If the rocks wanted us to pay attention that night, they'd have to hit us. My dreams were of YMCA showers with steam rising from the floor, a way of accounting for the tingling in my feet.

The next day we found that the mountain hadn't done with us yet. The rappels were sloppy. Without the two long ropes, we'd lost flexibility in setting up belay positions. The fussing to set up a solid position seemed interminable, like the rappels of beginners. We were a long way down the mountain now, so there were plenty of places for the rocks to come from and plenty of time for them to achieve terminal velocity. At one point, out of sheer perversity, I calculated the amount of rock falling around us. During one lowering, two hundred pounds of rock landed within thirty feet of me. I didn't see how we could escape taking a hit. This continuous assault from above, combined with fatigue and hunger, developed in us a condition which can be called rock shock. The most dramatic instance of what we'd become like occurred after Rick made the last, difficult overhanging lowering from the Grandstand to the snow at the top of the glacier. As the helicopter, carrying Gay to the hospital, started its engine, the roar crashed down on us from off the mountain walls. Those of us who were still on the mountain instantly cowered as if overtaken by the largest and last rockfall, believing that the mountain had waited until this last moment to get us.

The last two rappels, with the taste of beer practically in our mouths, turned out to be three.

It was here that we regained a small measure of dignity. Someone suggested that we just leave the ropes on the last two rappels in order to save time.

"No need to leave ropes behind," said Leigh. He wasn't thinking of their value. They were so chewed up they'd have to be discarded anyway. It was a question of style. The mountain had thrashed us to the bones, but in our retreat we would walk, not run.

The helicopter returned and carried, in relays, to the meadow outside our cabins, knowledge in Leigh, strength in Rick, reason in Bob, foresight in Mike, selflessness in Ralph, and compassion in Ted, courage in all, my comrades, who had made this the noblest adventure of my life, and given me, finally, self-possession.

from Working on the Edge
by Spike Walker

Crew members of the St. Patrick were used to to the rigors of fishing in the Gulf of Alaska where each icy day presents challenges that most people cannot even imagine. But nothing could prepare them for the ordeal they faced when monstrous waves pounded their scalloper in the winter of 1981. Spike Walker (born 1950), himself a veteran of more than twelve seasons of fishing for king crab, gives us this account.

.

I f the deaths of men off the fishing vessels *Vestfjord, Golden Pisces,* and *Cougar* hadn't been enough to shake up the fleet during the 1981 fall season, the dramatic incidents involving the crew of the "ghost ship" scalloper *St. Patrick* were.

On the gray and wintry morning of November 29, 1981, the 158-foot fishing vessel *St. Patrick* slipped her Kodiak moorings and slid east through the narrow passage of Near Island channel and moved out into the Gulf of Alaska. For the majority of the ten men and one woman on board, it would be a journey of no return.

On board was twenty-three-year-old Wallace Thomas. A few weeks earlier, he had ventured north to Alaska from his home in balmy St. Augustine, Florida. Like thousands of naive and adventurous hopefuls before him, he'd come in search of a berth on one of the fleet's high-paying crab boats. Unlike most, he had managed to land a job as a full-share deckhand on the *St. Patrick*, a scalloper that had arrived several months before from the East Coast by way of the Panama Canal.

That night, Thomas lay uneasily in one of the crew bunks housed forward in the bow of the ship. The *St. Patrick* had begun to plunge and leap beneath him. He could hear heavy seas crashing across the deck overhead, and each time the ship's bow buried itself in a wave, Thomas felt himself being pressed heavily into his mattress. Then as the bow rebounded, soaring high over the crest of the next wave, he would float upward, entirely free of his bedding.

Sensing that the storm was building, Thomas left his bunk, slipped into his rain gear, and in the chilling spray and darkness made his way across the deck to the wheelhouse mounted astern.

It was nearly midnight when Thomas entered the comforting warmth and light of the galley. What he saw stunned him. The kitchen was in shambles. The new tightly secured microwave oven had broken free and lay smashed on the floor. The cupboard doors were swinging open and a combination of catsup, pickles, grape juice, strawberry jam, buttermilk, and sugar was sliding this way and that with the G forces of the rolling ship, in a sticky, scrambled, flowing mass. Arthur "Art" Simonton, a former logger from the state of Washington (the most experienced deckhand on board), was standing with his back to the sink, clutching its edges, as he stared at the demolished kitchen. Other crew members were leaving as Simonton turned white-faced to Thomas. "We're going to put on our survival suits. This storm is getting out of hand."

Thomas felt sick with fright. He didn't own a survival suit! And he knew he didn't stand a chance in the thirty-nine-degree seas without one. Though he had never worn one in his short career at sea, he knew about their buoyant, heat-saving qualities.

The life raft! remembered Thomas. If the ship went down, it would be his only chance! He grabbed a flashlight and ran out on the back deck, where he managed to locate the tightly packaged self-inflating raft. He read the instructions.

Looks simple enough, he thought.

Thomas made his way back inside, where he ran into the ship's newly hired cook, twenty-three-year-old Vanessa Sandin. The blond-haired, green-eyed daughter of a Kodiak salmon fisherman was carrying her survival suit, an older variety that looked in poor shape. It didn't have a built-in flotation device or life vest attached. The normally cheerful Vanessa was terrified. "Wally! What should I do?" she asked.

"The wheelhouse would be the best place to be if the ship was to get in trouble," he told her. "I'll take you up there."

Thomas climbed the stairs into the wheelhouse, then jerked to a stop. Nearly the entire crew stood before him. Most were wearing survival suits.

There was thirty-four-year-old Jack Taylor and thirty-three-year-old Curt Nelson, both from the state of Virginia. It was only Taylor's second trip out as skipper of the *St. Patrick*. Nelson was his engineer. Then there was John Blessing, a hard-working youngster from Oregon. He'd come north to help finance his college education. And there was Harold Avery, Jim Harvey, and Ben Pruitt. All three of these tough, scrappy crewmen were from Virginia. Also there at the time was Robert Kidd. This incredibly strong and sinewy deckhand was from Rhode Island. And there was Paul Ferguson, a husky lad and former football player from Nebraska. Not in the room, but also on board at the time, was a youngster named Larry Sanders, as well as Arthur "Art" Simonton.

When Thomas looked out the wheelhouse window, he saw a mountainous wave rise out of the darkness and slam heavily into the *St. Patrick*'s port side, lifting and shaking the entire ship. Wave after wave broke over the tall handrailings and collapsed across the deck below him with a thundering crash.

The black foam streaked waves looked mammoth in the far-reaching beams of the mast lights. Some of the waves towered above the wheelhouse windows, more than twenty-five feet above the deck below.

To aid vision, the light at night in the wheelhouse was always kept to a minimum. In the near darkness, Thomas turned and looked at the others. Their wide eyes were filled with fear. The faces peering out from the sealed openings of the hoods of their survival suits looked bloated.

If anything happens to the *St. Patrick*, he thought, I'll have only the life raft to save me.

Back inside, Wallace Thomas helped Vanessa Sandin slip her legs into her survival suit. Then he rushed below to look for a suit for himself. The knot in the pit of his stomach continued to tighten. As he searched below, he felt a monstrous wave strike the *St. Patrick*. The boat shifted sharply and Thomas staggered against the wall.

Thomas crossed the floor at the bottom of the stairs and started down the next gangway into the engine room. He had gone only a few steps when another wave drove into the ship. In a steady motion, the engine room rotated before him, and suddenly he found himself lying on his back on what had been the wall. Stored canned goods, oil filters, tools, and supplies fell noisily from their shelves. Several fuel lines broke and diesel fuel began to spew everywhere. Then the *St. Patrick* partially righted herself.

Thomas struggled to his feet and raced back toward the wheelhouse. His heart pounded as he crossed the sloping galley floor. The entrance to the wheelhouse stairway was marked by two full-length swinging doors. As he approached, the doors burst open and were ripped from their hinges as a wall of rushing seawater exploded through them. The broad and powerful current carried with it charts and navigational equipment. The seawater slammed Thomas against the wall. When the hallway below quickly flooded, the waist-deep water began to empty down the second stairwell, which lead into the engine room.

Even before the torrent of water had finished draining from the wheel, house, Wallace Thomas raced tip the stairs. The scene there horrified him. A giant rogue wave had smashed through the *St. Patrick*'s "storm-proof" windows, tearing most of the ship's navigational equipment from its mounts. Equipment hung from the dripping ceiling, swaying from the ends of strands of wiring, while much of the ship's electronics lay broken and scattered across the flooded floor. A bone-chilling wind was gusting in through the holes where the windows had been.

The *St. Patrick* was listing about fifteen degrees to starboard at the time, making the wheelhouse floor slick and difficult for Thomas to cross. He spied his skipper lying amid the strewn equipment and broken window glass. Then he turned to Vanessa Sandin. She'd been only partially protected when the rogue wave shattered the windows and exploded into the room, and now she stood drenched and shaking.

Thomas had just finished helping Vanessa into her suit when the fuel-pressure alarm went off, clanging like an incessant fire bell. Then the main engines died and the lights aboard ship flickered, dimmed, and went dead. In the ghostly silence, a moaning wail became audible as winds approaching eighty knots howled through the steel cables of the mist rigging overhead and into the wheelhouse through the gaping window openings.

Jack Taylor found himself adrift at sea without steering or power. The only light aboard ship came from several battery-powered lamps two flights below. Then a second huge breaker drove into the side of the ship, rocking her sharply, and two crewmen were thrown to the floor. Thomas heard Taylor yell. "Hey! We've got to get off this damned thing! Let's get into the life raft before she goes down!"

An icy spray drenched them as they fled from the wheelhouse. Moving out in single file, they crawled along through the wet, cold darkness, climbing over the twisted, wave-bent handrailings and through tangles of rope and gear.

When Thomas reached the stern, he groped for the raft. "It's gone! The raft's gone!" he screamed above the howl of the wind. A few disbelieving groans met the news and then the group slipped into stunned silence. Thomas heard the skipper yell again. "We've got to get off this thing before it sinks! It'll flip over and suck us all down with her!"

A half-formed wave crashed against the far side of the *St. Patrick* and threw a wall of icy water over the crew. Those in survival suits paid scant attention. Clad only in his work clothes, Wallace Thomas was soaked and already ached with cold, however. He felt Vanessa grab him and heard her scream above the wind. "What are we going to do?" At that moment, Thomas spotted an amber beacon rising and failing off the stern. "It's the life raft!" he yelled. "It's got to be! Maybe we can swim for it!"

A crewman found a long length of rope and suggested that they tie themselves together to prevent getting separated once they were adrift in the ocean. The skipper agreed. Someone had located a waterproof flashlight, and periodically a voice would call out "Could you give me some light over here? I can't see!"

Suddenly, the realization of what he was about to do struck Thomas. The time twenty minutes pounded in his head. From his instruction in wilderness survival, he knew that a man without a survival suit seldom lasted longer than twenty minutes in seas of this temperature. *If you go into that water without a survival suit, he thought to himself, you'll be dead in twenty minutes!*

The stern deck grew steeper as the unrelenting velocity of the storm rolled the *Saint Pa'rick* farther on its side. Like the rest of the crew, Thomas was sure the ship was sinking. For one long moment, he stood on the stern at the water's edge, and as the water licked up the sloping deck and over his feet, he grappled with the insanity of panic. He pictured himself alone in the darkness of the wheelhouse, stretching for air as the wintery Gulf of Alaska seas rose slowly over his head.

Soon, the crew members finished tying themselves together. They were about to abandon ship, and, irrespective of logic, Thomas felt drawn to follow. As his skipper and crew edged closer to the water and prepared to jump, Thomas bolted, however.

"Taylor!" he shouted to his skipper. "I can't go in with you! I've got to stay with the ship as long as I can! I'll die if I go in that water!"

The skipper seemed dazed. "What?" he shouted back.

"I don't have a survival suit and I'm not going in that water without one! I'll stay aboard until the ship goes down and call out more Maydays!"

"I think there's another suit in the captain's cabin!" the skipper yelled back.

Thomas shook with fear as he hurried back toward the wheelhouse. He was frantic, and his legs drove him forward faster than his numbed hands could interpret the shape of things. But the suit meant life to him and he scarcely noticed the skinned shins and bruises he acquired as he stumbled along. Entering by the rear wheelhouse door, he crawled along the wall through the rubble, feeling his way to the captain's cabin.

Thomas was on the verge of hysteria. It was the prospect of being abandoned alone on board the sinking ship that terrified him. He wanted to get back to the others waiting on the stern before they became too fearful and left without him. His hands slapped frantically against the walls as he crawled through the darkness. He realized he was in the bathroom and quickly backed out. His hands shook uncontrollably as they fumbled through scattered socks, shirts, boots, pillows, a suitcase, and supplies that lay strewn about the room.

"Where is it? Where is it?" he yelled aloud.

Then as he groped in the darkness, he felt the distinctive shape of a survival-suit bag. There was nothing in it! The suit had been taken! His mind raced. Was the skipper mistaken? Could there possibly be another suit in all this junk? Had there ever been an extra suit in the first place?

He plodded ahead blindly, bumping into one wall and then another. He tore through a jumble of bedding and clothes. Reaching some cabinet doors, he jerked them open. Inside, he felt the soft bulk of another long vinyl bag. There was a survival suit inside.

Thomas wiggled into the suit and felt his way back to the stern, where he raced to tie himself between Vanessa Sandin and John Blessing. John was one of three crewmen without a survival suit. He had slipped on every piece of clothing he could wear and yet still fit into a bulky life jacket. "We've got to get off this thing!" yelled the skipper again. "She could go down any minute!"

As they prepared to jump, Thomas looked around him and caught brief glimpses of the crew in the flickering flashlight beams. Their slick, wet figures looked ghostly.

Then Chief Engineer Curt Nelson yelled a warning. "When the water hits those batteries, they're going to explode!" Just then, a loud *bang* sounded from below in the engine room. A massive wave rolled by, passing as a black hulk just off the stern. Water swept up the slanting deck and over the crew's feet.

As the stern of the *St. Patrick* dipped and swayed, the youthful six-foot four-inch frame of Art Simonton arrived. He had just returned from the bow. "Two guys just jumped overboard off the front deck!" he screamed, his eyes wide with terror. "We're going to capsize!"

"Okay," the skipper yelled. "Let's get off this thing!"

With the back deck constantly awash, Thomas could feel the ankle-deep water pulling at his legs. We're going down, he thought. We've got no choice but to abandon ship.

Bound together—around the waist and under the arms—by loosely tied loops for easy movement, the crew shuffled down the steep deck. The railing before them had been torn away and now, timing their move with the downward roll of the ship, the crew stepped off the stern deck.

As they struck the water, the crew went under briefly. When Thomas's head bobbed clear, he gulped in the precious air. I'm all right! he thought, his mind racing. I can breathe! I'm not dead!

In the next moment, the massive steel hull of the *St. Patrick* flashed before his eyes as it plunged down beside him, narrowly missing crushing the entire crew. Thomas screamed, "Paddle! Paddle!" and the group stroked furiously to get clear of the ship's deadly stern.

They were afloat in the stormy darkness and except for the fragile beam of a lone flashlight, vision was impossible. Looking back, only a few yards into their journey, not a hint of the ship's outline remained. Yet distinctly visible in the battering night were two small portholes. Power still generating from the engine-room batteries filled the round windows with warm light, and now the circles soared and dived in the blackness. Moments later, the porthole lights disappeared. She finally sank, thought Thomas. We got off just in time.

No sooner had the nine drifting crewmen of the *St. Patrick* swum clear of her deadly stern than a wave began to lift them. Up and up it carried them. Thomas was certain they had neared the top of the steep, sloping wave when he heard a loud thundering roar coming from behind him and far overhead. He turned toward the booming rumble just as the first monstrous wave top collapsed down upon them.

The body of the wave carried whole fathoms of sea over them. It drove the struggling crew under and tossed them end over end. Like Thomas, some of the crew members had turned toward the wave when it overtook them and caught the full force of its fury directly in their faces.

No one could have imagined such a wave. Some in the party were washed out of their rope loops. They bobbed to the surface, gasping for air, and fought to remain upright as they groped blindly for the rope.

Hundreds of feet of floating excess line had become tangled around them. And seventy-knot winds whipped an icy spray across the water, blinding those who had forgotten to turn away and stinging any face not protected with a sheltering hand.

Wallace Thomas soon discovered that two people were hanging on to him. Vanessa clung to an arm and John Blessing was hugging him around a thigh. Blessing was already shaking violently from the effects of the cold.

Thomas shouted to him.

"You're going to be all right, buddy! Just hang on!"

"Count off! Count off!" someone screamed.

Some of the crew seemed too disoriented to obey, while others were perhaps unable to hear the command.

Thomas felt another wave begin to lift him. It swept him up into the wind-torn blackness, ever higher and higher. Then he heard one end of the wave begin to roar as it folded over and collapsed through the darkness toward him.

"Look out! Look out!" he screamed. "It's another big one!"

The gigantic breaker rolled over the crew, submerging and tumbling them upside down as it passed. A few in the group had prepared for the approaching swell. Holding their breaths, they had turned their backs to it. Though they still found themselves tossed and wrenched violently about, their recovery, once the wave had passed, was surprisingly rapid. Suffering repeated dunkings, others of the drifting crew soon adapted—except, that is, for those without survival suits.

Thomas could feel John Blessing shivering violently as he clung to his leg. Less than twenty minutes had passed when his friend became delirious, moaning and speaking irrationally.

"It's cold! It's so cold!" he gasped in a painful rasping voice.

Thomas tried to encourage him. "Hang on, John! You've got to ride it out!"

But the mountainous waves continued to sweep them high. And each time the wave crests folded over, they smashed down upon the ragged group of fishermen like concrete walls.

Then one of the crewmen cried out above the noise of the storm.

"So you guys think we should pray?"

Thomas was quick to respond.

"Now is the time if there ever was one!"

They recited the Lord's Prayer then, their voices dissipating quickly in the storm-lashed night.

"Our Father, who art in heaven, hallowed be Thy name; Thy kingdom come, Thy will be done, on earth . . ."

They had completed less than half of the prayer when, without warning, another enormous wave broke directly over their heads, driving them deep beneath the surface.

The moment their heads again cleared the surface, there was heavy retching and gagging. Those tangled in the excess line fought frantically to free themselves before the next wave found them.

Wallace Thomas could see that John Blessing was in serious trouble. He wrapped his arm around the shaking man.

"Come on, John! Stay with us," he begged.

John stammered out his reply.

"My legs . . . arms . . . stiff . . . so cold."

John's moaning increased. Several times, Thomas felt his friend's quivering body go limp. When another large wave struck them, John was swept from Thomas's tiring grip and began to drift off. Stretching behind him in the wet darkness, Thomas managed to snag John with one hand. Then as he drew him near, he saw a small beacon attached to John's life jacket. He worked hard in the clumsy two-fingered gloves of his survival suit to grip the beacon and yank it alive. His aching arm muscles told him he couldn't carry his friend much longer.

The tiny beacon had just begun flashing when John spasmodically flailed his arms and floundered out of control. Almost immediately, the wind and current swept him away. Thomas was horrified to realize he could no longer reach him. He watched helplessly as the tiny amber beacon light weaved off into the darkness and disappeared.

Someone yelled, "Was that John?"

"My God, yes!" Thomas answered.

As he watched John disappear, Thomas felt Vanessa reattach herself to his arm. From the outset, Vanessa's suit had leaked steadily. It was becoming an ever-increasing struggle for her to keep her head above water. Together, they floated up and over the endless series of waves.

Vanessa Sandin prided herself in never getting seasick, even in the toughest weather. Several of her predecessors had lasted but a single trip. When Vanessa came on board, she was confronted by a galley that was dingy, dirty, and disorganized. She scrubbed the place from floor to ceiling. She emptied the cupboards and completely reorganized them. Then came the burned pots and pans, the oven interior, covered with burned grease and food, and finally the kitchen table, some twenty feet long.

She soon became known for having a good heart, and mischievous sense of humor. When Wallace Thomas had his twenty-third birthday shortly before shoving off on their fateful final journey, Vanessa had prepared him a huge birthday cake. When he tried to cut into it, however, his knife chinked to a stop. Vanessa had taken a twelve-pack of beer, wrapped it in cardboard, and camouflaged it with a thick spread of canned frosting.

She could also cook. Each summer, she fished right along with her father on his gillnet boat in Bristol Bay. One day, when she had decided to prepare a dinner of sockeye salmon, her father, a long-time Alaskan fisherman, made the mistake of trying to tell her how to go about cooking it.

"You run the boat," she scolded him, "and I'll fry the fish. Now get out of here!"

The salmon proved to be the best he had ever eaten.

Vanessa, her father recalled, could not only cook but also tie knots, mend webbing, make a drift set, pick tangled salmon out of the gillnet, and navigate. One day, it came to him that she learned more quickly and with greater ease than he had as a young man. But now this adventurous young woman could only cling to Thomas through the night and pray to be rescued at first light.

As they passed over the top of another immense swell, Thomas felt something bump heavily into his back. Fearful that a log had drifted up on them out of the night, he shouted, "Get that light over here! Something just hit me!"

Thomas searched the darkness with the dim beam of light. Suddenly, he reeled in the water. There, adrift beside him, floated the body of Larry Saunders, another crewman who had abandoned ship without a survival suit. He was still tied to the crew's rope line. "Turn off the light and save it!" shouted Thomas. The light flicked off.

Close by, Thomas overheard the muffled conversation between Ben Pruitt and Jim Harvey. Harvey had been on his first voyage to sea in Alaska. He was the last of the original three without survival suits. Now he turned numbly to his crewmate and pleaded.

"Ben! Ben, I'm so cold! Could I borrow your suit for a little while?"

"Jim, I'm cold, too! And the suit's leaking, anyway! Just try to hang on!"

"Ben! What am I going to do? Help me! Please, help me, Ben!"

Thomas knew that there was nothing anyone could do. Hypothermia was the dangerous lowering of one's body temperature; more specifically, the temperature of one's core, comprised of the heart, lungs, and brain. The moment the three frantic young men jumped from the stern of the *St. Patrick* without survival suits, they were doomed. Under such conditions, no man could live more than an hour.

A short time later, Jim Harvey began to moan and jabber incoherently. Eventually, he grew motionless and, still bound to the group by the rope line, his body drifted amongst them.

Eight hours after they had first abandoned ship, dawn slowly replaced the smothering black veil of darkness. In the dim gray light, Wallace Thomas could finally take in the unbelievable size of the massive seas. Raw winds whipped thin white streaks of foam across the moss green water. The waves moved under a bleak ceiling of sky, and he could make out blue-black rain squalls, squatting low as they moved across the horizon.

Each time he passed over the crest of another wave, his eyes swept the desolate expanse of water. Then something caught his eye.

"I can see somebody swimming over there!" he yelled. The six remaining crew members soon spotted him, too

"Hey, it's the skipper!"

They yelled and waved and blew metal whistles that came attached to their suits, but Jack Taylor showed no sign of having heard them. He backstroked slowly away from them and was lost from sight.

Then Vanessa began to yell excitedly.

"I can see land! I can see it! I'm sure of it!"

As he crested another twenty-five-foot wave, Thomas caught sight of it, too. Before long, he was able to make out two separate points of land. The spirits of the numb, pain-racked crew soared.

"When I get back," promised Vanessa, "I'm going to eat the biggest pizza I can order!"

Hours later, when the low-lying clouds cleared adequately, a steep rock coastline loomed large before them. Its uppermost slopes were covered with rich shades of winter-browned grass and crowned with dark green stands of spruce trees.

The crew members decided to paddle for the nearest outcropping of land but wave after wave struck them from the side, throwing them off course, and fog intermittently obliterated all sight of land.

"We're never going to make it this way!" Thomas called out. "We've got to swim more in line with the way the waves are moving! Then we can angle a little bit at a time in toward land!"

Swimming with the waves, they made steady progress, but soon Ben began to speak in fragmented phrases and suddenly collapsed face-down. The two crewmen on either side rolled him over.

"Come on, Ben! You've got to swim!" they screamed at him. "You've got to help us! We're not going to make it if you don't swim!"

Ben Pruitt tried. He flopped one weak arm and then the other out in front of him, but he was nearly unconscious. His two friends continued to encourage him as they pulled him along between them, kicking their numb legs and stroking with one hand while clutching Jay by the arm with the other.

Vanessa, too, was nearing the point of exhaustion. With her leaking survival suit now nearly full of the icy seawater, her body ached with cold. If she was to survive, she would need constant help.

Then Wallace Thomas and Harold Avery devised a method. One of them would paddle on his back, carrying Vanessa on top of him, while the other trailed the pair, watching for land and verbally guiding them.

Paul Ferguson and Curt Nelson soon adopted this technique to carry Ben. Gradually, they grew weaker and their progress slowed appreciably. Their bodies were chilled from nearly fourteen hours in the near-freezing water. Hunger cramped their stomachs and they were becoming dehydrated.

The survivors had decided to save the bodies for decent burial. But then, under the sinking weight of the body of Larry Sanders, Thomas saw how Ferguson was struggling to remain afloat.

"We've got to untie him!" he yelled.

Thomas swam forward through a tangle of floating lines and loosened the rope line. The corpse quickly sank from sight. Without comment, the six remaining crew members regrouped and pushed on.

Ever since they had first spotted land that morning, the struggling crew had been swimming. Now, some eight hours later, the coastline seemed much closer. Thomas could see the black flat faces of cliffs, perhaps a hundred feet high, lining the shore, but he could not see an accessible or calm stretch of beach. As they closed to within perhaps two miles, Thomas spotted the white explosions of waves bursting along the cliff bottoms.

The sight petrified him. He knew the deadly power of coastal breakers from years of surfing in Florida. Such seas were frightening enough, but to become entangled with one another in the rope lines in a heavy breaking surf would be suicidal.

"Before we try to go in, we've got to untie!" he called out to the others. "It's too dangerous! We won't make it this way!" The exhausted, floundering members numbly agreed.

Now Ben Pruitt seemed on the edge of collapse. The two who had carried him no longer appeared to be able to do so. Thomas left Vanessa with Harold Avery and swam to Jay and held his blue face out of the frigid water. He was still breathing.

Then off to his right, Thomas caught a flash of something white on the water. As it rose over the crest of the next wave, he saw it clearly. "There's a ship!"

Those who were able began to wave wildly and blow their whistles. They swung their shivering arms back and forth till they could no longer hold them aloft. Thomas wore his tongue raw whistling and the taste of blood filled his mouth. The ship closed toward them for nearly a half hour. Wallace and the rest of the crew members were sure it was coming for them.

Then they watched in disbelief as their rescue ship began to turn away. As it changed course, Thomas could see the distinct lines of the ship's wooden hull.

"No! No!" he cried. "Why can't they see us? Please, please see us!"

But the vessel was soon lost from sight.

The collective disappointment was almost too much. Wallace Thomas was the first to break the silence.

"We've got to get swimming again, you guys. He didn't see us."

With disappointment showing in every stroke, the remnant crew once again began to plod ahead toward shore. They had hardly begun, however, when Ben Pruitt rolled facedown in the water. Paul Ferguson and Curt Nelson summoned all their remaining strength to roll him back over and give him mouth-to-mouth resuscitation, but there was no response.

"Come on, you two!" Thomas finally called, his voice breaking. "You've got to let him go now. You've got to save yourselves. We've done everything we could. We've got to take care of the living now!"

The remaining survivors of the *St. Patrick* were too exhausted to untie Ben's body, so they left it in tow and resumed swimming.

Less than an hour later, the five remaining survivors closed to within what they believed was a half mile of the shoreline. "I'll go on in," yelled Harold Avery, "and if it's all right, I'll wave for you to follow on in after me! I've got some waterproof matches and I'll get a warm fire going. So just watch for my signal and then follow me in!"

Thoughts of a crackling-hot fire lifted the spirits of the four remaining crewmen. Vanessa was shaking constantly from the cold water seeping into her suit. She was growing visibly weaker. With Vanessa lying across his lap, Thomas shuddered as he watched Harold swim away.

They were able to stop paddling then and, sighing with relief, settled back to await the signal from shore. As they drifted nearer to shore, they decided to untie themselves from each other in preparation for the swim in through the surf. Freed from the rope line, Vanessa and Thomas found themselves drifting away from Paul Ferguson and Curt Nelson. But the two couples were too fatigued to reunite.

Shortly, Thomas saw the two men drop into a hollow in the sea and disappear. That afternoon, he caught his last brief glimpse of them. They appeared to have stopped swimming.

Now, with Vanessa completely dependent upon him for her survival, Thomas drifted and waited in anticipation for a signal from Harold Avery. Each time, as he rose up and over another wave, he would search for his good friend and deckmate's wave from the distant banks. Drifting ever nearer, he studied the soaring rock precipices. He could see the ghastly black form of the cliffs, slickened with spray and rising abruptly from out of a pounding misty-gray surf, with fog rolling across its sheer granite face.

He contemplated that perhaps he had underestimated the size of the surf and cliffs along the shore.

Suddenly, he caught the flicker of something tiny and orange in the thundering surf. It looked toylike, about the size of a petite orange buoy as it was lifted up and tossed against the wet face of the rock cliffs. He watched it being swept out by the surf, only to be gathered by another massive wave and flung high against the stone walls.

Then as he drifted nearer, the true dimensions of the terrain ahead finally struck Thomas. The rock cliffs were not a mere one hundred feet high, as he had estimated, but in frightening reality towered more than a thousand feet overhead!

When he spotted the minute orange object again, it was suspended in a wave and being swept some thirty feet up the face of the cliffs, with spray exploding far above it. And at that moment, it dawned on him—the object he had been studying so intently as it surged back and forth against the cliffs was not a buoy. It was the lifeless body of Harold Avery.

The sight took his breath. His heart felt like lead. All seemed lost and utterly hopeless. The safety they had associated with the first sighting of land had been only another cruel illusion. Vanessa hadn't seen the body. Thomas decided not to tell her.

"We can't get in here!" he yelled to her.

But what if there isn't any accessible beach on this island's entire shoreline? he worried secretly.

As Vanessa lay across his lap, Thomas noticed that her condition was worsening. She could no longer move her legs, the feeling had gone out of her arms, and her lips had turned a dark blue. As he paddled on his back over the waves, he tried to parallel the coastline.

He, too, had begun to shake uncontrollably, and his legs felt stiff and weighted. Toward evening, Wallace Thomas's back and arms began to cramp badly. He felt he couldn't carry Vanessa much longer. As he lay back, he thought he'd close his eyes and doze for a moment. It seemed only seconds before Vanessa rattled him awake.

"Wally! Wally, are you all right? You're looking pretty bad!"

"I'm fine, Vanessa," he reassured her. "I was just trying to relax for a few minutes."

Then a loud thumping noise began to pound in their ears. As if out of nowhere, an orange and white helicopter roared past them, close by overhead. In an adrenaline-pumping rush of excitement, Thomas waved his arms wildly; Vanessa raised one quivering hand.

"It's the Coast Guard! My God, they've finally come for us! They knew we're here! We've done it! We're going to be rescued! We're going to live!"

The helicopter sped out of sight, though. A few minutes later, they saw it making another pass in the distance.

Vanessa was too exhausted to wave.

"Did he spot us?" she asked in a weak voice.

"No. And he's too far away now."

He'd hardly finished speaking when another helicopter flew directly over them. As it passed, the side door slid open and Thomas could see a crewman standing in the doorway. He appeared to be looking right at them.

Thomas tried to rock forward, thereby rising slightly in the water, but Vanessa lay heavily across his lap. He screamed and waved frantically.

"Come on, Vanessa! We've got to signal to them! This might be the one time they see us!"

"I don't think I can anymore, Wally," she replied weakly.

The helicopter flew on out of sight.

"They didn't see us, did they?"

Thomas answered with silence.

"I don't think I'm going to make it, Wally," said Vanessa, her voice straining with pain and fatigue.

"Come on, Vanessa. We can still get out of this mess alive. We can float a good while longer if we have to."

"Oh, Wally," she replied in a disheartened voice, "I don't know. I'm awfully cold and there's a lot of water getting into my suit."

"Look over there," argued Thomas. "See that point of rock? Look past it. The waves aren't even breaking. There's a cove. We'll swim in around there somewhere."

Suddenly, Vanessa began to cough roughly. Then she jerked forward out of his arms and rolled facedown in the water.

Thomas was horrified. He jerked her back upright and shook her violently.

"Vanessa! Wake up! Say something to me! Answer me!"

There was no response. Her face was chalk blue. Her eyes were glassy.

She hacked deeply then and again wrenched free of Thomas's grip. Summoning what little strength he could, Thomas paddled to her side. He lifted her head and held her close. Her eyes were closed. Her body hung limply in his arms. She was no longer breathing. Vanessa was gone.

Thomas turned and slowly swam away. He was weary and heartbroken, and darkness was closing fast. His entire body ached with cold and now shook uncontrollably. He had been awake for more than thirty-six hours, twenty of them spent battling the stormy Alaskan seas. Now he wanted only to close his eyes and be done with it. His movements had grown sluggish to the point of immobility, but he fought to keep his tired mind on the task at hand.

I'm dead! I'm going to die! he concluded.

Shortly after nightfall, Wallace Thomas spotted a ship's mast lights. He did not grow overly excited. The lights were miles off. Each time, as he rose over another wave top, he caught glimpses of them. They appeared to be headed in his direction.

As the ship drew closer, Thomas tried to gather his failing strength. He lifted his leaden arms and began waving, drawing an arm back down to rest now and again. Occasionally, he called out, hoping his voice would somehow carry to those on board the ship. Then the vessel pulled up even with Thomas, and he screamed, "My God, I'm here! I'm right here!"

He fumbled for his whistle and began blowing it frantically. Then he held his breath and listened for a reply. He could hear the sounds of men's voices above the low rumble of the diesel engines. He could see the figures of crewmen working outside under the back deck lights. Yet the ship slowly lunged past him and disappeared into the night.

I'm dead, a goner. I'm going to die, he thought.

He struggled to come to terms with the finality of his predicament. He thought of his parents—how sad and wasteful losing their son this way would seem to them.

I'm sorry, Mom! I'm sorry, Dad! he thought, picturing them now in his mind. Such a lousy way to die, he pondered.

Thomas's shuddering body throbbed with cold. Then as he rode over the crest of a wave, he spotted tiny lights flickering in the distance.

Only a few hours before, Thomas would have known that they repre-
sented another ship miles away, but his thinking had become disoriented. He was sure they were the lights of Kodiak. "I'll swim in there,"
he decided. But seconds later, he'd forgotten the idea and paddled
numbly ahead.

Thomas knew he had to get out of the water. His body was just too
cold to remain in it much longer. Several times, his legs grew so stiff
that he was sure he no longer could use them. He knew he would soon
pass out from the relentless cold. His wilderness training in hypothermia flashed through his mind. If you got cold, you didn't try to ignore
it, he remembered. You act!

He crouched up into the fetal position then, and as he drifted in the
darkness, he tucked his mouth down into his suit and for a time
breathed heavily into it. His debilitating numbness and shivering
seemed to diminish slightly.

Then, as he came off the peak of a big loping wave, Thomas saw
something large in the moon-tinted darkness. It was floating beside
him. It looked like a huge buoy, partially covered with dark green
blotches of algae or seaweed, but its dimensions puzzled Thomas.

Maybe I can hang on to that and get some rest, he reasoned. I'll just
float along for a little while.

He paddled toward the object, but oddly, he didn't seem to be getting any closer. A moment later, Thomas drew back, frightened of the
thing. Now it looked like a whale, and, retreating, he splashed water at
the massive creature in an attempt to frighten it away.

Eventually, Thomas came to realize that the whale he had feared was
actually a point of land less than a half mile away. Maybe it's not your
time, he thought hopefully. You've got to at least try to swim for it! At
least you can do that! He turned then and using the breaststroke
headed in toward land.

"It's not your turn. It's not your time," he chanted to himself. "Going
to die if you stay out here any longer. May be the last thing you ever do.
Might as well swim for it. Got to try."

Shortly, Thomas found his movement impeded. A swaying tangle of

slimy fingers was bobbing about him, while others wrapped themselves around his arms and legs. Fear began to build. Oh, kelp, he realized suddenly. Must be getting closer. Must be.

He struggled on toward the shore, and on either side of him, in the
faint light, he spied tall pillars of blue-gray rock and moon-silvered
breakers fanning out and bursting high against them. When he heard
the roar of the breakers exploding along the shore, he grew sick with
fear. The vision of Harold Avery's body as it washed up against the cliff
kept shooting through his groggy mind. Aim yourself in between those
two pillars, he told himself. It's your only chance.

Wallace Thomas had no sooner decided upon his new course than
he felt an immense wave pick him up and hurl him forward through
the night. The wind blew sharply in his face and the water churned
beneath him as it heaved him along toward shore. Then, without warning, the wave crest he was riding curled forward.

He felt suspended in air as he fell down its folding face. When he
landed, the tremendous force of the pounding water shoved him
under the surface and held him there. The boiling torrent of ocean surf
pulled and pounded on him as if nothing short of his total destruc-
tion would satisfy it. It twisted him upside down, jerked him sideways,
and rolled him about. The smothering black surf seemed to pull at his
suit from all directions, and he could feel icy rivulets of water jetting
in around the facial opening of his hood.

Thomas fought to right himself and return to the surface. His lungs
burned for air. He had already begun the involuntary inhalation of the
icy salt water when his head finally cleared the surface. Thomas choked
violently and gasped in a lungful of the damp sea air. Then another
huge wave caught him and once again launched him swiftly forward
through the night.

He threw his battered arms out in front of him and attempted to
swim along with the thrusting power of the wave. Then he thought he
felt a hand strike a rock, and the foaming rush of water that had carried him there seemed to disappear from beneath him.

Thomas found himself lying facedown on the steep face of a solid rock bank. He clung to the steely cold surface in disbelief, his chest heaving for air. He felt too weak to move, but he knew if the next mammoth wave was to catch him still lying there, it might very well crush him with a single paralyzing blow.

In his mind, he stood to run, but his legs refused to move. It was as if they were no longer part of him! "Oh God! Dear God, help me!" he cried, pawing wildly at the slick bare rock of the bank.

Thomas had managed to crawl only a single body length up the surf-slickened bank when the next wave exploded at his feet, drenching him.

A bitter cold wind was gusting along the shoreline and soon it chilled Thomas to his core. The short stretch of rock he had lucked upon was only a few yards wide. Too weak to stand, and shivering uncontrollably, he pulled himself along with his hands, and, lucking upon a shallow rock crevice, he instinctively rolled into it. There, out of the direct assault of the wind, Thomas closed his weighted eyes and almost instantly fell asleep.

Yet it was a fitful rest. The surf pounded loudly only a few yards away, and even in the naturally protected chasm, the razor-sharp wind found him.

Wallace Thomas awoke with a start, to see the figure of Art Simonton standing close by and staring at him. His former crewmate and friend wore street clothes and seemed unaffected by the arctic wind racing along the shore. Was it the visible apparition of a dead and departed friend, or had he survived?

"Art!" he called out. "What are you doing here?"

When no answer came, Thomas took a moment to reposition himself and draw closer. But when he looked again, the figure had disappeared. He slumped back down and slipped into unconsciousness, lost in a merciful slumber.

The excruciating pain in his hands awakened him next. The arms of his suit were bloated with salt water forced in by the pummeling surf. He rolled onto his back, lifted his arms, drained the stinging water into the lower half of his suit, and fell back to sleep. When he awoke later, he found his hands had warmed to a point where he could at least open them.

The Coast Guard was finally able to verify that twelve crewmen had been aboard the fishing vessel *St. Patrick*. At first light, U.S. Coast Guard helicopter pilot Lt. Jimmy Ng lifted off from his base on Kodiak Island. Along with several other helicopters, C-130 SAR planes, and the Coast Guard cutter *Boutwell*, they began searching the area off Afognak Island for signs of survivors.

Lt. Ng worked his way around the steep rock shoreline of Marmot Island (positioned approximately four miles from the shores of Afognak Island). Some of the shoreline cliffs he encountered rose up in a sheer vertical climb more than twelve hundred feet above the water. A short time later, Lt. Ng located the first body. It was floating facedown in a small cliff-encircled cove. Oddly, the man wore neither rain gear nor a survival suit. The cliffs were too high and the cove too small to maneuver safely, so Lt. Ng hovered approximately fifty feet away and watched for signs of life. There were none, so he resumed his search around Marmot Island, and he soon came upon several more bodies.

"One body was off in the surf," he recalled. "He was bouncing around in the rocks. And two others were lying up on the beach. All were dead."

With the discovering of the first body, the Coast Guard search for the missing crew of the *St. Patrick* intensified. Soon, USCG helicopters, planes, and cutters were scanning the waters and shoreline from Whale Island, just offshore from Kodiak, to Marmot Bay, to Iszuit Bay, and completely around the northern tip of Afognak island, all in the hope of finding someone still alive.

Shortly after dawn, Wallace Thomas propped himself upright on a boulder. He sat shivering and studied the world around him. Overhead, rock walls rose as sheer and apparently inaccessible as those of a prison. More than one thousand feet above him, Thomas could see convoluted outcroppings of bare granite rock jutting into the sky, and beyond that, clinging to thin layers of soil, weather-stunted spruce trees bent in the wind. On either side of him, short stretches of narrow shoreline cut into the cliff rock and were strewn with boulders the size of dump trucks.

The cloud ceiling appeared to have lifted slightly but the freezing thirty-knot winds continued to blow without pause. The sea rushing up at him wore a blinding silver sheen. His pain-wracked legs still refused to support him, so he rubbed them furiously in an effort to restore circulation.

Thomas felt groggy and exhausted, miserably cold and hungry. But it was a maddening thirst that drove him finally to rise on wobbly legs and stagger stiff-legged along the cliff bottoms in search of fresh water. With water sloshing about inside, his survival suit hung heavily on him. He wanted to shed the suit but knew that to stand exposed to the Siberian-born winds in soaked clothing would mean death within hours.

Maybe I'll make it if I stay in the suit, he reasoned.

Thomas could find no fresh water close at hand. Walking only a few steps exhausted him.

If I'm going to survive, I've got to locate water, he told himself.

But there appeared to be no escaping the cliffs lining the beach. The sharp-crested outcroppings of rock extended well out into the surf. They loomed impossibly steep and dangerous to climb.

The pounding surf before him, which had taken the lives of so many of his companions and nearly his own, now petrified him. He would remain trapped on the shore and take his chances with hunger and thirst and exposure before he would return to the ocean again.

Then as the surf receded to near-dead low tide, he saw an opportunity. The tide had receded enough to allow passage around the base of the jutting column on his left. Wallace did not hesitate. Leaning against the rock walls, he hurried around them as quickly as his buckling legs would carry him.

He discovered an even shorter stretch of enclosed shoreline. Large boulders covered most of it. He stumbled forward and fell on the bank, panting. Slowly, a faint dribbling sound struck his consciousness. He spun and his eyes caught the movement of a tiny stream of water trickling off the face of a vertical rock bluff.

He rose staggering and fell. He crawled the last few feet but found a small pond formed where the droplets had landed. He dipped his glove-covered hands anxiously into the clear pool and sipped the bounty. The water tasted salty and he spit it back out. His heart fell.

Damn! A tide pool! he thought angrily.

Then he sampled the pool again.

It was fresh water!

Thomas felt foolish. The salt he had tasted had come from the gloves of his survival suit. The water in the pool was fresh and cold. He drank down a few eager swallows and then stopped abruptly. He could feel the water cool him and he wanted to allow his body time to catch up.

Even with fresh water, Thomas doubted he could make it through another night in his wet clothes without food or a fire. It had been nearly forty-five hours since his last meal and he was sick with hunger.

In an effort to hide from the painful and life-sapping cold of the December winds, Thomas hunched down between two huge boulders. From there, he could still command a view of a good portion of the ocean. As he waited, he shook so hard it felt as if all the bones in his body were rattling. Gradually, he thought he could make out the faint rumble of an engine. The noise dimmed, then grew stronger, only to fade once more. He debated whether to stand and look, exposing himself fully to the draining cold of the wind.

He had to try, he decided. His body was fast growing colder. He wavered as he stood, and his eyes squinted into the wind and swept quickly over the ocean before him. He was about to crouch back down when he spotted movement. It was the bow of a ship nosing its way through heavy seas off a point of land on his far right. Almost crippled with cold yet frantic with excitement, Thomas struggled up the side of a large boulder and began flailing his weary arms.

"They must be out looking for me! They've got to spot me! They've just got to see me now!" he cried out loud.

The one-hundred-foot ship drove nearly halfway across the open stretch of water in front of him before Thomas thought he saw it slow.

Through watering eyes, he saw quick flashes of light coming from the wheelhouse.

Were those really signals? Have they actually spotted me? Or am I only imagining things again?

Every few seconds, the ship would crest the top of another swell and then slide into a deep trough, and then, except for the radar scanner spinning steadily atop the wheelhouse, it would disappear as if swallowed whole.

The waving seemed to take the last of Thomas's strength. A sudden gust of wind staggered him, nearly toppling him from the rock. He dropped to his knees to maintain his balance. If they did see me, what will they do next? What could they do? his fuzzy mind puzzled.

On the horizon, Thomas caught sight of a small black dot moving directly toward him low over the water. Moments later, a four-engined C-130 U.S. Coast Guard plane roared by overhead. Its deep, growling engines shook his insides like the blast from a cannon. Thomas was ecstatic. He blew kisses and screamed excitedly. "Yes! Yes, they've seen me! Thank God, at least they know where I am!"

Soon, he spied a U.S. Coast Guard helicopter moving toward him. "I'm here! I'm alive!" he called out.

The wind was blowing hard against the one-thousand-foot cliffs behind him. The helicopter flew in twice over Thomas and hovered, only to clack noisily away.

Dear God, he can't get to me! he thought. I'm too cold! I've got to get out of here!

Then the bright orange, black, and white helicopter returned and hovered not fifty feet above him. The 10-knot wind churned up by the copter's blades whipped a mist off the water.

Thomas was thrilled when he saw the large steel body basket descend from out of the side door. But it landed well out in the breaking surf, and the pilot seemed reluctant to move in closer to the cliffs.

Gradually, the helicopter pilot maneuvered the craft closer, resting the basket in the surf on the edge of the shoreline. Though terrified of the water, Thomas shuffled down the embankment and fell into the basket. Fear that the next wave would catch him and batter him to death now that he was so near to being rescued raged in his mind. Yet almost instantly, the helicopter plucked Thomas up and out of the surf.

Thomas watched the shoreline grow minute in the distance. A cutting wind whipped over him as the upward acceleration of the helicopter pressed his body hard against the wire-meshed basket's bottom. Then the helicopter leveled off and stood away from the shore, hovering noisily. Thomas could feel himself being lifted toward the door.

Far below, he could see the ship that had first spotted him and radioed his location. It was the *Nelle Belle*. She was throwing off heavy sheets of bow spray as she plowed through the waves.

The helicopter crew hoisted him in through the door and checked him for serious injuries. Next a radio headset was fitted over his head, and Thomas heard the voice of the chief pilot.

"Are you all right, young man?"

"Yes. I think so."

"How do you feel?"

"Well, you got me out of there! I feel so much better now."

"Look, you've got hypothermia! Do you understand that?"

"I kind of figured as much."

"Okay, so now listen to what I'm telling you! Do not relax! Keep yourself charged up until we can get you into the hospital. You could go into shock right now and you could die before we could get you there! That has happened to us before. "

The helicopter pilot was worried about a dangerous phenomenon called "after drop," the process in which a hypothermia victim's core temperature continues to plunge even after he has been rescued and wrapped in wool blankets. If not halted, this downward slide will continue until the victim suffers a heart attack from the cool blood circulating through his heart.

"Have you found anyone else besides me?" asked Thomas.

"No. You're the only one so far," answered the pilot.

The somber news shook Thomas. He had hoped that Paul Ferguson or Curt Nelson had somehow found a way safely ashore. He wondered about Bob Kidd and Arthur "Art" Simonton, whom he'd seen in his dreams the night before. Bob Kidd had jumped overboard with Simonton from up near the bow minutes before Thomas and the rest of the crew had abandoned the *St. Patrick* off the stern.

When Wallace Thomas arrived at the hospital, his body temperature was ninety-three degrees Fahrenheit. Death can occur from heart failure at ninety degrees. The medical staff placed heated blankets and hot towels across his body and forced him to breathe heated oxygen. But it took little coaxing. The warm devices felt wonderful to Thomas's numb, sea-ravaged body.

The next day, Thomas learned that one other crewmate had survived the ordeal. As he lay recovering in a Kodiak hospital bed, nurses wheeled in Bob Kidd for a visit. "I can't believe it," Thomas finally confided to his good friend.

"I would never have believed that a ship built like the *St. Patrick* could have gone down as quickly as she did!"

Bob Kidd sat upright and turned and looked at Wally Thomas in astonishment. "Wally," said Kidd, "it didn't go down. It didn't sink. They found the *St. Patrick* floating the day after we abandoned ship. They're towing it in right now!"

from Wind, Sand and Stars
by Antoine de Saint-Exupéry

When pilot Antoine de Saint-Exupéry (1900-1944) and his mechanic Prévot crash landed in the desert of northern Africa, they were far from their intended flight path, so it was unlikely that anyone would find them. The pair had a pint of coffee, half a pint of wine, some grapes and an orange. They had to start walking—but neither man knew which way to go.

We crawled into the cabin and waited for dawn. I stretched out, and as I settled down to sleep I took stock of our situation. We didn't know where we were; we had less than a quart of liquid between us; if we were not too far off the Benghazi-Cairo lane we should be found in a week, and that would be too late. Yet it was the best we could hope for. If, on the other hand, we had drifted off our course, we shouldn't be found in six months. One thing was sure—we could not count on being picked up by a plane; the men who came out for us would have two thousand miles to cover.

"You know, it's a shame," Prévot said suddenly.

"What's a shame?"

"That we didn't crash properly and have it over with."

It seemed pretty early to be throwing in one's hand. Prévot and I pulled ourselves together. There was still a chance, slender as it was, that we might be saved miraculously by a plane. On the other hand, we couldn't stay here and perhaps miss a near-by oasis. We would walk all day and come back to the plane before dark. And before going off we would write our plan in huge letters in the sand.

With this I curled up and settled down to sleep. I was happy to go to sleep. My weariness wrapped me round like a multiple presence. I was not alone in the desert: my drowsiness was peopled with voices and memories and whispered confidences. I was not yet thirsty; I felt strong; and I surrendered myself to sleep as to an aimless journey. Reality lost ground before the advance of dreams.

Ah, but things were different when I awoke!

In times past I have loved the Sahara. I have spent nights alone in the path of marauding tribes and have waked up with untroubled mind in the golden emptiness of the desert where the wind like a sea had raised sandwaves upon its surface. Asleep under the wing of my plane I have looked forward with confidence to being rescued next day. But this was not the Sahara!

Prévot and I walked along the slopes of rolling mounds. The ground was sand covered over with a single layer of shining black pebbles. They gleamed like metal scales and all the domes about us shone like coats of mail. We had dropped down into a mineral world and were hemmed in by iron hills.

When we reached the top of the first crest we saw in the distance another just like it, black and gleaming. As we walked we scraped the ground with our boots, marking a trail over which to return to the plane. We went forward with the sun in our eyes. It was not logical to go due east like this, for everything—the weather reports, the duration of the flight—had made it plain that we had crossed the Nile. But I had started tentatively towards the west and had felt a vague foreboding I could not explain to myself. So I had put off the west till tomorrow. In the same way, provisionally, I had given up going north, though that led to the sea.

Three days later, when scourged by thirst into abandoning the plane and walking straight on until we dropped in our tracks, it was still eastward that we tramped. More precisely, we walked east-northeast. And this too was in defiance of all reason and even of all hope. Yet after we had been rescued we discovered that if we had gone in any other direction we should have been lost.

Northward, we should never have had the endurance to reach the sea. And absurd as it may appear, it seems to me now, since I had no other motive, that I must have chosen east simply because it was by going eastward that Guillaumet had been saved in the Andes, after I had hunted for him everywhere. In a confused way the east had become for me the direction of life.

We walked on for five hours and then the landscape changed. A river of sand seemed to be running through a valley, and we followed this river-bed, taking long strides in order to cover as much ground as possible and get back to the plane before night fell, if our march was in vain. Suddenly I stopped.

"Prévot!"

"What's up?"

"Our tracks!"

How long was it since we had forgotten to leave a wake behind us? We had to find it or die.

We went back, bearing to the right. When we had gone back far enough we would make a right angle to the left and eventually intersect our tracks where we had still remembered to mark them.

This we did and were off again. The heat rose and with it came the mirages. But these were still the commonplace kind—sheets of water that materialized and then vanished as we neared them. We decided to cross the valley of sand and climb the highest dome in order to look round the horizon. This was after six hours of march in which, striding along, we must have covered twenty miles.

When we had struggled up to the top of the black hump we sat down and looked at each other. At our feet lay our valley of sand, opening into a desert of sand whose dazzling brightness seared our eyes. As far as the eye could see lay empty space. But in that space the play of light created mirages which, this time, were of a disturbing kind, fortresses and minarets, angular geometric hulks. I could see also a black mass that pretended to be vegetation, overhung by the last of those clouds that dissolve during the day only to return at night. This mass of vegetation was the shadow of a cumulus.

It was no good going on. The experiment was a failure. We would have to go back to our plane, to that red and white beacon which, perhaps, would be picked out by a flyer. I was not staking great hopes on a rescue party, but it did seem to me our last chance of salvation. In any case, we had to get back to our few drops of liquid, for our throats were parched. We were imprisoned in this iron circle, captives of the curt dictatorship of thirst.

And yet, how hard it was to turn back when there was a chance that we might be on the road to life! Beyond the mirages the horizon was perhaps rich in veritable treasures, in meadows and runnels of sweet water. I knew I was doing the right thing by returning to the plane, and yet as I swung round and started back I was filled with portents of disaster.

We were resting on the ground beside the plane. Nearly forty miles of wandering this day. The last drop of liquid had been drained. No sign of life had appeared to the east. No plane had soared overhead. How long should we be able to hold out? Already our thirst was terrible.

We had built up a great pyre out of bits of the splintered wing. Our gasoline was ready, and we had flung on the heap sheets of metal whose magnesium coating would burn with a hard white flame. We were waiting now for night to come down before we lighted our conflagration. But where were there men to see it?

Night fell and the flames rose. Prayerfully we watched our mute and radiant fanion mount resplendent into the night. As I looked I said to myself that this message was not only a cry for help, it was fraught also with a great deal of love. We were begging water, but we were also begging the communion of human society. Only man can create fire: let another flame light up the night; let man answer man!

I was haunted by a vision of my wife's eyes under the halo of her hat. Of her face I could see only the eyes, questioning me, looking at me yearningly. I am answering, answering with all my strength! What flame could leap higher than this that darts up into the night from my heart?

What I could do, I have done. What we could do, we have done. Nearly forty miles, almost without a drop to drink. Now there was no water left. Was it our fault that we could wait no longer? Suppose we had sat quietly by the plane, taking suck at the mouths of our water-bottles? But from the moment I breathed in the moist bottom of the tin cup, a clock had started up in me. From the second when I had sucked up the last drop, I had begun to slip downhill. Could I help it if time like a river was carrying me away? Prévot was weeping. I tapped him on the shoulder and said, to console him:

"If we're done for we're done for, and that's all there is to it."

He said:

"Do you think it's me I'm bawling about?"

I might have known it. It was evident enough. Nothing is unbearable. Tomorrow, and the day after, I should learn that nothing was really unbearable. I had never really believed in torture. Reading Poe as a kid, I had already said as much to myself. Once, jammed in the cabin of a plane, I thought I was going to drown; and I had not suffered much. Several times it had seemed to me that the final smash-up was coming, and I don't remember that I thought of it as a cosmic event. And I didn't believe this was going to be agonizing either. There will be time tomorrow to find out stranger things about it. Meanwhile, God knows that despite the bonfire I had decidedly given up hope that our cries would be heard by the world.

"Do you think it's me . . ." There you have what is truly unbearable! Every time I saw those yearning eyes it was as if a flame were searing me. They were like a scream for help, like the flares of a sinking ship. I felt that I should not sit idly by: I should jump up and run—anywhere! straight ahead of me!

What a strange reversal of roles! But I have always thought it would be like this. Still, I needed Prévot beside me to be quite sure of it. Prévot was a level-headed fellow. He loved life. And yet Prévot no more than I was wringing his hands at the sight of death the way we are told men do. But there did exist something that he could not bear any more than I could. I was perfectly ready to fall asleep, whether for a night or for eternity. If I did fall asleep, I could not even know whether it was for the one or for the other. And the peace of sleep! But that cry that would be sent up at home, that great wail of desolation—that was what I could not bear. I could not stand idly by and look on at that disaster. Each second of silence drove the knife deeper into someone I loved. At the thought, a blind rage surged up in me. Why do these chains bind me and prevent me from rescuing those who are drowning? Why does our conflagration not carry our cry to the ends of the world? Hear me, you out here! Patience. We are coming to save you.

The magnesium had been licked off and the metal was glowing red. There was left only a heap of embers round which we crouched to warm ourselves. Our flaming call had spent itself. Had it set anything in the world in motion? I knew well enough that it hadn't. Here was a prayer that had of necessity gone unheard.

That was that.

I ought to get some sleep.

At daybreak I took a rag and mopped up a little dew on the wings. The mixture of water and paint and oil yielded a spoonful of nauseating liquid which we sipped because it would at least moisten our lips. After this banquet Prévot said:

"Thank God we've got a gun."

Instantly I became furious and turned on him with an aggressiveness which I regretted directly I felt it. There was nothing I should have loathed more at that moment than a gush of sentimentality. I am so made that I have to believe that everything is simple. Birth is simple. Growing up is simple. And dying of thirst is simple. I watched Prévot out of the corner of my eye, ready to wound his feelings, if that was necessary to shut him up.

But Prévot had spoken without emotion. He had been discussing a matter of hygiene, and might have said in the same tone, "We ought to wash our hands." That being so, we were agreed. Indeed already yester-day, my eye falling by chance on the leather holster, the same thought had crossed my mind, and with me too it had been a reasonable reflex, not an emotional one. Pathos resides in social man, not in the individual; what was pathetic was our powerlessness to reassure those for whom we were responsible, not what we might do with the gun.

There was still no sign that we were being sought; or rather they were doubtless hunting for us elsewhere, probably in Arabia. We were to hear no sound of plane until the day after we had abandoned our own. And if ships did pass overhead, what could that mean to us? What could they see in us except two black dots among the thousand shadowy dots in the desert? Absurd to think of being distinguishable from them. None of the reflections that might be attributed to me on the score of this torture would be true. I should not feel in the least tortured. The aerial rescue party would seem to me, each time I sighted one, to be moving through a universe that was not mine. When searchers have to cover two thousand miles of territory, it takes them a good two weeks to spot a plane in the desert from the sky.

They were probably looking for us all along the line from Tripoli to Persia. And still, with all this, I clung to the slim chance that they might pick us out. Was that not our only chance of being saved? I changed my tactics, determining to go reconnoitering by myself. Prévot would get another bonfire together and kindle it in the event that visitors showed up. Put we were to have no callers that day.

So off I went without knowing whether or not I should have the stamina to come back. I remembered what I knew about this Libyan desert. When, in the Sahara, humidity is still at forty percent of saturation, it is only eighteen here in Libya. Life here evaporates like a vapor. Bedouins, explorers, and colonial officers all tell us that a man may go nineteen hours without water. Thereafter his eyes fill with light, and that marks the beginning of the end. The progress made by thirst is swift and terrible. But this northeast wind, this abnormal wind that had blown us out off our course and had marooned us on this plateau, was now prolonging our lives. What was the length of the reprieve it would grant us before our eyes began to fill with light? I went forward with the feeling of a man canoeing in mid-ocean.

I will admit that at daybreak this landscape seemed to me less infernal, and that I began my walk with my hands in my pockets, like a tramp on a highroad. The evening before we had set snares at the mouths of certain mysterious burrows in the ground, and the poacher in me was on the alert. I went first to have a look at our traps. They were empty.

Well, this meant that I should not be drinking blood today; and indeed I hadn't expected to. But though I was not disappointed, my curiosity was aroused. What was there in the desert for these animals to live on? These were certainly the holes of fennecs, a long-eared carnivorous sand-fox the size of a rabbit. I spotted the tracks made by one of them, and gave way to the impulse to follow them. They led to a narrow stream of sand where each footprint was plainly outlined and where I marveled at the pretty palm formed by the three toes spread fanwise on the sand.

I could imagine my little friend trotting blithely along at dawn and licking the dew off the rocks. Here the tracks were wider apart: my fennec had broken into a run. And now I see that a companion has joined him and they have trotted on side by side. These signs of a morning stroll gave me a strange thrill. They were signs of life, and I loved them for that. I almost forgot that I was thirsty.

Finally I came to the pasture-ground of my foxes. Here, every hundred yards or so, I saw sticking up out of the sand a small dry shrub, its twigs heavy with little golden snails. The fennec came here at dawn to do his marketing. And here I was able to observe another of nature's mysteries.

My fennec did not stop at all the shrubs. There were some weighed down with snails which he disdained. Obviously he avoided them with some wariness. Others he stopped at but did not strip of all they bore. He must have picked out two or three shells and then gone on to another restaurant. What was he up to? Was he nurseryman to the snails, encouraging their reproduction by refraining from exhausting the stock on a given shrub, or a given twig? Or was he amusing himself

by delaying repletion, putting off satiety in order to enhance the pleasure he took from his morning stroll?

The tracks led me back to the hole in which he lived. Doubtless my
fennec crouched below, listening to me and startled by the crunching
of my footsteps. I said to him:

"Fox, my little fox, I'm done for; but somehow that doesn't prevent
me from taking an interest in your mood."

And there I stayed a bit, ruminating and telling myself that a man
was able to adapt himself to anything. The notion that he is to die in
thirty years has probably never spoiled any man's fun. Thirty years . . .
or thirty days: it's all a matter of perspective.

Only, you have to be able to put certain visions out of your mind.

I went on, finally, and the time came when, along with my weariness,
something in me began to change. If those were not mirages, I was
inventing them.

"Hi! Hi, there!"

I shouted and waved my arms, but the man I had seen waving at me
turned out to be a black rock. Everything in the desert had grown ani-
mate. I stooped to waken a sleeping Bedouin and he turned into the
trunk of a black tree. A tree-trunk? Here in the desert? I was amazed
and bent over to lift a broken bough. It was solid marble.

Straightening up I looked round and saw more black marble. An
antediluvian forest littered the ground with its broken tree-tops. How
many thousand years ago, under what hurricane of the time of Genesis,
had this cathedral of wood crumbled in this spot? Countless centuries
had rolled these fragments of giant pillars at my feet, polished them
like steel, petrified and vitrified them and indued them with the color
of jet.

I could distinguish the knots in their branches, the twistings of their
once living boughs, could count the rings of life in them. This forest
had rustled with birds and been filled with music that now was struck
by doom and frozen into salt. And all this was hostile to me. Blacker
than the chain-mail of the hummocks, these solemn derelicts rejected

me. What had I, a living man, to do with this incorruptible stone? Perishable as I was, I whose body was to crumble into dust, what place had I in this eternity?

Since yesterday I had walked nearly fifty miles. This dizziness that I felt came doubtless from my thirst. Or from the sun. It glittered on these hulks until they shone as if smeared with oil. It blazed down on this universal carapace. Sand and fox had no life here. This world was a gigantic anvil upon which the sun beat down. I strode across this anvil and at my temples I could feel the hammer-strokes of the sun.

"Hi! Hi, there!" I called out.

"There is nothing there," I told myself. "Take it easy. You are delirious."

I had to talk to myself aloud, to bring myself to reason. It was hard for me to reject what I was seeing, hard not to run towards that caravan plodding on the horizon. There! Do you see it?

"Fool! You know very well that you are inventing it."

"You mean that nothing in the world is real?"

Nothing in the world is real if that cross which I see ten miles off on the top of a hill is not real. Or is it a lighthouse? No, the sea does not lie in that direction. Then it must be a cross.

I had spent the night studying my map—but uselessly, since I did not know my position. Still, I had scrutinized all the signs that marked the marvelous presence of man. And somewhere on the map I had seen a little circle surmounted by just such a cross. I had glanced down at the legend to get an explanation of the symbol and had read: "Religious institution."

Close to the cross there had been a black dot. Again I had run my finger down the legend and had read: "Permanent well." My heart had jumped and I had repeated the legend aloud: "Permanent well, permanent well." What were all of Ali Baba's treasures compared with a permanent well? A little farther on were two white circles. "Temporary wells," the legend said. Not quite so exciting. And round about them was nothing . . . unless it was the blankness of despair.

But this must be my "religious institution"! The monks must certainly have planted a great cross on the hill expressly for men in our plight! All I had to do was to walk across to them. I should be taken in by those Dominicans. . . .

"But there are only Coptic monasteries in Libya!" I told myself.

. . . by those learned Dominicans. They have a great cool kitchen with red tiles, and out in the courtyard a marvelous rusted pump. Beneath the rusted pump; beneath the rusted pump . . . you've guessed it! . . . beneath the rusted pump is dug the permanent well! Ah, what rejoicing when I ring at their gate, when I get my hands on the rope of the great bell.

"Madman! You are describing a house in Provence; and what's more, the house has no bell!"

. . . on the rope of the great bell. The porter will raise his arms to Heaven and cry out, "You are the messenger of the Lord! " and he will call aloud to all the monks. They will pour out of the monastery. They will welcome me with a great feast, as if I were the Prodigal Son. They will lead me to the kitchen and will say to me, "One moment, my son, one moment. We'll just be off to the permanent well." And I shall be trembling with happiness.

No, no! I will *not* weep just because there happens to be no cross on the hill.

The treasures of the west turned out to be mere illusion. I have veered due north. At least the north is filled with the sound of the sea.

Over the hilltop. Look there, at the horizon! The most beautiful city in the world!

"You know perfectly well that is a mirage."

Of course I know it is a mirage! Am I the sort of man who can be fooled? But what if I *want* to go after that mirage? Suppose I enjoy indulging my hope? Suppose it suits me to love that crenelated town all beflagged with sunlight? What if I choose to walk straight ahead on light feet—for you must know that I have dropped my weariness behind me, I am happy now. . . . Prévot and his gun! Don't make me laugh! I prefer my drunkenness. I am drunk. I am dying of thirst.

It took the twilight to sober me. Suddenly I stopped, appalled to think how far I was from our base. In the twilight the mirage was dying. The horizon had stripped itself of its pomp, its palaces, its priestly vestments. It was the old desert horizon again.

"A fine day's work you've done! Night will overtake you. You won't be able to go on before daybreak, and by that time your tracks will have been blown away and you'll be properly nowhere."

In that case I may as well walk straight on. Why turn back? Why should I bring my ship round when I may find the sea straight ahead of me?

"When did you catch a glimpse of the sea? What makes you think you could walk that far? Meanwhile there's Prévot watching for you beside the *Simoon*. He may have been picked up by a caravan, for all you know."

Very good. I'll go back. But first I want to call out for help.

"Hi! Hi!"

By God! You can't tell me this planet is not inhabited. Where are its men?

"Hi! Hi!"

I was hoarse. My voice was gone. I knew it was ridiculous to croak like this, but—one more try:

"Hi! Hi!"

And I turned back.

I had been walking two hours when I saw the flames of the bonfire that Prévot, frightened by my long absence, had sent up. They mattered very little to me now.

Another hour of trudging. Five hundred yards away. A hundred yards. Fifty yards.

"Good Lord!"

Amazement stopped me in my tracks. Joy surged up and filled my heart with its violence. In the firelight stood Prévot talking to two Arabs who were leaning against the motor. He had not noticed me, for he was too full of his own joy. If only I had sat still—and waited with him! I should have been saved already. Exultantly I called out:

"Hi! Hi!"

The two Bedouins gave a start and stared at me. Prévot left them standing and came forward to meet me. I opened my arms to him. He caught me by the elbow. Did he think I was keeling over? I said:

"At last, eh?"

"What do you mean?"

"The Arabs!"

"What Arabs?"

"Those Arabs there, with you."

Prévot looked at me queerly, and when he spoke I felt as if he was very reluctantly confiding a great secret to me:

"There are no Arabs here."

This time I know I am going to cry.

A man can go nineteen hours without water, and what have we drunk since last night? A few drops of dew at dawn. But the northeast wind is still blowing, still slowing up the process of our evaporation. To it, also, we owe the continued accumulation of high clouds. If only they would drift straight overhead and break into rain! But it never rains in the desert.

"Look here, Prévot. Let's rip up one of the parachutes and spread the sections out on the ground, weighed down with stones. If the wind stays in the same quarter till morning, they'll catch the dew and we can wring them out into one of the tanks."

We spread six triangular sections of parachute under the stars, and Prévot unhooked a fuel tank. This was as much as we could do for ourselves till dawn. But, miracle of miracles! Prévot had come upon an orange while working over the tank. We shared it, and though it was little enough to men who could have used a few gallons of sweet water, still I was overcome with relief.

Stretched out beside the fire I looked at the glowing fruit and said to myself that men did not know what an orange was. "Here we are, condemned to death," I said to myself, "and still the certainty of dying cannot compare with the pleasure I am feeling. The joy I take from this half of an orange which I am holding in my hand is one of the greatest joys I have ever known."

I lay flat on my back, sucking my orange and counting the shooting stars. Here I was, for one minute infinitely happy. "Nobody can know anything of the world in which the individual moves and has his being," I reflected. "There is no guessing it. Only the man locked up in it can know what it is."

For the first time I understood the cigarette and glass of rum that are handed to the criminal about to be executed. I used to think that for a man to accept these wretched gifts at the foot of the gallows was beneath human dignity. Now I was learning that he took pleasure from them. People thought him courageous when he smiled as he smoked or drank. I knew now that he smiled because the taste gave him pleasure. People could not see that his perspective had changed, and that for him the last hour of his life was a life in itself.

We collected an enormous quantity of water—perhaps as much as two quarts. Never again would we be thirsty! We were saved; we had a liquid to drink!

I dipped my tin cup into the tank and brought up a beautifully yellow-green liquid the first mouthful of which nauseated me so that despite my thirst I had to catch my breath before swallowing it. I would have swallowed mud, I swear; but this taste of poisonous metal cut keener than thirst.

I glanced at Prévot and saw him going round and round with his eyes fixed to the ground as if looking for something. Suddenly he leaned forward and began to vomit without interrupting his spinning. Half a minute later it was my turn. I was seized by such convulsions that I went down on my knees and dug my fingers into the sand while I puked. Neither of us spoke, and for a quarter of an hour we remained thus shaken, bringing up nothing but a little bile.

After a time it passed and all I felt was a vague, distant nausea. But our last hope had fled. Whether our bad luck was due to a sizing on the parachute or to the magnesium lining of the tank, I never found out. Certain it was that we needed either another set of cloths or another receptacle.

Well, it was broad daylight and time we were on our way. This time we should strike out as fast as we could, leave this cursed plateau, and tramp till we dropped in our tracks. That was what Guillaumet had done in the Andes. I had been thinking of him all the day before and had determined to follow his example. I should do violence to the pilot's unwritten law, which is to stick by the ship; but I was sure no one would be along to look for us here.

Once again we discovered that it was not we who were shipwrecked, not we but those who were waiting for news of us, those who were alarmed by our silence, were already torn with grief by some atrocious and fantastic report. We could not but strive towards them. Guillaumet had done it, had scrambled towards his lost ones. To do so is a universal impulse.

"If I were alone in the world," Prévot said, "I'd lie down right here. Damned if I wouldn't."

East-northeast we tramped. If we had in fact crossed the Nile, each step was leading us deeper and deeper into the desert.

I don't remember anything about that day. I remember only my haste. I was hurrying desperately towards something—towards some finality. I remember also that I walked with my eyes to the ground, for the mirages were more than I could bear. From time to time we would correct our course by the compass, and now and again we would lie down to catch our breath. I remember having flung away my waterproof, which I had held on to as covering for the night. That is as much as I recall about the day. Of what happened when the chill of evening came, I remember more. But during the day I had simply turned to sand and was a being without mind.

When the sun set we decided to make camp. Oh, I knew as well as anybody that we should push on, that this one waterless night would finish us off. But we had brought along the bits of parachute, and if the poison was not in the sizing, we might get a sip of water next morning. Once again we spread our trap for the dew under the stars.

But the sky in the north was cloudless. The wind no longer had the same taste on the lip. It had moved into another quarter. Something was rustling against us, but this time it seemed to be the desert itself. The wild beast was stalking us, had us in its power. I could feel its breath in my face, could feel it lick my face and hands. Suppose I walked on: at the best I could do five or six miles more. Remember that in three days I had covered one hundred miles, practically without water.

And then, just as we stopped, Prévot said:

"I swear to you I see a lake!"

"You're crazy."

"Have you ever heard of a mirage after sunset?" he challenged.

I didn't seem able to answer him. I had long ago given up believing my own eyes. Perhaps it was not a mirage; but in that case it was a hallucination. How could Prévot go on believing? But he was stubborn about it.

"It's only twenty minutes off. I'll go have a look."

His mulishness got on my nerves.

"Go ahead!" I shouted. "Take your little constitutional. Nothing better for a man. But let me tell you, if your lake exists it is salt. And whether it's salt or not, it's a devil of a way off. And besides, there is no damned lake! "

Prévot was already on his way, his eyes glassy. I knew the strength of these irresistible obsessions. I was thinking: "There are somnambulists who walk straight into locomotives." And I knew that Prévot would not come back. He would be seized by the vertigo of empty space and would be unable to turn back. And then he would keel over. He somewhere, and I somewhere else. Not that it was important.

Thinking thus, it struck me that this mood of resignation was doing me no good. Once when I was half drowned I had let myself go like this. Lying now flat on my face on the stony ground, I took this occasion to write a letter for posthumous delivery. It gave me a chance, also, to take stock of myself again. I tried to bring up a little saliva: how long was it since I had spit? No saliva. If I kept my mouth closed, a kind of glue sealed my lips together. It dried on the outside of the lips and formed a hard crust. However, I found I was still able to swallow, and

I bethought me that I was still not seeing a blinding light in my eyes. Once I was treated to that radiant spectacle I might know that the end was a couple of hours away.

Night fell. The moon had swollen since I last saw it. Prévot was still not back. I stretched out on my back and turned these few data over in my mind. A familiar impression came over me, and I tried to seize it. I was . . . I was . . . I was at sea. I was on a ship going to South America and was stretched out, exactly like this, on the boat deck. The tip of the mast was swaying to and fro, very slowly, among the stars. That mast was missing tonight, but again I was at sea, bound for a port I was to make without raising a finger. Slave-traders had flung me on this ship.

I thought of Prévot who was still not back. Not once had I heard him complain. That was a good thing. To hear him whine would have been unbearable. Prévot was a man.

What was that! Five hundred yards ahead of me I could see the light of his lamp. He had lost his way. I had no lamp with which to signal back. I stood up and shouted, but he could not hear me.

A second lamp, and then a third! God in Heaven! It was a search party and it was me they were hunting!

"Hi! Hi!" I shouted.

But they had not heard me. The three lamps were still signaling me.

"Tonight I am sane," I said to myself. "I am relaxed. I am not out of my head. Those are certainly three lamps and they are about five hundred yards off." I stared at them and shouted again, and again I gathered that they could not hear me.

Then, for the first and only time, I was really seized with panic. I could still run, I thought. "Wait! Wait!" I screamed. They seemed to be turning away from me, going off, hunting me elsewhere! And I stood tottering, tottering on the brink of life when there were arms out there ready to catch me! I shouted and screamed again and again.

They had heard me! An answering shout had come. I was strangling, suffocating, but I ran on, shouting as I ran, until I saw Prévot and keeled over.

When I could speak again I said: "Whew! When I saw all those lights . . ."

"What lights? "

God in Heaven, it was true! He was alone!

This time I was beyond despair. I was filled with a sort of dumb fury.

"What about your lake?" I rasped.

"As fast as I moved towards it, it moved back. I walked after it for about half an hour. Then it seemed still too far away, so I came back. But I am positive, now, that it is a lake."

"You're crazy. Absolutely crazy. Why did you do it? Tell me. Why?"

What had he done? Why had he done it? I was ready to weep with indignation, yet I scarcely knew why I was so indignant. Prévot mumbled his excuse:

"I felt I had to find some water. You . . . your lips were awfully pale."

Well! My anger died within me. I passed my hand over my forehead as if I were waking out of sleep. I was suddenly sad. I said:

"There was no mistake about it. I saw them as clearly as I see you now. Three lights there were. I tell you, Prévot, I saw them!"

Prévot made no comment.

"Well," he said finally, "I guess we're in a bad way."

In this air devoid of moisture the soil is swift to give off its temperature. It was already very cold. I stood up and stamped about. But soon a violent fit of trembling came over me. My dehydrated blood was moving sluggishly and I was pierced by a freezing chill which was not merely the chill of night. My teeth were chattering and my whole body had begun to twitch. My hand shook so that I could not hold an electric torch. I who had never been sensitive to cold was about to die of cold. What a strange effect thirst can have!

Somewhere, tired of carrying it in the sun, I had let my waterproof drop. Now the wind was growing bitter and I was learning that in the desert there is no place of refuge. The desert is as smooth as marble. By day it throws no shadow; by night it hands you over naked to the wind. Not a tree, not a hedge, not a rock behind which I could seek shelter.

The wind was charging me like a troop of cavalry across open country. I turned and twisted to escape it: I lay down, stood up, lay down again, and still I was exposed to its freezing lash. I had no strength to run from the assassin and under the sabrestroke I tumbled to my knees, my head between my hands.

A little later I pieced these bits together and remembered that I had struggled to my feet and had started to walk on, shivering as I went. I had started forward wondering where I was and then I had heard Prévot. His shouting had jolted me into consciousness.

I went back towards him, still trembling from head to foot—quivering with the attack of hiccups that was convulsing my whole body. To myself I said: "It isn't the cold. It's something else. It's the end." The simple fact was that I hadn't enough water in me. I had tramped too far yesterday and the day before when I was off by myself, and I was dehydrated.

The thought of dying of the cold hurt me. I preferred the phantoms of my mind, the cross, the trees, the lamps. At least they would have killed me by enchantment. But to be whipped to death like a slave! . . .

Confound it! Down on my knees again! We had with us a little store of medicines—a hundred grammes of ninety percent alcohol, the same of pure ether, and a small bottle of iodine. I tried to swallow a little of the ether: it was like swallowing a knife. Then I tried the alcohol: it contracted my gullet. I dug a pit in the sand, lay down in it, and flung handfuls of sand over me until all but my face was buried in it.

Prévot was able to collect a few twigs, and he lit a fire which soon burnt itself out. He wouldn't bury himself in the sand, but preferred to stamp round and round in a circle. That was foolish.

My throat stayed shut, and though I knew that was a bad sign, I felt better. I felt calm. I felt a peace that was beyond all hope. Once more, despite myself, I was journeying, trussed up on the deck of my slave-ship under the stars. It seemed to me that I was perhaps not in such a bad pass after all.

So long as I lay absolutely motionless, I no longer felt the cold. This allowed me to forget my body buried in the sand. I said to myself that I would not budge an inch, and would therefore never suffer again. As a matter of fact, we really suffer very little. Back of all these torments there is the orchestration of fatigue or of delirium, and we live on in a kind of picture-book, a slightly cruel fairy-tale.

A little while ago the wind had been after me with whip and spur, and I was running in circles like a frightened fox. After that came a time when I couldn't breathe. A great knee was crushing in my chest. A knee. I was writhing in vain to free myself from the weight of the angel who had overthrown me. There had not been a moment when I was alone in this desert. But now I have ceased to believe in my surroundings; I have withdrawn into myself, have shut my eyes, have not so much as batted an eyelid. I have the feeling that this torrent of visions is sweeping me away to a tranquil dream: so rivers cease their turbulence in the embrace of the sea.

Farewell, eyes that I loved! Do not blame me if the human body cannot go three days without water. I should never have believed that man was so truly the prisoner of the springs and freshets. I had no notion that our self-sufficiency was so circumscribed. We take it for granted that a man is able to stride straight out into the world. We believe that man is free. We never see the cord that binds him to wells and fountains, that umbilical cord by which he is tied to the womb of the world. Let man take but one step too many . . . and the cord snaps.

Apart from your suffering, I have no regrets. All in all, it has been a good life. If I got free of this I should start right in again. A man cannot live a decent life in cities, and I need to feel myself live. I am not thinking of aviation. The airplane is a means, not an end. One doesn't risk one's life for a plane any more than a farmer ploughs for the sake of the plough. But the airplane is a means of getting away from towns and their bookkeeping and coming to grips with reality.

Flying is a man's job and its worries are a man's worries. A pilot's business is with the wind, with the stars, with night, with sand, with the sea. He strives to outwit the forces of nature. He stares in expectancy for the coming of dawn the way a gardener awaits the coming of spring. He looks forward to port as to a promised land, and truth for him is what lives in the stars.

I have nothing to complain of. For three days I have tramped the desert, have known the pangs of thirst, have followed false scents in the sand, have pinned my faith on the dew. I have struggled to rejoin my kind, whose very existence on earth I had forgotten. These are the cares of men alive in every fibre, and I cannot help thinking them more important than the fretful choosing of a night-club in which to spend the evening. Compare the one life with the other, and all things considered this is luxury! I have no regrets. I have gambled and lost. It was all in the day's work. At least I have had the unforgettable taste of the sea on my lips.

I am not talking about living dangerously. Such words are meaningless to me. The toreador does not stir me to enthusiasm. It is not danger I love. I know what I love. It is life.

The sky seemed to me faintly bright. I drew up one arm through the sand. There was a bit of the torn parachute within reach, and I ran my hand over it. It was bone dry. Let's see. Dew falls at dawn. Here was dawn risen and no moisture on the cloth. My mind was befuddled and I heard myself say: "There is a dry heart here, a dry heart that cannot know the relief of tears."

I scrambled to my feet. "We're off, Prévot," I said. "Our throats are still open. Get along, man!"

The wind that shrivels up a man in nineteen hours was now blowing out of the west. My gullet was not yet shut, but it was hard and painful and I could feel that there was a rasp in it. Soon that cough would begin that I had been told about and was now expecting. My tongue was becoming a nuisance. But most serious of all, I was beginning to see shining spots before my eyes. When those spots changed into flames, I should simply lie down.

The first morning hours were cool and we took advantage of them to get on at a good pace. We knew that once the sun was high there would be no more walking for us. We no longer had the right to sweat. Certainly not to stop and catch our breath. This coolness was merely the coolness of low humidity. The prevailing wind was coming from the desert, and under its soft and treacherous caress the blood was being dried out of us.

Our first day's nourishment had been a few grapes. In the next three days each of us ate half an orange and a bit of cake. If we had had anything left now, we couldn't have eaten it because we had no saliva with which to masticate it. But I had stopped being hungry. Thirsty I was, yes, and it seemed to me that I was suffering less from thirst itself than from the effects of thirst. Gullet hard. Tongue like plaster-of-Paris. A rasping in the throat. A horrible taste in the mouth.

All these sensations were new to me, and though I believed water could rid me of them, nothing in my memory associated them with water. Thirst had become more and more a disease and less and less a craving. I began to realize that the thought of water and fruit was now less agonizing than it had been. I was forgetting the radiance of the orange, just as I was forgetting the eyes under the hat-brim. Perhaps I was forgetting everything.

We had sat down after all, but it could not be for long. Nevertheless, it was impossible to go five hundred yards without our legs giving way. To stretch out on the sand would be marvelous—but it could not be.

The landscape had begun to change. Rocky places grew rarer and the sand was now firm beneath our feet. A mile ahead stood dunes and on those dunes we could see a scrubby vegetation. At least this sand was preferable to the steely surface over which we had been trudging. This was the golden desert. This might have been the Sahara. It was in a sense my country.

Two hundred yards had now become our limit, but we had determined to carry on until we reached the vegetation. Better than that we could not hope to do. A week later, when we went back over our traces in a car to have a look at the *Simoon*, I measured this last lap and found that it was just short of fifty miles. All told we had done one hundred and twenty-four miles.

The previous day I had tramped without hope. Today the word "hope" had grown meaningless. Today we were tramping simply because we were tramping. Probably oxen work for the same reason.

Yesterday I had dreamed of a paradise of orange-trees. Today I would not give a button for paradise; I did not believe oranges existed. When I thought about myself I found in me nothing but a heart squeezed dry. I was tottering but emotionless. I felt no distress whatever, and in a way I regretted it: misery would have seemed to me as sweet as water. I might then have felt sorry for myself and commiserated with myself as with a friend. But I had not a friend left on earth.

Later, when we were rescued, seeing our burnt-out eyes men thought we must have called aloud and wept and suffered. But cries of despair, misery, sobbing grief are a kind of wealth, and we possessed no wealth. When a young girl is disappointed in love she weeps and knows sorrow. Sorrow is one of the vibrations that prove the fact of living. I felt no sorrow. I was the desert. I could no longer bring up a little saliva; neither could I any longer summon those moving visions towards which I should have loved to stretch forth arms. The sun had dried up the springs of tears in me.

And yet, what was that? A ripple of hope went through me like a faint breeze over a lake. What was this sign that had awakened my instinct before knocking on the door of my consciousness? Nothing had changed, and yet everything was changed. This sheet of sand, these low hummocks and sparse tufts of verdure that had been a landscape, were now become a stage setting. Thus far the stage was empty, but the scene was set. I looked at Prévot. The same astonishing thing had happened to him as to me, but he was as far from guessing its significance as I was.

I swear to you that something is about to happen. I swear that life has sprung in this desert. I swear that this emptiness, this stillness, has suddenly become more stirring than a tumult on a public square.

"Prévot! Footprints! We are saved!"

We had wandered from the trail of the human species; we had cast ourselves forth from the tribe; we had found ourselves alone on earth and forgotten by the universal migration; and here, imprinted in the sand, were the divine and naked feet of man!

"Look, Prévot here two men stood together and then separated."

"Here a camel knelt."

"Here . . ."

But it was not true that we were already saved. It was not enough to squat down and wait. Before long we should be past saving. Once the cough has begun, the progress made by thirst is swift.

Still, I believed in that caravan swaying somewhere in the desert, heavy with its cargo of treasure.

We went on. Suddenly I heard a cock crow. I remembered what Guillaumet had told me: "Towards the end I heard cocks crowing in the Andes. And I heard the railway train." The instant the cock crowed I thought of Guillaumet and I said to myself: "First it was my eyes that played tricks on me. I suppose this is another of the effects of thirst. Probably my ears have merely held out longer than my eyes." But Prévot grabbed my arm:

"Did you hear that?"

"What?"

"The cock."

"Why . . . why, yes, I did."

To myself I said: "Fool! Get it through your head! This means life!"

I had one last hallucination—three dogs chasing one another. Prévot looked, but could not see them. However, both of us waved our arms at a Bedouin. Both of us shouted with all the breath in our bodies, and laughed for happiness.

But our voices could not carry thirty yards. The Bedouin on his slow-moving camel had come into view from behind a dune and now he was moving slowly out of sight. The man was probably the only Arab in this desert, sent by a demon to materialize and vanish before the eyes of us who could not run.

We saw in profile on the dune another Arab. We shouted, but our shouts were whispers. We waved our arms and it seemed to us that they must fill the sky with monstrous signals. Still the Bedouin stared with averted face away from us.

At last, slowly, slowly he began a right angle turn in our direction. At the very second when he came face to face with us, I thought, the curtain would come down. At the very second when his eyes met ours, thirst would vanish and by this man would death and the mirages be wiped out. Let this man but make a quarter-turn left and the world is changed. Let him but bring his torso round, but sweep the scene with a glance, and like a god he can create life.

The miracle had come to pass. He was walking towards us over the sand like a god over the waves.

The Arab looked at us without a word. He placed his hands upon our shoulders and we obeyed him: we stretched out upon the sand. Race, language, religion were forgotten. There was only this humble nomad with the hands of an archangel on our shoulders.

Face to the sand, we waited. And when the water came, we drank like calves with our faces in the basin, and with a greediness which alarmed the Bedouin so that from time to time he pulled us back. But as soon as his hand fell away from us we plunged our faces anew into the water.

· Water, thou hast no taste, no color, no odor; canst not be defined, art relished while ever mysterious. Not necessary to life, but rather life itself, thou fillest us with a gratification that exceeds the delight of the senses. By thy might, there return into us treasures that we had abandoned. By thy grace, there are released in us all the dried-up runnels of our heart. Of the riches that exist in the world, thou art the rarest and also the most delicate—thou so pure within the bowels of the earth! A man may die of thirst lying beside a magnesian spring. He may die within reach of a salt lake. He may die though he hold in his hand a jug of dew, if it be inhabited by evil salts. For thou, water, art a proud divinity, allowing no alteration, no foreignness in thy being. And the joy that thou spreadest is an infinitely simple joy.

You, Bedouin of Libya who saved our lives, though you will dwell for ever in my memory yet I shall never be able to recapture your features. You are Humanity and your face comes into my mind simply as man incarnate. You, our beloved fellowman, did not know who we might be, and yet you recognized us without fail. And I, in my turn, shall recognize you in the faces of all mankind. You came towards me in an aureole of charity and magnanimity bearing the gift of water. All my friends and all my enemies marched towards me in your person. It did not seem to me that you were rescuing me: rather did it seem that you were forgiving me. And I felt I had no enemy left in all the world.

This is the end of my story. Lifted on to a camel, we went on for three hours. Then, broken with weariness, we asked to be set down at a camp while the cameleers went on ahead for help. Towards six in the evening a car manned by armed Bedouins came to fetch us. A half hour later we were set down at the house of a Swiss engineer named Raccaud who was operating a soda factory beside saline deposits in the desert. He was unforgettably kind to us. By midnight we were in Cairo.

I awoke between white sheets. Through the curtains came the rays of a sun that was no longer an enemy. I spread butter and honey on my bread. I smiled. I recaptured the savor of my childhood and all its marvels. And I read and re-read the telegram from those dearest to me in all the world whose three words had shattered me:

"So terribly happy!"

from The Perfect Storm
by Sebastian Junger

In his best-selling book, The Perfect Storm, *Sebastian Junger (born 1962) followed the crew of a fishing boat that ran into a hurricane in the North Atlantic. His narrative included another, equally riveting story: Team members of a rescue helicopter found their craft running out of fuel as they raced back to base in the storm.*

For the next twenty minutes Ruvola keeps the helicopter in a hover over the sailboat while the crew peers out the jump door, discussing what to do. They finally agree that the boat looks pretty good in the water—she's riding high, relatively stable—and that any kind of rescue attempt will put Tomizawa in more danger than he is already in. He should stay with his boat. *We're out of our league, boys,* Ruvola finally says over the intercom. *We're not going to do this.* Ruvola gets the C-130 pilot on the radio and tells him their decision, and the C-130 pilot relays it to the sailboat. Tomizawa, desperate, radios back that they don't have to deploy their swimmers at all— just swing the basket over and he'll rescue himself *No, that's not the problem,* Buschor answers. *We don't mind going in the water; we just don't think a rescue is possible.*

Ruvola backs away and the tanker plane drops two life rafts connected by eight hundred feet of line, in case Tomizawa's boat starts to founder, and then the two aircraft head back to base. (Tomizawa was eventually picked up by a Romanian freighter.) Ten minutes into the return flight Ruvola lines up on the tanker for the third time, hits the drogue immediately and takes on 1,560 pounds of fuel. They'll need one more refueling in order to make shore. Spillane settles into the portside spotter's seat and stares down at the ocean a thousand feet below. If Mioli hadn't spoken up, he and Rick Smith might be swimming around down there, trying to get back into the rescue basket. They'd have died. In conditions like these, so much water gets loaded into the air that swimmers drown simply trying to breathe.

Months later, after the Air National Guard has put the pieces together, it will determine that gaps had developed in the web of resources designed to support an increased-risk mission over water. At any given moment *someone* had the necessary information for keeping Ruvola's helicopter airborne, but that information wasn't disseminated correctly during the last hour of Ruvola's flight. Several times a day, mission or no mission, McGuire Air Force Base in New Jersey faxes weather bulletins to Suffolk Airbase for their use in route planning. If Suffolk is planning a difficult mission, they might also call McGuire for a verbal update on flight routes, satellite information, etc. Once the mission is underway, one person—usually the tanker pilot—is responsible for obtaining and relaying weather information to all the pilots involved in the rescue. If he needs more information, he calls Suffolk and tells them to get it; without the call, Suffolk doesn't actively pursue weather information. They are, in the words of the accident investigators, "reactive" rather than "proactive" in carrying out their duties.

In Ruvola's case, McGuire Air Force Base has real-time satellite information showing a massive rain band developing off Long Island between 7:30 and 8:00 p.m.—just as he is starting back for Suffolk. Suffolk never calls McGuire for an update, though, because the tanker pilot never asks for one; and McGuire never volunteers the information because they don't know there is an Air Guard helicopter out there in the first place. Were Suffolk to call McGuire for an update, they'd learn that Ruvola's route is blocked by severe weather, but that he can avoid it by flying fifteen minutes to westward. As it is, the tanker pilot calls Suffolk for a weather update and gets a report of an 8,000-foot ceiling, fifteen-mile visibility, and low-level wind shear. He passes that information on to Ruvola, who—having left the worst of the storm behind him—reasonably assumes that conditions will only improve as he flies westward. All he has to do is refuel before hitting the wind shear that is being recorded around the air field. Ruvola—they all—are wrong.

The rain band is a swath of clouds fifty miles wide, eighty miles long, and 10,000 feet thick. It is getting dragged into the low across the northwest quadrant of the storm; winds are seventy-five knots and the visibility is zero. Satellite imagery shows the rain band swinging across Ruvola's flight path like a door slamming shut. At 7:55, Ruvola radios the tanker pilot to confirm a fourth refueling, and the pilot rogers it. The refueling is scheduled for five minutes later, at precisely eight o'clock. At 7:56, turbulence picks up a little, and at 7:58 it reaches moderate levels. *Let's get this thing done*, Ruvola radios the tanker pilot. At 7:59 he pulls the probe release, extends it forward, and moves into position for contact. And then it hits.

Headwinds along the leading edge of the rain band are so strong that it feels as if the helicopter has been blown to a stop. Ruvola has no idea what he's run into; all he knows is that he can barely control the aircraft. Flying has become as much a question of physical strength as of finesse; he grips the collective with one hand, the joystick with the other, and leans forward to peer through the rain rattling off the windscreen. Flight manuals bounce around the cockpit and his copilot starts throwing up in the seat next to him. Ruvola lines up on the tanker and tries to hit the drogue, but the aircraft are moving around so wildly that it's like throwing darts down a gun barrel; hitting the target is pure dumb luck. In technical terms, Ruvola's aircraft is doing things "without inputs from the controls"; in human terms, it's getting batted around the sky. Ruvola tries as low as three hundred feet—"along the ragged edges of the clouds," as he says—and as high as 4,500 feet, but he can't find clean air. The visibility is so bad that even with night-vision goggles on, he can barely make out the wing lights of the tanker plane in front of him. And they are right—*right*—on top of it; several times they overshoot the drogue and Spillane thinks they are going to take the plane's rudder off.

Ruvola has made twenty or thirty attempts on the drogue—a monstrous feat of concentration—when the tanker pilot radios that he has to shut down his number one engine. The oil pressure gauge is fluctuating wildly and they are risking a burnout. The pilot starts in on the shutdown procedure, and suddenly the left-hand fuel hose retracts; shutting off the engine has disrupted the air flow around the wing, and the reel-in mechanism has mistaken that for too much slack. It performs what is known as an "uncommanded retraction." The pilot finishes shutting down the engine, brings Ruvola back in, and then reextends the hose. Ruvola lines up on it and immediately sees that something is wrong. The drogue is shaped like a small parachute, and ordinarily it fills with air and holds the hose steady; now it is just convulsing behind the tanker plane. It has been destroyed by forty-five minutes of desperate refueling attempts.

Ruvola tells the tanker pilot that the left-hand drogue is shot and that they have to switch over to the other side. In these conditions refueling from the right-hand drogue is a nightmarish, white-knuckle business because the helicopter probe also extends from the right-hand side of the cockpit, so the pilot has to come even tighter into the fuselage of the tanker to make contact. Ruvola makes a run at the right-hand drogue, misses, comes in again, and misses again. The usual technique is to watch the tanker's wing flaps and anticipate where the drogue's going to go, but the visibility is so low that Ruvola can't even see that far; he can barely see past the nose of his own helicopter. Ruvola makes a couple more runs at the drogue, and on his last attempt he comes in too fast, overshoots the wing, and by the time he's realigned himself the tanker has disappeared. They've lost an entire C-130 in the clouds. They are at 4,000 feet in zero visibility with roughly twenty minutes of fuel left; after that they will just fall out of the sky. Ruvola can either keep trying to hit the drogue, or he can try to make it down to sea level while they still have fuel.

We're going to set up for a planned ditching, he tells his crew. *We're going to ditch while we still can.* And then Dave Ruvola drops the nose of the helicopter and starts racing his fuel gauge down to the sea.

John Spillane, watching silently from the spotter's seat, is sure he's just heard his death sentence. "Throughout my career I've always managed—just barely—to keep things in control," says Spillane. "But now, suddenly, the risk is becoming totally uncontrollable. We can't get fuel, we're going to end up in that roaring ocean, and we're not gonna be in control anymore. And I know the chances of being rescued are practically zero. I've been on a lot of rescue missions, and I know they can hardly even *find* someone in these conditions, let alone recover them. We're some of the best in the business—best equipped, best trained. We couldn't do a rescue a little while earlier, and now we're in the same situation. It looks real bleak. It's not going to happen."

While Ruvola is flying blindly downward through the clouds, copilot Buschor issues a mayday on an Air National Guard emergency frequency and then contacts the *Tamaroa,* fifteen miles to the northeast. He tells them they are out of fuel and about to set up for a planned ditching. Captain Brudnicki orders the *Tam's* searchlights turned up into the sky so the helicopter can give them a bearing, but Buschor says he can't see a thing. *Okay, just start heading towards us,* the radio dispatcher on the *Tam* says. *We don't have time, we're going down right now,* Buschor replies. Jim McDougall, handling the radios at the ODC in Suffolk, receives—simultaneously—the ditching alert and a phone call from Spillane's wife, who wants to know where her husband is. She'd had no idea there was a problem and just happened to call at the wrong moment; McDougall is so panicked by the timing that he hangs up on her. At 9:08, a dispatcher at Coast Guard headquarters in Boston takes a call that an Air National Guard helicopter is going down and scrawls frantically in the incident log: *"Helo [helicopter] & 130 enroute Suffolk. Can't refuel helo due visibility. May have to ditch. Stay airborne how long? 20-25 min. LAUNCH!"* He then notifies Cape Cod Air Base, where Karen Stimpson is chatting with one of her rescue crews. The five airmen get up without a word, file into the bathroom, and then report for duty out on the tarmac.

Ruvola finally breaks out of the clouds at 9:28, only two hundred feet above the ocean. He goes into a hover and immediately calls for the ditching checklist, which prepares the crew to abandon the aircraft. They have practiced this dozens of times in training, but things are happening so fast that the routines start to fall apart. Jim Mioli has trouble seeing in the dim cabin lighting used with night-vision gear, so he can't locate the handle of the nine-man life raft. By the time he finds it, he doesn't have time to put on his Mustang survival suit. Ruvola calls three times for Mioli to read him the ditching checklist, but Mioli is too busy to answer him, so Ruvola has to go through it by memory. One of the most important things on the list is for the pilot to reach down and eject his door, but Ruvola is working too hard to remove his hands from the controls. In military terminology he has become "task-saturated," and the door stays on.

While Ruvola is trying to hold the aircraft in a hover, the PJs scramble to put together the survival gear. Spillane slings a canteen over his shoulder and clips a one-man life raft to the strap. Jim Mioli, who finally manages to extract the nine-man raft, pushes it to the edge of the jump door and waits for the order to deploy. Rick Smith, draped in survival gear, squats at the edge of the other jump door and looks over the side. Below is an ocean so ravaged by wind that they can't even tell the difference between the waves and the troughs; for all they know they are jumping three hundred feet. As horrible as that is, though, the idea of staying where they are is even worse. The helicopter is going to drop into the ocean at any moment, and no one on the crew wants to be anywhere nearby when it does.

Only Dave Ruvola will stay on board; as pilot, it is his job to make sure the aircraft doesn't fall on the rest of his crew. The chances of his escaping with his door still in place are negligible, but that is beside the point. The ditching checklist calls for a certain procedure, a procedure that insures the survival of the greatest number of crew. That Mioli neglects to put on his survival suit is also, in some ways, suicidal, but he has no choice. His duty is to oversee a safe bailout, and if he stops to put his survival suit on, the nine-man raft won't be ready for deployment. He jumps without his suit.

At 9:30, the number one engine flames out; Spillane can hear the turbine wind down. They've been in a low hover for less than a minute. Ruvola calls out on the intercom: *The number one's out! Bail out! Bail out!* The number two is running on fumes; in theory, they should flame out at the same time. This is it. They are going down.

Mioli shoves the life raft out the right-hand door and watches it fall, in his words, "into the abyss." They are so high up that he doesn't even see it hit the water, and he can't bring himself to jump in after it. Without telling anyone, he decides to take his chances in the heli-copter. Ditching protocol calls for copilot Buschor to remain on board as well, but Ruvola orders him out because he decides Buschor's chances of survival will be higher if he jumps. Buschor pulls his door-release lever but the door doesn't pop off the fuselage, so he just holds it open with one hand and steps out onto the footboard. He looks back at the radar altimeter, which is fluctuating between ten feet and eighty, and realizes that the timing of his jump will mean the difference between life and death. Ruvola repeats his order to bail out, and Buschor unplugs the intercom wires from his flight helmet and flips his night-vision goggles down. Now he can watch the waves roll under-neath him in the dim green light of enhanced vision. He spots a huge crest, takes a breath, and jumps.

Spillane, meanwhile, is grabbing some last-minute gear. "I wasn't terrified, I was scared," he says. "Forty minutes before I'd been more scared, thinking about the possibilities, but at the end I was totally committed. The pilot had made the decision to ditch, and it was a great decision. How many pilots might have just used up the last twenty minutes of fuel trying to hit the drogue? Then you fall out of the sky and everyone would die."

The helicopter is strangely quiet without the number one engine. The ocean below them, in the words of another pilot, looks like a lunar landscape, cratered and gouged and deformed by wind. Spillane spots Rick Smith at the starboard door, poised to jump, and moves towards him. "I'm convinced he was sizing up the waves," Spillane says. "I wanted desperately to stick together with him. I just had time to sit down, put my arm around his shoulders, and he went. We didn't have time to say anything—you want to say goodbye, you want to do a lot of things, but there's no time for that. Rick went, and a split second later, I did."

According to people who have survived long falls, the acceleration of gravity is so heart-stoppingly fast that it's more like getting shot downward out of a cannon. A body accelerates roughly twenty miles an hour for every second it's in the air; after one second it's falling twenty miles an hour; after two seconds, forty miles an hour, and so on, up to a hundred and thirty. At that point the wind resistance is equal to the force of gravity, and the body is said to have reached terminal velocity. Spillane falls probably sixty or seventy feet, two and a half seconds of acceleration. He plunges through darkness without any idea where the water is or when he is going to hit. He has a dim memory of letting go of his one-man raft, and of his body losing position, and he thinks: My God, what a long way down. And then everything goes blank.

John Spillane has the sort of handsome, regular features that one might expect in a Hollywood actor playing a pararescueman—playing John Spillane, in fact. His eyes are stone-blue, without a trace of hardness or indifference, his hair is short and touched with grey. He comes across as friendly, unguarded, and completely sure of himself. He has a quick smile and an offhand way of talking that seems to progress from detail to detail, angle to angle, until there's nothing more to say on a topic. His humor is delivered casually, almost as an afterthought, and seems to surprise even himself. He's of average height, average build, and once ran forty miles for the hell of it. He seems to be a man who has long since lost the need to prove things to anyone.

Spillane grew up in New York City and joined the Air Force at seventeen. He served as a teletype maintenance repairman for four years, joined the Air National Guard, "guard-bummed" around the world for a year, and then signed up for PJ school. After several years of active duty he scaled back his commitment to the National Guard, went through the police academy, and became a scuba diver for the New

York City Police Department. For three years he pulled bodies out of submerged cars and mucked guns out of the East River, and finally decided to go back to school before his G.I. Bill ran out. He got a degree in geology—"I wanted to go stomp mountaintops for a while"—but he fell in love instead and ended up moving out to Suffolk to work full-time for the Guard. That was in 1989. He was thirty-two, one of the most widely experienced PJs in the country.

When John Spillane hits the Atlantic Ocean he is going about fifty miles an hour. Water is the only element that offers more resistance the harder you hit it, and at fifty miles an hour it might as well be concrete. Spillane fractures three bones in his right arm, one bone in his left leg, four ribs in his chest, ruptures a kidney, and bruises his pancreas. The flippers, the one-man raft, and the canteen all are torn off his body. Only the mask, which he wore backward with the strap in his mouth, stays on as it is supposed to. Spillane doesn't remember the moment of impact, and he doesn't remember the moment he first realized he was in the water. His memory goes from falling to swimming, with nothing in between. When he understands that he is swimming, that is *all* he understands—he doesn't know who he is, why he is there or how he got there. He has no history and no future; he is just a consciousness at night in the middle of the sea.

When Spillane treats injured seamen offshore, one of the first things he evaluates is their degree of consciousness. The highest level, known as "alert and oriented times four," describes almost everyone in an everyday situation. They know who they are, where they are, what time it is, and what's just happened. If someone suffers a blow to the head, the first thing they lose is recent events—"alert and oriented times three"—and the last thing they lose is their identity. A person who has lost all four levels of consciousness, right down to their identity, is said to be "alert and oriented times zero." When John Spillane wakes up in the water, he is alert and oriented times zero. His understanding of the world is reduced to the fact that he exists, nothing more. Almost simultaneously, he understands that he is in excruciating pain. For a long time, that is all he knows. Until he sees the life raft.

Spillane may be alert and oriented times zero, but he knows to swim for a life raft when he sees one. It has been pushed out by Jim Mioli, the flight engineer, and has inflated automatically when it hits the water. Now it is scudding along on the wave crests, the sea anchors barely holding it down in the seventy-knot wind. "I lined up on it, intercepted it, and hung off the side," says Spillane. "I knew I was in the ocean, in a desperate situation, and I was hurt. I didn't know anything else. It was while I was hanging onto the raft that it all started coming back to me. We were on a mission. We ran out of fuel. I bailed out. I'm not alone."

While Spillane is hanging off the raft, a gust of wind catches it and flips it over. One moment Spillane is in the water trying to figure out who he is, the next moment he is high and dry. Instantly he feels better. He is lying on the wobbly nylon floor, evaluating the stabbing pain in his chest—he thinks he's punctured his lungs—when he hears people shouting in the distance. He kneels and points his diver's light in their direction, and just as he is wondering how to help them— whoever they are—the storm gods flip the raft over again. Spillane is dumped back into the sea. He clings to the safety line, gasping and throwing up sea water, and almost immediately the wind flips the raft over a third time. He has now gone one-and-a-half revolutions. Spillane is back inside, lying spread-eagle on the floor, when the raft is flipped a fourth and final time. Spillane is tossed back into the water, this time clinging to a rubberized nylon bag that later turns out to contain half a dozen wool blankets. It floats, and Spillane hangs off it and watches the raft go cartwheeling off across the wave crests. He is left alone and dying on the sea.

"After I lost contact with the raft I was by myself and I realized my *only* chance of survival was to make it until the storm subsided," he says. "There was no way they could pick us up, I'd just ditched a perfectly good helicopter and I knew our guys would be the ones to come out and get us if they could, but they couldn't. They couldn't refuel. So I'm contemplating this and I know I cannot make it through the storm. They might have somebody on-scene when light breaks, but I'm not going to make it that long. I'm dying inside."

For the first time since the ordeal began, Spillane has the time to contemplate his own death. He isn't panicked so much as saddened by the idea. His wife is five months pregnant with their first child, and he's been home very little recently—he was in paramedic school, and in training for the New York City marathon. He wishes that he'd spent more time at home. He wishes—incredibly—that he'd cut the grass one more time before winter. He wishes there was someone who could tell his wife and family what happened in the end. It bothers him that Dave Ruvola probably died taking the helicopter in. It bothers him they're all going to die for lack of five hundred pounds of jet fuel. The shame of it all, he thinks; we have this eight-million-dollar helicopter, nothing's wrong with it, nobody's shooting at us, we're just out of fuel.

Spillane has regained his full senses by this point, and the circumstances he finds himself in are nightmarish beyond words. It is so dark that he can't see his hand in front of his face, the waves just rumble down on him out of nowhere and bury him for a minute at a time. The wind is so strong it doesn't blow the water so much as fling it; there is no way to keep it out of his stomach. Every few minutes he has to retch it back up. Spillane has lost his one-man life raft, his ribs are broken, and every breath feels like he is being run through with a hot fire poker. He is crying out in pain and dawn isn't for another eight hours.

After an hour of making his farewells and trying to keep the water out of his stomach, Spillane spots two strobes in the distance. The Mustang suits all have strobe lights on them, and it is the first real evidence he has that someone else has survived the ditching. Spillane's immediate reaction is to swim toward them, but he stops himself. There is no way he is going to live out the night, he knows, so he might as well just die on his own. That way he won't inflict his suffering on anyone else. "I didn't want them to see me go," he says. "I didn't want them to see me in pain. It's the same with marathons—don't talk to me, let me just suffer through this by myself. What finally drove me to them was survival training. It emphasizes strength in numbers, and I know that if I'm with them, I'll try harder not to die. But I couldn't let them see me in pain, I told myself. I couldn't let them down."

Believing that their chances will be slightly less negligible in a group, Spillane slowly makes his way toward the lights. He is buoyed up by his life vest and wetsuit and swimming with his broken arm stretched out in front of him, gripping the blanket bag. It takes a long time and the effort exhausts him, but he can see the lights slowly getting closer. They disappear in the wave troughs, appear on the crests, and then disappear again. Finally, after a couple of hours of swimming, he gets close enough to shout and then to make out their faces. It is Dave Ruvola and Jim Mioli, roped together with parachute cord. Ruvola seems fine, but Mioli is nearly incoherent with hypothermia. He only has his Nomex flight suit on, and the chances of him lasting until dawn are even lower than Spillane's.

Ruvola had escaped the helicopter unscathed, but barely. He knew that the rotors would tear him and the helicopter apart if they hit the water at full speed, so he moved the aircraft away from his men, waited for the number two engine to flame out, and then performed what is known as a hovering auto-rotation. As the helicopter fell, its dead rotors started to spin, and Ruvola used that energy to slow the aircraft down. Like downshifting a car on a hill, a hovering auto-rotation is a way of dissipating the force of gravity by feeding it back through the engine. By the time the helicopter hit the water it had slowed to a manageable speed, and all the torque had been bled out of the rotors; they just smacked the face of an oncoming wave and stopped.

Ruvola found himself in a classic training situation, only it was real life: He had to escape from a flooded helicopter upside-down in complete darkness. He was a former PJ, though, and a marathon swimmer, so being underwater was something he was used to. The first thing he did was reach for his HEEDS bottle, a three-minute air supply strapped to his left leg, but it had been ripped loose during the ditching; all he had was the air in his lungs. He reached up, pulled the quick-release on his safety belt, and it was then that he realized he'd never kicked the exit door out. He was supposed to do that so it wouldn't get jammed shut on impact, trapping him inside. He found the door handle, turned it, and pushed.

To his amazement, the door fell open; Ruvola kicked his way out from under the fuselage, tripped the CO_2 cartridge on his life vest, and shot ten or fifteen feet to the surface. He popped up into a world of shrieking darkness and landsliding seas. At one point the crest of a wave drove him so far under the surface that the pressure change damaged his inner ear. Ruvola started yelling for the other crew members, and a few minutes later flight engineer Mioli—who'd also managed to escape the sinking helicopter—answered him in the darkness. They started swimming toward each other, and after five or ten minutes Ruvola got close enough to grab Mioli by his survival vest. He took the hood off his survival suit, put it on Mioli's head, and then tied their two bodies together with parachute cord.

They've been in the water for a couple of hours when Spillane finally struggles up, face locked up with pain. The first thing Ruvola sees is a glint of light on a face mask, and he thinks that maybe it's a Navy SEAL who has airlocked out of a U.S. submarine and is coming to save them. It isn't. Spillane swims up, grabs a strap on Ruvola's flotation vest, and clamps his other arm around the blanket bag. What's that? Ruvola screams. I don't know, I'll open it tomorrow! Spillane yells back. Open it now! Ruvola answers. Spillane is in too much pain to argue about it, so he opens the bag and watches several dark shapes—the blankets— go snapping off downwind.

He tosses the bag aside and settles down to face the next few hours as best he can.

One can tell by the very handwriting in the District One incident log that the dispatcher—in this case a Coast Guardsman named Gill— can't quite believe what he's writing down. The words are large and sloppy and salted with exclamation points. At one point he jots down, a propos of nothing: *"They're not alone out there,"* as if to reassure himself that things will turn out all right. That entry comes at 9:30, seconds after Buschor calls in the first engine loss. Five minutes later Gill writes down: *"39-51 North, 72-00 West, Ditching here, 5 POB [people on board]."* Seven minutes after that the tanker plane—which will circle the area until their fuel runs low—reports hearing an EPIRB signal for fifteen seconds, then nothing. From Gill's notes:

> *9:30—Tamaroa in area, launched H-65*
> *9:48—Cape Cod 60!*
> *9:53— CAA [Commander of Atlantic Area]/brfd—ANYTHING YOU WANT—NAVY SHIP WOULD BE GREAT—WILL LOOK.*

Within minutes of the ditching, rescue assets from Florida to Massachusetts are being readied for deployment. The response is massive and nearly instantaneous. At 9:48, thirteen minutes into it, Air Station Cape Cod launches a Falcon jet and an H-3 helicopter. Half an hour later a Navy P-3 jet at Brunswick Naval Air Station is requested and readied. The P-3 is infrared-equipped to detect heat-emitting objects, like people. The *Tamaroa* has diverted before the helicopter has even gone down. At 10:23, Boston requests a second Coast Guard cutter, the *Spencer*. They even consider diverting an aircraft carrier.

The survivors are drifting fast in mountainous seas and the chances of spotting them are terrible. Helicopters will have minimal time on-scene because they can't refuel, it's unlikely conditions would permit a hoist rescue anyway, and there's no way to determine if the guardsmen's radios are even working. That leaves the *Tamaroa* to do the job, but she wasn't even able to save the *Satori* crew, during less severe conditions. The storm is barreling westward, straight toward the ditch point, and wave heights are climbing past anything ever recorded in the area.

If things look bad for Ruvola's crew, they don't look much better for the people trying to rescue them. It's not inconceivable that another helicopter will have to ditch during the rescue effort, or that a Coast Guardsman will get washed off the *Tamaroa*. (For that matter the *Tamaroa* herself, at 205 feet, is not necessarily immune to disaster. One freak wave could roll her over and put eighty men in the water.) Half a dozen aircraft, two ships, and two hundred rescuers are heading for 39 north, 72 west; the more men out there, the higher the chances are of someone else getting into trouble. A succession of disasters could draw the rescue assets of the entire East Coast of the United States out to sea.

A Falcon jet out of Air Station Cape Cod is the first aircraft on-scene. It arrives ninety minutes after the ditching, and the pilot sets up what is known as an expanding-square search. He moves slightly downsea of the last known position—the "splash point"—and starts flying ever-increasing squares until he has covered an area ten miles across. He flies at two hundred feet, just below cloud cover, and estimates the probability of spotting the survivors to be one-in-three. He turns up nothing. Around 11:30 he expands his search to a twenty-mile square and starts all over again, slowly working his way southwest with the direction of drift. The infrared-equipped P-3 is getting ready to launch from Brunswick, and a Coast Guard helicopter is pounding its way southward from Cape Cod.

And then, ten minutes into the second square, he picks up something: a weak signal on 243 megahertz. That's a frequency coded into Air National Guard radios. It means at least one of the airmen is still alive.

The Falcon pilot homes in on the signal and tracks it to a position about twenty miles downsea of the splash point. Whoever it is, they're drifting fast. The pilot comes in low, scanning the sea with night-vision goggles, and finally spots a lone strobe flashing below them in the darkness. It's appearing and disappearing behind the huge swell. Moments later he spots three more strobes half a mile away. All but one of the crew are accounted for. The pilot circles, flashing his lights, and then radios his position in to District One. An H-3 helicopter, equipped with a hoist and rescue swimmer, is only twenty minutes away. The whole ordeal could be over in less than an hour.

The Falcon circles the strobes until the H-3 arrives, and then heads back to base with a rapidly falling fuel gauge. The H-3 is a huge machine, similar to the combat helicopters used in Vietnam, and has spare fuel tanks installed inside the cabin. It can't refuel in midflight, but it can stay airborne for four or five hours. The pilot, Ed DeWitt, tries to establish a forty-foot hover, but wind shear keeps spiking him downward. The ocean is a ragged white expanse in his searchlights and there are no visual reference points to work off of. At one point he turns downwind and almost gets driven into the sea.

DeWitt edges his helicopter to within a hundred yards of the three men and tells his flight engineer to drop the rescue basket. There's no way he's putting his swimmer in the water, but these are experienced rescuemen, and they may be able to extract themselves. It's either that or wait for the storm to calm down. The flight engineer pays out the cable and watches in alarm as the basket is blown straight back toward the tail rotors. It finally reaches the water, swept backward at an angle of forty-five degrees, and DeWitt tries to hold a steady hover long enough for the swimmers to reach the basket. He tries for almost an hour, but the waves are so huge that the basket doesn't spend more than a few seconds on each crest before dropping to the end of its cable. Even if the men could get themselves into the basket, a shear pin in the hoist mechanism is designed to fail with loads over 600 pounds, and three men in waterlogged clothing would definitely push that limit. The entire assembly—cable, basket, everything—would let go into the sea.

DeWitt finally gives up trying to save the airmen and goes back up to a hover at two hundred feet. In the distance he can see the *Tamaroa*, searchlights pointed straight up, plunging through the storm. He vectors her in toward the position of the lone strobe in the distance—Graham Buschor—and then drops a flare by the others and starts back for Suffolk. He's only minutes away from "bingo," the point at which an aircraft doesn't have enough fuel to make it back to shore. He's only minutes away from "bingo," the point at which an aircraft doesn't have enough fuel to make it back to shore.

Two hundred feet below, John Spillane watches his last hope clatter away toward the north. He hadn't expected to get rescued, but still, it's hard to watch. The only benefit he can see is that his family will know for sure that he died. That might spare them weeks of false hope. In the distance, Spillane can see lights rising and failing in the darkness. He assumes it's a Falcon jet looking for the other airmen, but its lights are moving strangely; it's not moving like an aircraft. It's moving like a ship.

● ● ●

The *Tamaroa* has taken four hours to cover the fifteen miles to the splash point; her screws are turning for twelve knots and making three. Commander Brudnicki doesn't know how strong the wind is because it rips the anemometer off the mast, but pilot Ed DeWitt reports that his airspeed indicator hit eighty-seven knots—a hundred miles an hour—while he was in a stationary hover. The *Tamaroa's* course to the downed airmen puts them in a beam sea, which starts to roll the ship through an arc of 110 degrees; at that angle, bulkheads are easier to walk on than floors. In the wheelhouse, Commander Brudnicki is surprised to find himself looking *up* at the crest of the waves, and when he orders full rudder and full bell, it takes thirty or forty seconds to see any effect at all. Later, after stepping off the ship, he says, "I certainly hope that was the high point of my career."

The first airman they spot is Graham Buschor, swimming alone and relatively unencumbered a half mile from the other three. He's in a Mustang survival suit and has a pen-gun flare and the only functional radio beacon of the entire crew. Brudnicki orders the operations officer, Lieutenant Kristopher Furtney, to maneuver the *Tamaroa* upsea of Buschor and then drift down on him. Large objects drift faster than small ones, and if the ship is upwind of Buschor, the waves won't smash him against the hull. The gunner's mate starts firing flares off from cannons on the flying bridge, and a detail of seamen crouch in the bow with throwing ropes, waiting for their chance. They can hardly keep their feet in the wind.

The engines come to a full stop and the *Tamaroa* wallows beam-to in the huge seas. It's a dangerous position to be in; the *Tamaroa* loses her righting arm at seventy-two degrees, and she's already heeling to fifty-five. Drifting down on swimmers is standard rescue procedure, but the seas are so violent that Buschor keeps getting flung out of reach. There are times when he's thirty feet higher than the men trying to rescue him. The crew in the bow can't get a throwing rope anywhere near him, and Brudnicki won't order his rescue swimmer overboard because he's afraid he won't get him back. The men on deck finally realize that if the boat's not going to Buschor, Buschor's going to have to go to it. *SWIM!* they scream over the rail. *SWIM!* Buschor rips off his gloves and hood and starts swimming for his life.

He swims as hard as he can; he swims until his arms give out. He claws his way up to the ship, gets swept around the bow, struggles back within reach of it again, and finally catches hold of a cargo net that the crew have dropped over the side. The net looks like a huge rope ladder and is held by six or seven men at the rail. Buschor twists his hands into the mesh and slowly gets hauled up the hull. One good wave at the wrong moment could take them all out. The deck crewmen land Buschor like a big fish and carry him into the deckhouse. He's dry-heaving seawater and can barely stand; his core temperature has dropped to ninety-four degrees. He's been in the water four hours and twenty-five minutes. Another few hours and he may not have been able to cling to the net.

It's taken half an hour to get one man on board, and they have four more to go, one of whom hasn't even been sighted yet. It's not looking good. Brudnicki is also starting to have misgivings about putting his men on deck. The larger waves are sweeping the bow and completely burying the crew; they keep having to do head counts to make sure no one has been swept overboard. "It was the hardest decision I've ever had to make, to put my people out there and rescue that crew," Brudnicki says. "Because I knew there was a chance I could lose some of my men. If I'd decided not to do the rescue, no one back home would've said a thing—they knew it was almost impossible. But can you really make a conscious decision to say, 'I'm just going to watch those people in the water die?'"

Brudnicki decides to continue the rescue; twenty minutes later he has the *Tamaroa* in a beam sea a hundred yards upwind of the three Guardsmen. Crew members are lighting off flares and aiming search-lights, and the chief quartermaster is on the flying bridge radioing Furtney when to fire the ship's engine. Not only do they have to maneuver the drift, but they have to time the roll of the ship so the gunwale rides down toward the waterline while the men in the water grab for the net. As it is, the gunwales are riding from water level to twenty feet in the air virtually every wave. Spillane is injured, Mioli is incoherent, and Ruvola is helping to support them both. There's no way they'll be able to swim like Buschor.

Spillane watches the ship heaving through the breaking seas and for the life of him can't imagine how they're going to do this. As far as he's concerned, a perfectly likely outcome is for all three of them to drown within sight of the ship because a pickup is impossible. "My muscles were getting rigid, I was in great pain," he says. "The *Tam* pulled up in front of us and turned broadside to the waves and I couldn't believe they did that—they were putting themselves in terrible risk. We could hear them all screaming on the deck and we could see the chemical lights coming at us, tied to the ends of the ropes."

The ropes are difficult to catch, so the deck crew throw the cargo net over the side. Lieutenant Furtney again tries to ease his ship over to the swimmers, but the vessel is 1,600 tons and almost impossible to control. Finally, on the third attempt, they snag the net. Their muscles are cramping with cold and Jim Mioli is about to start a final slide into hypothermia. The men on deck give a terrific heave—they're pulling up 600 pounds deadweight—and at the same time a large wave drops out from underneath the swimmers. They're exhausted and desperate and the net is wrenched out of their hands.

The next thing Spillane knows, he's underwater. He fights his way to the surface just as the boat rolls inward toward them and he grabs the net again. This is it; if he can't do it now, he dies. The deck crew heaves again, and Spillane feels himself getting pulled up the steel hull. He climbs up a little higher, feels hands grabbing him, and the next thing he knows he's being pulled over the gunwale onto the deck. He's in such pain he cannot stand. The men pin him against the bulkhead, cut off his survival suit, and then carry him inside, staggering with the roll of the ship. Spillane can't see Ruvola and Mioli. They haven't managed to get back onto the net.

The waves wash the two men down the hull toward the ship's stern, where the twelve-foot screw is digging out a cauldron of boiling water.

Furtney shuts the engines down and the two men get carried around the stern and then up the port side of the ship. Ruvola catches the net for the second time and gets one hand into the mesh. He clamps the other one around Mioli and screams into his face, You got to do this, Jim! There aren't too many second chances in life! This is gonna take everything you got!

Mioli nods and wraps his hands into the mesh. Ruvola gets a foothold as well as a handhold and grips with all the strength in his cramping muscles. The two men get dragged upward, penduluming in and out with the roll of the ship, until the deck crew at the rail can reach them. They grab Ruvola and Mioli by the hair, the Mustang suit, the combat vest, anything they can get their hands on, and pull them over the steel rail. Like Spillane they're retching seawater and can barely stand. Jim Mioli has been in sixty-degree water for over five hours and is severely hypothermic. His core temperature is 90.4, eight degrees below normal; another couple of hours and he'd be dead.

The two airmen are carried inside, their clothing is cut off, and they're laid in bunks. Spillane is taken to the executive officer's quarters and given an IV and catheter and examined by the ship's paramedic. His blood pressure is 140/90, his pulse is a hundred, and he's running a slight fever. *Eyes PERLA abdomen and chest tenderness, pain to quadricep,* the paramedic radios SAR OPS [Search-and-Rescue Operations] Boston. *Fractured wrist, possibly ribs, suspect internal injury. Taking Tylenol-3 and seasick patch.* Boston relays the information to an Air National Guard flight surgeon, who says he's worried about internal bleeding and tells them to watch the abdomen carefully. If it gets more and more tender to the touch, he's bleeding inside and has to be evacuated by helicopter. Spillane thinks about dangling in a rescue litter over the ocean and says he'd rather not. At daybreak the executive officer comes in to shave and change his clothes, and Spillane apologizes for bleeding and vomiting all over his bed. Hey, whatever it takes, the officer says. He opens the porthole hatch, and Spillane looks out at the howling grey sky and the ravaged ocean. Ah, could you close that? he says. I can't take it.

The crew, unshaven and exhausted after thirty-six hours on deck, are staggering around the ship like drunks. And the mission's far from over: Rick Smith is still out there. He's one of the most highly trained pararescue jumpers in the country, and there's no question in anyone's mind that he's alive. They just have to find him. *PJ wearing black 1/4" wetsuit, went out door with one-man life-raft and spray sheet, two 12-oz. cans of water, mirror, flare kit, granola bar, and whistle,* the Coast Guard dispatcher in Boston records. *Man is in great shape—can last quite a while, five to seven days.*

A total of nine aircraft are slated for the search, including an E2 surveillance plane to coordinate the air traffic on-scene. Jim Dougherty, a PJ who went through training with Smith and Spillane, throws a tin of Skoal chewing tobacco in his gear to give Smith when they find him. *This guy's so good,* Guardsmen are saying, *he's just gonna come through the front door at Suffolk Airbase wondering where the hell we all were.*

from Three Years Among
the Indians and Mexicans
by Thomas James

John Colter was a valuable member of Lewis and Clark's expedition to the Pacific. But as the party headed back to St. Louis, Colter decided to remain in the West as a trapper and a trader. He became one of the first mountain men, and his courage and skill were by all accounts unsurpassed. In 1808, Colter and another trapper blundered into a party of Blackfeet, whose tribe members habitually tortured and killed their captives. Thomas James (1782-1847) was a fellow trapper who heard the story from Colter himself.

When Colter was returning in 1807 with Lewis & Clark, from Oregon, he met a company of hunters ascending the Missouri, by whom he was persuaded to return to the trapping region, to hunt and trap with them. Here he was found by Liza in the following year, whom he assisted in building the Fort at the Big Horn. In one of his many excursions from this post to the Forks of the Missouri, for beaver, he made the wonderful escape adverted to in the last chapter and which I give precisely as he related it to me. His veracity was never questioned among us and his character was that of a true American backwoodsman. He was about thirty-five years of age, five feet ten inches in height and wore an open, ingenious, and pleasing countenance of the Daniel Boone stamp. Nature had formed him, like Boone, for hardy endurance of fatigue, privations and perils. He had gone with a companion named Potts to the Jefferson river, which is the most western of the three Forks, and runs near the base of the mountains. They were both proceeding up the river in search of beaver, each in his own canoe, when a war party of about eight hundred Black-Feet Indians suddenly appeared on the east bank of the river. The Chiefs ordered them to come ashore, and apprehending robbery only, and knowing the utter hopelessness of flight and having dropped his traps over the side of the canoe from the Indians, into the water, which was here quite shallow, he hastened to obey their mandate. On reaching the shore, he was seized, disarmed and stripped entirely naked. Potts was still in his canoe in the middle of the stream, where he remained stationary, watching the result. Colter requested him to come ashore, which he refused to do, saying he might as well lose his life at once, as he stripped and robbed in the manner Colter had been. An Indian immediately fired and shot him about the hip; he dropped down in the, canoe, but instantly rose with his rifle in his hands. "Are you hurt," said Colter. "Yes," said he, "too much hurt to escape; if you can get away do so. I will kill at least one of them." He leveled his rifle and shot an Indian dead. In an instant, at least a hundred bullets pierced his body and as many savages rushed into the stream and pulled the canoe, containing his riddled corpse, ashore. They dragged the body up onto the bank, and with their hatchets and knives cut and hacked it all to pieces, and limb from limb. The entrails, heart, lungs, etc., they threw into Colter's face. The relations of the killed Indian were furious with rage and struggled, with tomahawk in hand, to reach Colter, while others held them back. He was every moment expecting the death blow or the fatal shot that should lay him beside his companion. A council was hastily held over him and his fate quickly determined upon. He expected to die by tomahawk, slow, lingering and horrible. But they had magnanimously determined to give him a chance, though a slight one, for his life. After the council, a Chief pointed to the prairie and motioned him away with his hand, saying in the Crow language, "go—go away." He supposed they intended to shoot him as soon as he was out of the crowd and presented a fair mark to their guns. He started in a walk, and an old Indian with impatient signs and exclamations, told him to go faster, and as he still kept a walk, the same Indian manifested his wishes by still more violent gestures and adjurations. When he had gone a distance of eighty or a hundred yards from the army of his enemies, he saw the younger Indians throwing off their blankets, leggings, and other incumbrances, as if for a race. Now he knew their object. He was to run a race, of which the prize was to be his own life and scalp. Off he started with the speed of the wind. The war-whoop and yell immediately arose behind him; and looking back, he saw a large company of young warriors, with spears, in rapid pursuit. He ran with all the strength that nature, excited to the utmost, could give; fear and hope lent a supernatural vigor to his limbs and the rapidity of his flight astonished himself. The Madison Fork lay directly before him, five miles from his starting place. He had run half the distance when his strength began to fail and the blood to gush from his nostrils. At every leap the red stream spurted before him, and his limbs were growing rapidly weaker and weaker. He stopped and looked back; he had far outstripped all his pursuers and could get off if strength would only hold out. One solitary Indian, far ahead of the others, was rapidly approaching, with a spear in his right hand, and a blanket streaming behind from his left hand and shoulder. Despairing of escape, Colter awaited his pursuer and called to him in the Crow language, to save his life. The savage did not seem to hear him, but letting go his blanket, and seizing his spear with both hands, he rushed at Colter, naked and defenseless as he stood before him and made a desperate lunge to transfix him. Colter seized the spear, near the head, with his right hand, and exerting his whole strength, aided by the weight of the falling Indian, who had lost his balance in the fury of the onset, he broke off the iron head or blade which remained in his hand, while the savage fell to the ground and lay prostrate and disarmed before him. Now was *his* turn to beg for his life, which he did in the Crow language, and held up his hands imploringly, but Colter was not in a mood to remember the golden rule, and pinned his adversary through the body to the earth one stab with the spear head. He quickly drew the weapon from the body of the now dying Indian, and seizing his blanket as lawful spoil, he again set out with renewed strength, feeling, he said to me, as if he had not run a mile. A shout and yell arose from the pursuing army in his rear as from a legion of devils, and he saw the prairie behind him covered with Indians in full and rapid chase. Before him, if any where was life and safety; behind him certain death; and running as never man before sped the foot, except, perhaps, at the Olympic Games, he reached his goal, the Madison river and the end of his five mile heat. Dashing through the willows on the bank he plunged into the stream and saw close beside him a beaver house, standing like a coal-pit about ten feet above the surface of the water, which was here of about the same depth. This presented to him a refuge from his ferocious enemies of which he immediately availed himself. Diving under the water he arose into the beaver house, where he found a dry and comfortable resting place on the upper floor or story of this singular structure. The Indians soon came up, and in their search for him they stood upon the roof of his house of refuge, which he expected every moment to hear them breaking open. He also feared that they would set it on fire. After a diligent search on that side of the river, they crossed over, and in about two hours returned again to his temporary habitation in which he was enjoying bodily rest, though with much anxious foreboding. The beaver houses are divided into two stories and will generally accommodate several men in a dry and comfortable lodging. In this asylum Colter kept fast till night. The cries of his terrible enemies had gradually died away, and all was still around him, when he ventured out of his hiding place, by the same opening under the water by which he entered and which admits the beavers to their building. He swam the river and hastened towards the mountain gap or ravine, about thirty miles above on the river, through which our company passed in the snow with so much difficulty. Fearing that the Indians might have guarded this pass, which was the only outlet from the valley, and to avoid the danger of a surprise, Colter ascended the almost perpendicular mountain before him, the tops and sides of which a great way down, were covered with perpetual snow. He clambered up this fearful ascent about four miles below the gap, holding on by the rocks, shrubs and branches of trees, and by morning had reached the top. He lay there concealed all that day, and at night proceeded on in the descent of the mountain, which he accomplished by dawn. He now hastened on in the open plain towards Manuel's Fort on the Big Horn, about three hundred miles ahead in the north-east. He travelled day and night, stopping only for necessary repose, and eating roots and the bark of trees for eleven days. He reached the Fort, nearly exhausted by hunger, fatigue and excitement. His only clothing was the Indian's blanket, whom he had killed in the race, and his only weapon, the same Indian's spear which he brought to the Fort as a trophy. His beard was long, his face and whole body were thin and emaciated by hunger, and his limbs and feet swollen and sore. The company at the Fort did not recognize him in this dismal plight until he had made himself known. Colter now with me passed over the scene of his capture and wonderful escape, and described his emotions during the whole adventure with great minuteness. Not the least of his exploits was the scaling of the mountain, which seemed to me impossible even by the mountain goat. As I looked at its rugged and perpendicular sides I wondered how he ever reached the top—a feat probably never performed before by mortal man. The whole affair is a fine example of the quick and ready thoughtfulness and presence of mind in a desperate situation, and the power of endurance, which characterise the western pioneer. As we passed over the ground where Colter ran his race, and listened to his story an undefinable fear crept over all. We felt awe-struck by the nameless and numerous dangers that evidently beset us on every side. Even Cheek's courage sunk and his hitherto buoyant and cheerful spirit was depressed at hearing of the perils of the place. He spoke despondingly and his mind was uneasy, restless and fearful. "I am afraid," said he, "and I acknowledge it. I never felt fear before but now I feel it." A melancholy that seemed like a presentiment of his own fate, possessed him, and to us he was serious almost to sadness, until he met his death a few days afterwards from the same Blackfeet from whom Colter escaped. Colter told us the particulars of a second adventure which I will give to the reader. In the winter when he had recovered from the fatigues of his long race and journey, he wished to recover the traps which he had dropped into the Jefferson Fork on the first appearance of the Indians who captured him. He supposed the Indians were

all quiet in winter quarters, and retraced his steps to the Gallatin Fork.
He had just passed the mountain gap, and encamped on the bank of
the river for the night and kindled a fire to cook his supper of buffalo
meat when he heard the crackling of leaves and branches behind him
in the direction of the river. He could see nothing, it being quite dark,
but quickly he heard the cocking of guns and instantly leaped over the
fire. Several shots followed and bullets whistled around him, knocking
the coals off his fire over the ground. Again he fled for life, and for the
second time, ascended the perpendicular mountain which he had
gone up in his former flight fearing now as then, that the pass might
be guarded by Indians. He reached the top before morning and resting for the day descended the next night, and then made his way with
all possible speed, to the Fort. He said that at the time, he promised
God Almighty that he would never return to this region again if he were
only permitted to escape once more with his life. He did escape once
more, and was now again in the same country, courting the same dangers, which he had so often braved, and that seemed to have for him a
kind of fascination. Such men, and there are thousands of such, can
only live in a state of excitement and constant action. Perils and danger
are their natural element and their familiarity with them and indifference to their fate, are well illustrated in these adventures of Colter.

from The Everest Years
by Chris Bonington

Climbers know that the most difficult part of many climbs is not getting up, but getting down. Veteran British climbers Chris Bonington (born 1934) and Doug Scott were descending from the summit of the Ogre, a 23,900-foot peak nestled in the Himalayas, when disaster struck. As often happens in the mountains, when one thing goes wrong, everything goes wrong in a hurry.

D oug was already sorting out the ropes, pulling them down to a small rock outcrop a couple of metres below the summit. I followed and helped set up the abseil.

'Do you want me to go down first?' I asked.

'I'm off now, youth.'

He set off down into the gloom. Waiting, I could just pick out the pyramid of K2, etched black against the eastern horizon, dominating the peaks around it. That surely must be the Mustagh Tower and closer were the fierce upthrusts of the Latok peaks, black teeth against the sky. To the south-west the afterglow of the setting sun threw the great mass of Nanga Parbat into clear relief. I felt a sense of contentment at being on this high summit, a satisfaction that washed away all my earlier frustration. I loved the beauty of the still cold clear evening.

And then from below came a moan that built up into a penetrating scream. Then suddenly was cut off and it was as silent as it had been before. I was sure Doug had gone off the end of the rope. I tugged at it for confirmation. It was taut. He was still on the rope. I shouted down but there was no reply. Was he unconscious? If he didn't get his weight off the end of the rope I couldn't abseil down to join him but I could jumar. It's a slow painstaking process in reverse but perfectly possible. I felt very very lonely standing on the Ogre's summit in the gloom of the night. 'You might not get out of this one, Bonington,' I thought.

And then there was a distant shout from below: 'I've broken my leg.'

I felt a flood of relief. He was alive and conscious and I was no longer alone. I had a role to play.

'Can you get your weight off the rope?'

'I'll try. There's a ledge just below me.'

Another pause, and the rope went slack in my hand. I could abseil down to join him but how on earth were we going to get a man with a broken leg back across the West Summit and all the way down that long and complex route? Even the three of us couldn't possibly carry him. As I came in sight of Doug, I assumed a confidence I didn't feel.

'What ho, mate.'

He was sitting on a tiny ledge, belayed to a piton he had just hammered in. 'I slipped on some ice,' he told me.

Later I gathered he had just finished traversing the snow ridge leading to the top of the long rock pitch that had provided the crux of the climb. He was stepping down to clip into the piton we had left in place and had braced his foot against the rock. In the gathering dark he hadn't seen the thin film of ice and, because he wasn't wearing crampons, his boot skidded off, sending him swinging like the weight on the end of a pendulum into space across the rock wall. He must have been a good forty metres out horizontally from the anchor point, yet only twenty metres or so below it. As he swung through the dark he instinctively raised his feet to act as buffers as he came crashing into a rock corner. The impact had in fact broken both his legs though neither of us realised this immediately. But perhaps this saved him from more complex injuries.

'We'll just work at getting you down,' I said cheerfully. 'Don't worry, you're a long way from being dead.'

Probably not the most tactful thing to say, but it was the thought uppermost in my mind. It hadn't remotely occurred to Doug, who felt extremely rational and remarkably clear about what to do. I pulled down the doubled rope and fixed another abseil. It was now very nearly pitch dark. We did not have head torches and I didn't fancy the prospect of trying to get all the way down in the dark. I could just see through the gloom a wider snow ledge about fifteen metres below. It might be suitable for a bivouac. On arriving, I hacked away at the snow. There was enough to clear a comfortable ledge that we could at least sit on.

'It's O.K., Doug, you might as well come on down.'

He slid down the rope, keeping his legs behind him, but once on the snow he had to traverse a metre or two to reach the ledge I had started to dig. He tried to stand. There was a distinct sound of bone scraping on bone. He let out a cry of pain and keeled over onto his knees where he paused slumped, then crawled over, his legs stuck out behind him clear of the snow, to join me on the ledge. Kneeling, he helped enlarge the ledge for the night. We might get out of this after all, I began to think.

We had nothing with us, no food or drink, no down clothing, just what we had climbed in during the day and the gear we had used. We took off our boots, though it was too dark to examine Doug's legs. Fortunately they did not hurt too much, provided he didn't put any weight on them and I didn't inadvertently lean on them. We tucked our stockinged feet into each others' crutches, massaged them from time to time through the night, occasionally talked. At one point Doug said, 'If you've got to get into this kind of predicament, I can't think of a better person to be with.' Most of the time we were wrapped in our own thoughts. The penetrating cold soon dominated everything. I rationalised it by telling myself that the discomfort was ephemeral, that it was just a few hours, a tiny fraction of my life span, and then the sun would rise and we would be warm once again. I limited my thoughts to the prospects of the haven of the snow cave just a hundred or so metres away, of hot drinks and a warm sleeping bag and the support of Mo and Clive.

I became aware of Doug rubbing my feet, a strong hint that he wanted his toes massaged. I did so with care, to avoid hurting him. He was particularly worried about the dangers of frostbite which would inevitably be increased by the injuries he had sustained. The night slowly dragged by until at last the sky began to lighten. We were on the western side of the Ogre and so couldn't expect the sun until late in the morning. We didn't wait. Doug managed to get his boots back on; another relief.

I set up the abseil and plunged down to a ledge nearly fifty metres below. Doug followed more slowly but very steadily. Three more abseils and we were on the snow at the foot of the summit block. With action and with Doug's absolute steadiness and quiet competence, I was becoming more optimistic about our chances. We now had our next test. The snow cave was about thirty metres higher and a hundred metres from us in a horizontal direction. Would Doug be able to crawl across fairly steep snow?

I left him at the foot of the abseil and set out to warn the other two whom I met just short of the snow cave. They had seen the fall the previous night and were coming over to see what they could do to help. I carried on into the welcome shelter of the cave, leaving them to collect Doug. They met him about a third of the way up the tracks I had left. Doug is not the kind of person to wait around. He had already started crawling. Clive picked up his sack while Mo started digging out great bucket steps for Doug to crawl in. Mercifully he did not have compound fractures or he would not have been able to crawl without acute pain, and we had no painkillers.

They got back to the snow cave two hours later. We all now felt confident that Doug would be able to cope with the descent, in spite of its length and complex nature. It was wonderful just to lie in the warmth of one's sleeping bag cocooned in the confines of the snow cave, brewing endless cups of tea. That day we ate and drank our fill but in the evening we finished our last freeze-dried meal. All we had left was some soup and a few tea bags. This didn't seem too serious, however, as surely we should get back down to Advance Base in a couple of days.

Mo had brought a pack of cards with him and we spent the rest of the day playing Min, or Black Bitch as it is called in some circles, a delightful trick-taking game that had had us entertained throughout the expedition. A bank of high cloud stretched across the western horizon but we had seen plenty of threats of a storm in the last few weeks and none of them had materialised. We settled down for the night confident that we would be able to get most of the way down the following morning.

When I woke I thought it was too early, the light was so dim. I glanced at my watch to see that it was six o'clock. It should have been broad daylight outside. I looked across the cave to see that Mo, who was on the outside nearest the door, was covered in spindrift. The entrance was completely blocked with fresh snow. It looked as if the weather had at last broken. We slowly crept into consciousness. Clive, who was next to the stove, scooped some snow from the wall and started brewing the first drink of the day. We had plenty of gas, which was a blessing. You can go for some days without food, but the effects of dehydration are much more serious. Without liquid we would deteriorate very quickly and to get liquid we needed fuel.

It was only after having a cup of tea, each using the last of our few cubes of sugar, that we dug out the entrance. A cloud of spindrift immediately blew in. Within the cave it was sepulchrally quiet; outside was an inferno of screaming wind and driving snow. But we had to move; Clive and I ventured out to see how bad it was and I belayed him while he ploughed up to his thighs using a swimming action to make any progress at all. He turned back after running out twenty metres of rope in a struggle that took over an hour. The furrow he ploughed on his return journey was covered almost instantly. Cold and wet, we crawled back into the snow cave. Our situation was now very much more serious but, whatever anyone thought privately, there was no sense of despondency within the party. Mo's humour was as sharp as ever and Doug only complained if someone sat on one of his damaged legs. We snuggled down in our sleeping bags and waited out the day.

Next morning the storm still raged. It had the feeling that a spell of extreme weather, either good or bad, brings—that it will last for ever.

This was our second day without food; we couldn't wait any longer. However bad the storm and the snow, we had to fight our way out. To assert our determination, we all packed our rucsacks, dividing Doug's gear between the three of us, and set out into the storm. Clive and Mo took turns forcing the route up towards the West Summit, leaving a rope behind them. Doug needed all his strength to crawl up through the deep snow, hauling himself bodily on the jumar. I stamped and shivered in the rear collecting the ropes. It took four hours for me to reach the top. I crouched on the West Summit while Doug painstakingly part-crawled, part-abseiled down the snow-plastered rocky ridge. It was so different from the two previous occasions when there had been a cloudless sky and brilliant sun. Visibility was down to a metre. There were glimpses of rock walls dropping darkly into the white of driving snow. Mo was out in front, setting up abseils, picking a route through this maze of snow and cloud and rock. All I had to do was follow the line of rope, the thread through the Minator's labyrinth. I could hear the great bull roar.

There was no question of abseiling down the ridge line. The rope would have caught in the rocks when I tried to pull it down. I therefore climbed down, coiling it as I went. The others were waiting below, having run out all the rope. They were like snowmen, faces rimed with ice, clothing plastered. Mo plunged on down with the ropes I had given him, while I squatted ready for another long cold wait. We were now descending the steep snow rake below the West Summit rocks. This in turn led to the ice slope that had been precarious even in perfect conditions. I couldn't help wondering how Doug would manage to crawl across it and the consequences of a fall.

But so much snow had fallen, even though it was still precarious, the snow just held Doug's weight as he edged across. Once again I brought up the rear, uncomfortably aware that no one was belaying me. I couldn't afford to fall. By the time I reached the site of our previous bivouac it was very nearly dark. Mo had already vanished into the snow cave he and I had excavated on the way up.

It had been only just big enough for the two of us. Now it was part filled with snow and was much too small for four. Only one person could work in it at a time. Another could shovel the excavated snow out, but the other two just stood and shivered in the dark and cold. Consequently we piled into the cave before it was big enough. Doug urged us to do some more work on it, but we were all too tired. We just wanted to slide into our sleeping bags and have something to drink, though it could only be milkless, sugarless tea with one tea bag between the four of us.

Just taking off our outer, snow-plastered clothes was a struggle. It was impossible to keep the snow off the sleeping bags. I was on the outside and tried to block the entrance with rucsacks and climbing gear but the spindrift sought out every chink. It blew into our little cave, covering everything in a cold white film that, as we tossed and turned to avoid it, melted on our sleeping bags, turning the down into a useless congealed mess, then penetrating our clothes until by morning everything was wet and soggy. We weren't cold in the night. There was a warmth in our very proximity but that morning, 17th July, four days after the accident and two days since we'd had any solid food, the cold penetrated as soon as we crawled out of the shelter of the cave into the storm that still screamed around the Ogre.

A knife-edged ridge led down to the top of the Pillar. Mo went on ahead to fix the first abseil, while Clive and I put Doug between us, as we slowly made our way down. We could do nothing to help Doug, other than carry his gear, dig big bucket steps for him where possible, and be ready to hold him on the rope should he slip. He went carefully, steadily, never complaining, never showing the pain and stress that he must have felt. At last we reached the top of the Pillar. Mo had fixed the doubled ropes of the abseil and had already vanished. At least we were going straight down—the steeper the better.

Doug went first. We peered down, his shape blurred into the driving snow and then vanished. There was a shout from below but we couldn't make out any words. The rope was slack and so Clive went down. Another long pause. Then I clipped in and slid down the doubled rope, blinded by the driving snow that seemed to be blown from every direction. My frozen clothing was like a suit of armour, restricting movement. But it was good to be on the rope. All I had to do was slide; I could relax my concentration for just a few minutes. I was nearly down and could see Clive's shape, opposite and just below me. That surely must be the top of the fixed rope. We were very nearly out of trouble.

And then I was falling, plummeting head downwards. Had the anchor come away? A stab of absolute horror surged through me; this was it. Then came a jarring, smashing pain in my chest. I was hanging suspended on the rope. I just hung there, shocked and frightened for a minute. Then my mind took over once again with an instinctive analysis of what had happened.

I was attached to a single rope by my abseil brake. The ends of the rope must have been uneven and I had come off one end, pulling the rope I was still on down, until I was brought to a halt after a fall of some seven metres or so by the loop on the longer end of the rope that had been placed over a spike of rock. I swung across and clipped in to the start of the fixed rope. My ribs ached but I had no idea that I had done anything more than hit something on the way down and would probably be badly bruised as a result. There was no time for worry. We had to get back to the tents that day. I could see Doug over to the left, secured to the fixed rope, working his way painstakingly over an awkward rock traverse. It wasn't too bad in cramponed boots but he had to crawl.

It was only that evening that I learnt that Doug had had an even narrower escape than I. When he abseiled neither of the ropes at the bottom had been anchored. He went straight off the ends and was plummetting down the gully. Fortunately the fixed rope we had left in place went across the gully about five metres below. As he shot passed it, he managed to grab it and arrest his fall. Otherwise he could have gone another 1300 metres to the glacier far below.

There was no time to linger over near misses. Slowly we worked our way back along the fixed ropes, abseiling and traversing, until at last we were just above the snow spur leading down to the tents. Mo had already got down and we could see him begin to dig them out. The fixed rope ended just above a bergschrund. It had been easy enough to climb up uninjured, in perfect conditions. Getting down in a storm with an injured man was very different. I had brought with me a short length of rope for this contingency. We tied Doug to the end of it and began to lower him. It wasn't quite long enough. The storm suddenly rose to a crescendo. Spindrift avalanched down the spur engulfing and blinding us; it was as if the Ogre didn't want to let us go. Could we die now, so very close to relative safety? And then the storm relented. Doug managed to establish himself on easier angled snow so that he could untie the rope. Clive and I followed and soon we were digging out our buried tents. At least we had some kind of shelter now, though our sleeping bags and clothing were soaked and we had only a few tea bags supplemented by a few cubes of curried Oxo and a packet of sugar. There was no solid food.

It was when I undressed that I realised my injuries were more serious than a few bruises. I could feel an uneven indentation on the right-hand side of my rib cage. I had probably broken some ribs. My left hand was also part paralysed and the wrist was swollen. Had I broken it? I crawled into my wet sleeping bag. Mo, who was sharing the tent with me, brought me a mug of tea. Hot and sweet, it tasted like nectar. I just curled up in the bag, trying to hold on to the little glimmer of warmth it had kindled, and wondered what the next day would bring.

I slept intermittently, listened to the wind screaming around the tent, and prayed for the weather to clear. But the storm was as fierce as ever in the morning. I dragged myself out to relieve myself and realised how weak I had become, I felt terrible and returned to my sleeping bag. It was beginning to dry out but was stealing my body heat to do so. I curled up and let the rest of the day slip away in a semi-coma. My chest didn't hurt as long as I didn't move or cough but every cough was like a fierce stab and my throat, raw from our ordeal, built up into a sore tickle until I broke out into a paroxysm of uncontrollable coughing. I crouched, hugging my ribs, trying to alleviate the pain.

I was coughing up a bubbly froth. Was this pulmonary, or perhaps pulmonary oedema caused by the trauma? As the day dragged on I became convinced that I could die if we didn't get down soon. In the dark blue gloom of the tent my fears built up. I staggered next door and expressed my worry about pulmonary oedema, urging that I needed to get down before it took a grip, yet feeling ashamed of the fuss I was making.

Mo pointed out that we would never be able to find our way across the plateau in a white-out. We had to wait for a clear day. He was right and I crawled back to the tent to wait out the rest of the day and the long night. Waiting was much worse than the struggle of the descent.

And then came dawn. The wind still hammered the tent but suddenly a finger of light touched its walls. It was the sun. The sky had cleared; we could see the plateau stretched out below us and escape from our trap.

Mo and Clive were now carrying colossal loads as we slowly abseiled down the steep slopes leading back to the plateau. One of the tents, secured under the straps of Clive's rucsack, slipped out and went bounding down the slope. Clive cursed but resigned himself to making the long detour to get it. At last we had reached the relative safety of the plateau. Under a clear blue sky we felt almost out of danger. Doug volunteered to take Clive's pack while Clive went for the tent. He set out on all fours, weighed down by the huge sack. I followed and was appalled to find I couldn't keep up with him. My strength had oozed away. I took a few steps, sat down and rested, then took a few more.

We had now been five days without solid food, but we just had the last thousand metres of descent, all safeguarded by fixed rope, and we would be back on the glacier. The others surely would have come to Advance Base to meet and help us, as they would be worried by now. Soon it would be their responsibility. The ordeal was nearly over.

On the morning of 20th July, Mo and I got away first. I had dumped every piece of gear that wasn't absolutely essential to lighten my rucsack. I even left my camera behind. Mo fix-roped the upper part of the ridge and I followed trying to cut bigger steps for Doug to crawl down. It was awkward work because I couldn't use my left hand at all. This made the descent difficult as well, particularly as the fixed ropes had deteriorated in the time we had been on the mountain, becoming

stretched in places and tangled in others. The descent seemed interminable. I kept gazing down at the glacier trying to see a welcoming
committee. There were no tents at Advance Base and no sign of any
kind of life.

The fixed ropes ended on the last of the rock. Below that was a snow
slope which in the intervening time had turned to ice. It was just a matter of cramponing down it but each kick of the crampons sent an agonising stab of pain into my chest. I couldn't bear it. To hell with it, I'd
slide. I threw my rucsack down the slope and then followed, sliding on
my backside, the classic sitting glissade. But I could only hold my ice
axe with one hand and was unable to use it as an effective brake. I
rapidly gained speed and was soon hurtling down towards the bottom,
doing what I could to protect my ribs. I arrived with a crunch and just
lay in the snow, exhausted and relieved that the worst of the descent
was over.

Mo was waiting. 'We'd better rope up for the glacier,' he said. 'After
all that I'd hate to end up in the bottom of a crevasse.'

I took the proffered rope and Mo set off, ploughing through deep
soft snow. He was like a tug boat towing a derelict ship. I could feel the
pull of the rope at my waist and wearily put one foot in front of the
other in the tracks that Mo had made. At last we reached the rocky
moraine at the end of the glacier.

'You should be all right from here,' Mo said. 'I'd better get down and
see what the others are up to.'

He quickly disappeared from view, leaving me to wander down the
moraine. I staggered a few paces at a time then sank down to revel in
the heat of the sun as it slowly penetrated the chill of my body.

The terrain changed from barren piled rock to the beginnings of
vegetation, a pink cluster of primula almost hidden in a crevice, and
then, round a corner, the little oasis formed by the meadow and lake
of our Base Camp—emerald green grass embraced by the arms of the
glacier moraine. But there were no tents, no sign of humanity. I
reached the boulder where we had our cooking shelter. There were
pots and pans and boxes of food stored under the overhang. There

was also a note. It was in Nick's hand, dated 20th July, that very day, and started:

> *Dear All,*
> *In the unlikely event of your ever reading this, I've gone down to try to catch up with Tut and the porters so that we can come back and look for you. We saw you come down off the summit on the 14th and assumed you'd be back down next morning. The porters had already arrived and we had neither the food nor the money to keep them. Tut and Aleem therefore went down with the porters and all the gear while I waited with six of them to help carry your stuff.*
> *I can only assume something has gone badly wrong but I couldn't come up to see for myself as I've sent away all my hill gear. Tut and I will get back up as quick as we can.*
>
> > *Nick*

There was another note in Mo's handwriting at the bottom:

> *I've pushed straight on to try to catch up with Nick. I'll go down with him to get the porters back up here as soon as possible to help you all down.*
>
> > *Mo*

We were still on our own. Would Doug be able to crawl all the way to Base? It was a good four miles. I should go back to help Clive but I was too tired, too tired even to eat. I had had no solid food for five days yet did not feel particularly hungry. I just lay down and felt the soft warm blades of grass against my face, could smell it, pungent with the scent of life; I could hear the buzz of flies and rustle of the wind in the reeds of the lake. I was alive and knew that I could hang on to life. I just had to be patient and soon I'd be home.

I summoned the energy to fetch some water from the stream and lit the stove. Soon I was sipping soup and nibbling at some biscuits. But I really should go back for the others. Just a little rest first. I pulled out my sleeping bag, crawled into it and dropped off to sleep. It was dark when I woke. Nine o'clock. I had been asleep for several hours. Still no sign of Doug and Clive. Full of foreboding, I pulled on my boots and, taking a head torch, slowly retraced my steps back up the glacier. To my immense relief I saw a little pool of light in the distance. It was Clive. Just behind him was Doug, slowly but steadily crawling on his hands and knees over the sharp and broken rocks of the moraine. Clive pushed on to the camp to start a brew while I walked with Doug the last few yards back to the boulder. We'd made it. We were alive and now, whatever the delays, whatever the discomfort, it was just a matter of time.

I might not have waxed so philosophical had I known just how long this would take in my case. It was four days before Nick arrived back with porters who carried Doug on a makeshift stretcher down to the Biafo Glacier where he was collected by a helicopter. Nick had had an appalling time waiting for us at Base Camp, seeing us intermittently near the West Summit, trying to guess what had gone wrong, and then not seeing us at all and having to decide what to do next. I had experienced the same emotion on Everest, waiting for Pete Boardman, Pertemba and Mick Burke to return, but I had only a matter of hours to wait, sharing my anxiety with friends, while Nick had suffered seven days in effective solitude. For he could barely communicate with the few porters who had stayed behind with him, his diary recorded his growing despair:

> *19th July: Fine morning. They* must *come down today.*
> *Still no sign of them at 5.30 in spite of fine weather all day. Preparing to go down to Askole tomorrow to collect Tut and form a search party.*
> *Beginning to give up—thinking of Wendy and other wives and how to get news to them. Spent whole day looking through binocs. Every stone on the glacier seems to move until you examine it. Also if you listen hard enough you can hear human voices in the sound of running water or falling stones.*

Summit appeared for half an hour in early afternoon—snow cave now invisible and no sign of tracks.
20th July: Hardly slept a wink—in the early morning I have hal-lucinations, or were they dreams? In the middle of the night I thought I saw a green flare up the glacier—also a distinct shout of 'Nick'. No further signs, though.

After the evacuation of Doug the rest of us plodded on down to Askole where Mo and Tut were waiting. That night had a good party atmosphere. An American expedition, on their way back from climbing the Trango Tower were also in the village. We had a camp fire, chupatties, apricots and endless cups of tea. But the following morning they were all anxious to get on their way, unhinderd by me.

'Don't worry, Chris, the helicopter pilot promised to come back for you today.'

They wanted to get out quickly, walking long days. They reminded me how painful the jeep journey would be with my broken ribs. I had no choice but to resign myself to waiting for the helicopter.

The Americans had a doctor. He dug his hand into his pocket and produced a handful of multi-coloured pills, giving me half a dozen striped ones as antibiotics, some little white ones for sleeping and red ones for pain. He also gave me a paperback to help pass the time while I waited to be evacuated.

I couldn't help feeling desperately lonely as they shouldered their rucsacks and all strode away down the path, leaving me propped against a tree just outside the village. Still, I was only going to have to wait an hour or so and I would be picked up and whisked into Skardu while they were still plodding down the Braldu Gorge.

I waited through the day but there was no sign of the helicopter. A few youngsters played in the dust around me but the rest of the village seemed to have forgotten my existence. As dusk fell and it became obvious that the helicopter was not coming back that day, I went in search of shelter, knocking on the door of one of our porter's houses and trying, with sign language, to show that I had nowhere to sleep.

Hadji Fezil, a middle-aged Balti, with a thin face and large very dirty, gap-teeth, took me in and let me lay my sleeping mat under an awning on the flat roof of his house.

The helicopter didn't come the next day. Nor did it come in the next five. I was weak and still felt very ill. I just lay in my sleeping bag, dragging myself once a day down through the house and along the path in search of a quiet spot to relieve myself. The village youngsters would follow me, whistling a whirring noise, grinning and calling, 'Helicopter no coming, helicopter no coming.' The cry reverberated round my brain, accompanied me back to my rooftop and crept round my head at night.

I became quite paranoid. 'They've left me. The whole bloody lot of them have just pushed off home.' It was just as well that the American doctor had given me a thick book. It was *Centennial* by Michener, one of those bumper chronicles about a patch of Colorado from the beginning of time to the present day—a good easy read for an invalid marooned on a flat mud roof in the middle of the Karakoram. The only other events of the day were meal times. These consisted of chupatties, a spinach-like vegetable and boiled eggs. I had to brush the flies away as I took each mouthful. Hadji Fezil and his family were very kind. I had no money, was unable to communicate, except by signs, and seemed to have been abandoned.

On the sixth day, I was so desperate I set out to walk accompanied by the faithful Hadji Fezil. If anything I had become even weaker in the intervening days. Walking was purgatory. That day we reached Chongo and stayed in the house of one of his relatives. We had now to get through the steep section of the Braldu Gorge. The river was in full spate, tearing at the boulders of the path. In places we had to wade through it or its subsidiary streams. I just hugged my ribs, terrified of the pain that the slightest stumble or sudden movement created. That night we reached the village of Kunul. The following day we should be at Dasso where we could get a jeep but I dreaded the thought of the jeep ride.

We had just started breakfast when the distant whine of an engine alerted us. It could only be a helicopter. I rushed out of the hut, followed by Hadji Fezil. We were in a grove of apricot trees at the side of the valley. The helicopter could not possibly see us. I dashed down into the flat valley bottom, the pain of my ribs ignored. The helicopter was already overhead, flying purposefully up to Askole. Would it see us on the way back? We lit a fire, made a marker of yellow foam mats and waited, full of a desperate uncertainty. An hour went by. And then the distant roar. It was flying down the valley floor. It dropped down beside us, and the smiling pilot flung open the door. My ordeal was over.

The pilot, a major in the Pakistan army, explained that the helicopter which had evacuated Doug had had a crash landing in Skardu that could easily have proved fatal, and there had been a delay in getting a replacement. He had flown up that morning from Islamabad.

'I might as well take you straight there if you want. I'm going back anyway.'

And so we flew all the way to Islamabad, down the great gorge of the Indus and across the foothills to Pakistan's capital.

'Where are you staying? Might as well get you as close as I can.'

'At the British Embassy.'

'I can't land there. The closest I can get is the golf course.'

We landed on the 18th green. A group of golfers eyed the helicopter respectfully, no doubt expecting to see a general descend. They must have been surprised to see the filthy, skeletal apparition that I had become climb out. My hair and beard were unkempt and tangled. I was wearing dirty red Lifa long-johns and vest and had one arm in a sling.

The helicopter took off and I walked over to the club house. People shrank away from me as I approached the desk and asked if I could phone the British Embassy. Half an hour later Carolyn, with whom we had stayed on our way out, came to pick me up.

It's easy to talk of heroism in describing a near catastrophe. Doug had shown extraordinary fortitude and endurance in crawling back down the mountain but that was a matter of survival. Mo and Clive, who had lost their chance to go for the summit, had risked their lives in helping Doug and me to get down, though they couldn't very well have left us and certainly the thought would have never entered their minds. But if one wants to talk of heroes, I believe that Nick came the closest to that role. He was landed with the grim task of sitting it out, of taking desperately difficult decisions armed with inadequate information, of organising first Doug's evacuation and then mine. This kind of role demands greater moral courage and fortitude than direct involvement in a crisis where the struggle for personal survival has a stimulus of its own.

As for the villain, that was the Ogre himself. He was to leave us all with wounds that were going to take a long time to heal. He had played cat and mouse with us. He had had his fun and then, having battered and mauled us, had let us go.

from To Timbuktu
by Mark Jenkins

Young people who engage in potentially dangerous sports like climbing take risks because they don't fully understand what's at stake. More seasoned participants push the edge because they know—or think they know—how far they can push. But somewhere on the journey from youth to experience, most people push too far. Mark Jenkins (born 1958) did just that, as he describes in two passages from his 1997 memoir.

We were working on the Eskimo roll before class. It was winter. The creeks and lakes around town were trapped under two feet of ice, so we were practicing in the pool.

The Eskimo roll is a fundamental maneuver in kayaking. Unlike all other boats man has invented, kayaks were designed to be rolled.

To hunt sea mammals through pack ice, maneuvering easily and swiftly along remote leads, Eskimos needed a craft as sleek and agile as their prey, something that could spin on a dime when a seal surfaced behind them. Consequently, they created a boat that was shaped like a seal—pointed at prow and stem, with a round, keelless belly. It was even sewn from sealskin. But a keelless boat is tipsy, so they cinched the deck tight around the paddler's waist. Now when the boat did tip over, it wouldn't swamp. The only trick was getting back up. It had to be done immediately. Humans freeze to death in a matter of minutes in Arctic water. Hence: the Eskimo roll.

A smooth sweep of the paddle underwater, a quick flick of hip and knee, and presto, back to the surface like a cork.

Mike got it right away. Rolling in full circles slick as a seal. Water was his natural habitat. He was a state champion swimmer, a "fish" in high school patois. Round head, orange hair tinted lime from the chlorine, foot-deep chest. He moved through the sapphire liquid like a submarine. His lungs were so powerful he could swim three lengths of the pool underwater without coming up for air.

It wasn't so easy for me. I swam with the swim team to stay in shape, but I wasn't a "fish." I was a gymnast. At least that's the sport I competed in. What I loved was climbing mountains. Rock was my natural habitat. In the water I tended to muscle things and you can't muscle the Eskimo roll; it takes technique.

Mike made it look easy. He'd pretend he was shot and slowly fall over sideways, sink under, hang upside down from his boat for a second, then explode back up. He could even do it without a paddle, perfectly timing the thrust of his shoulders, sweep of his arms, and snap of his knee. It's called a combat roll.

An ordinary roll was enough for me. I usually hit it, but sometimes I had to bail—peeling out of the cockpit underwater, then ignominiously dogpaddling my capsized kayak to the side of the pool.

Of course we didn't make it easy on each other. That would have been unsporting. When one of us went under, the other would hold his boat down so he couldn't immediately roll back up. It got to be a game. Who could stay under longer.

After a while it became unnecessary to hold each other under; we did it to ourselves. Flipped over and just hung there, upside down underwater. This is an unnatural position for humans. You get disoriented beneath the water with your head pointing down. You can't breathe so you start to panic. Your lungs begin to burn and your heart starts thundering and your brain misfires and suddenly a chemical fear is coursing through your body. Adrenaline, pure animal instinct. Fight or flight—roll or bail. We were trying to teach ourselves how not to do both. How to control fear. After a while we weren't practicing the Eskimo roll anymore; we were practicing sangfroid.

One morning Coach caught us.

Coach was a compassionate, taciturn, merciless man. He looked like Clint Eastwood. He led the swim team to seven consecutive state titles. He was one of the few people on earth who expected more from himself than from you. Kids swam hard for Coach, swam to guthollow, limplimbed, red-eyed exhaustion.

With Coach there were different punishments for different crimes. If you pushed a kid into the pool, a minor offense, you'd get a few thousand yards. Snap someone with a towel leaving a welt big enough for Coach to notice, and after confessing, you'd get laps plus weights. For serious transgressions—arrogance, vanity, pride, or hubris—your sentence was something special. The Hallelujah.

There was a ritual to the Hallelujah. The guilty had to wait for an unforewarned day. It was always conducted directly following workout when you were already beat. No kids who couldn't take it ever got it.

We got it a week later. Coach blew the whistle and we all climbed out to shower and crawl into our clothes and bicycle home and fall asleep in our dinner plates, then he turned to us.

"Jenkins. Moe. Back in the pool."

We knew what to do. We dove back in and began treading water in the deep end under the diving board. Coach slowly walked down the length of the pool and stepped up onto the board. He moved out to the end, seated himself with his legs crossed like a black belt, which he was, and peered down at us.

Already the pool was strangely calm after suffering three hours of flogging. As if it were flesh preternaturally dosing over a wound.

"You two like to push it, don't you."

We grinned up at him like the adolescent fools we were.

"Okay. I want you to imagine that your hands are tied to a pole above your head."

We understood. We'd been here before. Even if it was the first time for some poor sucker, he would have already heard the rumors and would know what to do. We raised our arms up into the air.

"Elbows out of the water, gentlemen."

To tread water using both your arms and legs is not hard. You rotate your arms in wide flat ovals and frog-kick your legs one at a time. Everything is synchronized and your head stays well above the surface of the water. With practice you can do it for a long time.

To tread water without your arms, with your arms not only useless but raised above your head as extra weight, is different. You must frog-kick strenuously, but if you kick too hard, as if you're frightened that you might drown, you become exhausted within minutes and your head starts to go under and you do begin to drown. So there's a method. First you must lean your head back until your eyes are staring straight up at the ceiling. At the same time you must allow yourself to sink until only your face is above the surface. Then you must kick only enough to keep your mouth from filling with water. The liquid will be all around your face, splashing into the corners of your eyes, but you must stay calm.

We frog-kicked with our arms up in the air and Coach sat there. He did not say things to make us angry or inspire us. He simply sat there, above us.

For the first few minutes Mike and I razzed Coach. We shouted at him about how easy it was, how we could do it all night, how he should go out and get us a pizza so we could eat it while we were treading water.

Coach smiled.

We clapped our hands and shouted. We clapped our hands in unison as if we were at a rock concert. We sang lewd songs.

This didn't last long. Shenanigans used up too much strength. Besides, something else starts to happen after your body has been moving in a slow, powerful rhythm for a while: Your mind is set free. Your body is operating on its own, autonomous and self-governing, so you can go anywhere you want.

I don't know where Mike went, but I went off to Europe.

When I was thirteen, my family had moved to Holland. Just picked up and left. Mom and Dad were from the limitless ocean of South Dakota and had wanted to sail away since they met. Then I came along. Then Steve. Then Pam and Dan and Wendy Sue and Christopher. By then they had it figured out. Go even if you can't possibly go. Even if it will take a miracle.

We only lived in de Nederland for one year but nothing was ever the same again. We were just dirt and snow kids from the high plains of Wyoming when the rest of the world got lodged inside us like an arrowhead too close to the spine. I started dreaming about Europe the day we got back. I dreamed about it at night and daydreamed about it in class. This had been going on for three years. I got so good at slipping off to Europe I could get there in a matter of seconds.

So I was somewhere on a nude beach with a medieval castle doing heroic things when a wave of fatigue spilled over me and I realized that soon I wouldn't be able to talk anymore.

"Mike?"

"Buck?"

"I been thinking about escaping."

"Yeah."

"You want to go?"

"Sure. Where're we going?"

"Europe."

We had to stop talking after that. We had to conserve our energy.

We treaded through seconds and minutes. We treaded through dinnertime, our stomachs sucking up into our ribs. We treaded through pieces of memory that slipped away before we could find out what they were.

After a while everything started to turn blue. A deep melting blue. The water. The air. The concrete ceiling. The underside of the diving board. Even our arms drooping above our heads like limbs in a Salvador Dali painting.

Then we went past the point when you think you are too tired to go on for another second so you close your eyes and try to make time disappear. But even then, even when it started getting rough, it wasn't that bad really because Coach was right there. Right above our heads. He still is.

And time did disappear. It had to.

Just when we were empty, our arms still hanging on to the air but our legs sinking as if tied to cement blocks and our heads quietly going under, Coach spoke. We could hardly hear him.

"Hit the showers."

The day school got out we went down to the railroad office. We stood in line in workboots and workclothes and lowered baseball caps and lied through our teeth. We lied about our ages and our experience and fabricated Social Security numbers and the man spit lassos of tobacco juice on our feet and didn't believe a word but didn't give a damn either because he was shorthanded up in Medicine Bow.

It was a rail gang. We worked thirteen twelves—twelve hours a day, thirteen days on, one day off. Using crowbars and hand jacks we raised and straightened track buckled and splayed by the coal trains heaving down from Hanna. We were the only white guys on the crew. They called us *güeros* and *pendejos* and *cabrones* but we didn't give a shit because they were lifers and we were going to escape. They were working on the railroad out in the freezing burning prairie. We were working on the underground railroad, digging a tunnel out of Wyoming.

After we'd each saved a thousand bucks, enough to go clear around the world, we quit. Just packed up our tent and walked away with a roll of twenties bulging in our pockets like hard-ons.

Mike was a year ahead and had graduated that spring. I finished high school by Christmas, a semester early. For graduation Mom and Dad and the kids gave me a one-way bus ticket to New York City and Mike bought his own and our families came to the gas station to see us off. They waved at us and we waved at them until we lost each other in the whirling snow.

It was January 1977. Mike and I were eighteen.

Of course we didn't know it then, but there are only certain times in your life when you can do certain things. If you don't do them that very moment, they pass you by forever and you and your life become something else. Lighting out to see the world is one of those things. If you are too young, you will be hurt by the malformed people who prey on innocents, and never again feel safe or trust humans. If you are too old, the seeds of cynicism and fearfulness have already taken root and you shall be a loathsome traveler. You must be young enough to believe in your own immortality in a mysterious, ineluctable way, but old enough to understand that you could die if you got too messed up.

Sitting in the front seats of the bus staring at the storm burying the highway and the sagebrush and the antelope, Mike and I were trembling from an untaintable, undauntable expectancy.

It was still snowing when we landed in Europe. We couldn't believe the prices. We'd already shot half our wad on the plane ticket. We decided not to spend another dime of our hard-earned dinero. We'd live off the land. We set out on foot and walked across Luxembourg in one day, once taking refuge in a pub where old men in berets bought us mugs of warm beer.

We hitchhiked to Paris expecting it to be as beautiful as a songbird, but instead it was winter there too. In spring, when you're supposed to go to Paris, it's probably beautiful and romantic but in winter it is sleeting and the city is as ugly as a wet pigeon. An old man with a teal cravat and a red nose bought us dinner one night because he remembered weeping when the Americans marched down the Champs Élysées. We drank port and he cried, *"Le plus beau jour pour la France!"* and it made him weep again. The police arrested us for camping in the Bois de Boulogne. Then again for camping in the Montparnasse cemetery.

In Barcelona we got mixed up in a riot and had to run from soldiers with shields beating people with truncheons and firing rubber bullets.

In Madrid we tried to hop a freight train but failed and wound up sleeping in flower beds. We found out it was easier to hop passenger trains and just hide from the conductor. Once we fell in with some sailors and got so drunk we got off at different stations and didn't find each other for a couple of days.

In the south of Spain we fell in love and then left before dawn because we were going and they were staying and we thought that was the biggest difference there was.

We were having fun but Europe wasn't the adventure I'd remembered as a boy. I'd thought I knew where we were going but when we got there it was gone. Europe wasn't a mysterious land full of opportunities for valor and hardship. Europe was more like America's grandfather. Old and familiar with a few quirky traditions. That's not what we wanted. We didn't leave Wyoming to wind up at Grandpa's. We left home to be homeless. To be fugitives.

One afternoon while we were walking along the docks sharing half a loaf of bread we'd found on a bench and staring out at the ruffling green sea, it hit us.

Africa.

It was a word from the boundlessness of childhood. Big and deep as the sky. We couldn't believe we hadn't thought of it earlier.

We decided it was time for the beach. The next day we caught another bus and switchbacked out of the Atlas Mountains down to the Atlantic. When we saw the emerald-blue ocean, we dropped our packs and rushed into the water with our clothes on.

We pitched our tent in the thornbushes on shore and decided to stay forever.

Every morning we walked into the ocean naked. We had been told there were sharks but we paid no attention. Before our brains were even awake, our bodies were surfing. The waves were enormous. Dangerous. They attacked us. Rammed us into the sand and knocked the wind out of us. Rolled us into shore trying to break off our arms and legs. Dragged us across the sand rasping our sunburned bodies. We loved it.

In the middle of the day we hid from the sun in our hooch in the thornbushes and talked about girls and gazed at the crashing blue water.

In the evening, when the tide went out, we dug clams and tore up mussels and boiled them over driftwood for dinner. We listened to the pounding surf and talked about how far away we were. For breakfast we stole oranges from an orchard along the road, loading them into our shirts. Once every few days we walked to an Arab village down the coast and bought several round loaves of bread from black-robed women.

We couldn't imagine a better life. Living outdoors, living off the land. We were kings. Vagabond kings.

One night when we were lying in the sand around the campfire, Mike sprang to his feet.

"I got an idea. Let's swim out to the point."

"Right now? In the dark?"

"Why not?"

"The moon won't be up for at least an hour."

"That's right!"

Down on the beach noise surrounded us. The explosions of the surf were tremendous. They were so much louder when you couldn't see them. All we could make out were phosphorescent lines shimmering, then vanishing.

We kicked off our hiking boots and stripped off our clothes and walked into the invisible water. It was mercurial, molten and cold. We shivered, gasping involuntarily. When it rose to our thighs, we shouted and dove in.

The cold made us swim hard, the mass of black weight chopping into us. Farther out, walls broke over our shoulders and shoved us under. In the pandemonium, we lost each other.

I kept swimming, trying to duck the waves, but I couldn't see them coming. Sometimes I could feel one approaching and manage to dive under at the right moment; sometimes I got hit. Eventually I swam through. Beyond the breakers each swell raised me into the abyss of night, held me there for a second, then gently let me down as the force moved on.

I stopped swimming and let my legs swing down. I could see absolutely nothing. It was amazing. The air itself seemed to have turned to ink.

I opened my mouth to shout for Mike but instead a screech came out. Suddenly I was kicking and writhing and screaming. Something had bitten my leg.

I knew it was circling for another attack and I couldn't tell if I still had a foot or if it was just jagged bone dangling bleeding into the water and I was slamming my thighs up and down and punching into the nothingness with my fists and then I heard a splash behind me and spun around and couldn't see a fucking thing.

"You thought I was a shark!"

"*Goddamn* you, Michael!"

He was gurgling with mirth, choking on the salt water.

"Where are you?"

"Right here."

I stirred myself toward the voice, pulling my arms in circles and kicking my legs. My foot brushed against something.

"Mike, that you?"

"That's me."

I could just make out something in front of me.

"It's wild, huh?"

I calmed myself down. I knew how to do this. I leaned my head back and stared up into the blackness. It was so dark it didn't matter if my eyes were open or closed. I listened to the water at my ears. It made soft clucking noises.

"You know what it's like, Mike? Remember hiding in the closet with somebody when you were a kid. How it was so dark you had to reach out and touch them to make sure they were there."

I waited for a response.

"Mike?"

"What?"

His voice was far away. In the pitch dark, we had drifted apart.

"Over here."

I heard splashing.

"Where are you?"

"Right here."

I heard more splashing.

"We should maybe try to stay close to each other."

"Fine by me."

We treaded water beside each other for a few minutes.

"Mike, what are you thinking about?"

"What it would be like to be lost at sea."

"C'mon."

"No, I am."

So I thought about it too. About those people who fall overboard sailing around the world or folks who are just on a short voyage when their ship is caught in a storm and founders and they're left bobbing in the ocean.

"How about you?"

"Oh, I'm thinking about sharks."

I hadn't been, really, but then maybe I was. On shore in the bright light of day I didn't think about sharks at all. I could hardly imagine them. But now in the stygian darkness I could see them plainly. Their blunt snouts and beady eyes, their massive, powerful bodies, their teeth like row after row of razors. It made me think about all the scrapes I had on my body. I wondered if any of them was leaking blood.

"Ready to swim for the point, Mike?"

"Sure."

"We should swim left."

"Left?"

"My left."

"No. Your right, my left." He was goofing around. Doing his who's-on-first routine.

"No really. We should swim left, don't you think?"

"Which way are you facing?"

"I don't know. I think I hear the surf to my left."

"I don't think you do."

"Which direction is it then?"

"How should I know?" he laughed.

"Mike. Really. Which direction do you think the shore is?" I was expecting him to say something smart-aleck again. "Mike?"

"Shhhhhhh. I'm trying to listen."

I tried to listen too. I slowly rotated myself in a circle. I didn't want to say anything. I wanted just to wait and hear the safe voice of the shore calling us like a mother calling her sons.

"Well?"

"I don't know."

We had drifted apart again. We moved toward each other.

"So." Mike's voice was different now. "Can you see any stars?"

I looked up. The blackness was so complete it was uncanny. It was as if we were underground.

"There must be a haze or something."

I knew what he was thinking. Mike was an Eagle Scout. All we had to do was find a constellation we could recognize; then we could reconnoiter. Find the Big Dipper, go straight up off the top of the lip, find the Little Dipper, find the North Star at the end of the handle, rotate to the right a quarter turn, swim east to shore. Nothing to it.

"You're right, there must be fog. I can't see a thing."

The fear was beginning, insinuating itself slowly, like a needle into the flesh of my belly. I tried to ignore it.

"It's funny."

"What?"

"It's just funny. I mean we can't tell any direction from any other direction. It's never happened to me before."

"It's not so funny, Mike."

"C'mon, Buck. What's the big deal? We can tread water all night if we have to."

I loosened up a little. Mike was right. We were strong. We could tread water for hours if we had to. I tried to go back to the way I was feeling before and enjoy being out here but something wouldn't let me.

"Mike."

"Yeah."

"We can't really tread water all night."

"Sure we can."

"I mean we can, but it won't matter."

"Why?"

"Because we're not just staying in one place. We can't feel it but the current is moving us. There's nothing we can do about it. By the time the sun comes up we could be out in the middle of the ocean."

I waited for him to refute me. I wanted him to refute me. He didn't answer.

We were keeping close to each other now, both smoothly treading water, once in a while intentionally brushing against each other. For a long time we didn't speak.

"Mike. We went too far this time."

"Maybe. Maybe just a little."

We kept treading.

"We should send a postcard tomorrow." His voice was soft and quiet.

"Yeah, we should."

Mike and I sent postcards instead of letters. With postcards we didn't have to write so much. You could never explain to everybody back home what was really happening to you anyway. Some of it was what you saw and where you went but most of it was what was going on inside you. Every few weeks we sent one postcard from the both of us, alternating families. The family that got it was expected to pass it on after they read it.

"We could tell them about how we were saved by mermaids."

"Exactly."

"Mermaids used to save shipwrecked sailors all the time."

I put my head back. My eyes were open to the blackness. I treaded water. I tried to stay cool but I knew I was only pretending. It made me wonder if that was all staying cool really was.

Even though I didn't want it to, my mind kept returning to those people lost overboard. How they wouldn't have life jackets and so they would try to float but the waves would be too rough and they would have to tread water just like us. But then most of them wouldn't have much practice and wouldn't know how to conserve energy so they'd get tired fast. Then, too soon, they would start to think about what was going to happen to them.

Mike and I treaded for a long time without talking. I couldn't tell how long. I couldn't tell time anymore. Minutes, or maybe they were hours, kept expanding like balloons, then popping.

"Mark." Mike touched me with his foot. "I'm sorry."

I opened my eyes. "Yeah, we fucked up."

Just for a moment, the water and the air felt like the same substance. As if all I had to do was let myself sink and I would begin to breathe water as naturally as I breathed air.

"Hey listen." I touched Mike with my foot. "The sun'll come up and we'll see the shore and just swim for it, right."

"Sounds good."

Suddenly I thought I saw stars. My eyes were open and I was staring straight up into blackness and I thought I saw stars! But I wasn't sure. I didn't say anything. I could be wrong. I couldn't see them if I looked straight at them but if I looked kind of from the side I could see pricks of light in the black void.

"Mark?"

I was trying not to look right at them. I was desperate. I didn't want them to vanish. I was staring so hard my eyes were watering. I started trying to fill in the blank spaces between the stars. I was whispering inside myself over and over *God let that be the Big Dipper God let that be the Big Dipper.* But I didn't say anything. I still could be mistaken. Maybe it was all in my head. Maybe I was hallucinating. I'd read somewhere that sometimes that happened right before you died.

"Did you ever see those pictures of astronauts floating around in outer space?" Mike's voice was very calm. "The ones where the spaceship is far away and they're just out there with that long white string attached to them."

"Yeah, Mike, but—" I wanted to tell him to look up but I couldn't. I had to be certain.

Then two more stars sprang out. I was so ecstatic my rhythm got off and I wasn't treading water efficiently anymore and I started sinking, spitting water, laughing from the joy of hope.

"Well, Mark, it's like that string just broke."

Consequences, Part I
by Alan Kesselheim

Sometimes when things go wrong, the key players have to make an immediate decision and live with it. Alan Kesselheim's 1998 memoir, Threading the Currents, *includes this narration of a 1979 canoe capsize in the frigid waters of Opacopa Lake in northern Quebec. Kesselheim (born 1952) was thrust into the role of rescuer. Compare his account with the following piece (beginning on page 165), in which I tell the story from my perspective as one of the capsized paddlers.*

I

t's a sunny day in northern Quebec, sleepy with July warmth and slightly breezy. We've been dawdling down a tea-colored stream near the moss-deep divide between water that flows north to Hudson Bay and water that pours south across glacier-tempered rock to the Gulf of St. Lawrence. The stream connects two lakes, one with a crescent beach we camped on the night before and the other a north-south taper slashing through twenty miles of rockbound, spruce-stubbled fastness.

As we float along, we fish. Craig hooks a northern pike that he says feels, at first, like a waterlogged branch. It thrashes water only as it's hauled from the tannic liquid world and into the sun-washed air. There it lies, lifeless as a piece of stove-length firewood, in the bottom of their canoe; plenty for dinner.

Kris and I have leapt across the continent from New Mexico to join my brother and his partner for this expedition. We have been together for two years, but at the end of this trip I will be taking a teaching job at a small college in Wisconsin and Kris will be going to graduate school in California. Our first journey into the boreal wilds is also the watershed in our relationship. We pay lip service to a future with possibilities, but we both know that this is it.

Four days in. Two yellow canoes. The iron-dark, big-muscled Moisie River is coming up soon, only a day or two south. Until now the river has been a theoretical journey on maps down a snaking blue ribbon in a land full of ribbons, a southward meander crossing brown contour lines like stair steps, broken up by such a density of crosshatches that the cartographers resorted to space-saving R's and F's rather than writing out "Rapids" and "Falls." Even now, still dozens of miles distant, I listen for the river in winds from the south, in just the way I might wake late at night to a train whistle and strain for the last, far moan of the freight as it picks up speed leaving town. I lean toward the Moisie's sound, its pull, the funnel of frothy, dangerous velocity that will suck us south all the way to the ocean-swelled St. Lawrence.

It is still sunny when we break out along the shore of Opacopa Lake through a stream-wide gap in the woods. We rest there a minute, adjusting to the horizon, assessing the broad bulb of water, feeling the unhindered breeze.

A decision. Should we cross a mile-wide bay to save distance or hug the shoreline and stay safe? It is a decision like any of a dozen made each day: do we angle into waves or hit them straight, steer left or right of a mid-river rock, sneak along the edge of a rapid or portage, wait out a rain or pull on our gear and keep paddling? Each one can mean life or death. At the same time, each is as mundane as crossing a street.

The wind is blowing across the lake, broadside to our route. There are waves but few whitecaps. It looks as if the crossing would save us at least a mile, and the far point is a sharp line of spruce trees, tangible and within reach. We shrug into life vests, kneel on the bottom, and start paddling out.

The cadence changes. It is lake rhythm, wind and wave and deep-water music. The canoe rolls beneath us in time. Our knees shift, hips swing, and paddles hit in a rough beat. From the stern I watch the lift and drop of waves, adjusting to the larger ones. Some slap up the side of the boat right to the gunwale, but we don't take on water. The far point doesn't seem as close now. The waves are bigger than we thought. Craig and Dorcas are just ahead, their boat climbing and diving, paddles flashing.

I strike a balance between heading straight across and facing into the wind so that I slice waves at a slight angle and the wind pushes the hull sideways like a ferry in river current. There are whitecaps now, blinking around us like fla ˙ ˙s of liquid lightning.

It seems a long time, with wind snatching at my clothes and the heavy boat riding far from shore. But we are halfway. I can distinguish the larger boulders on the point, the ice-racked line of moss and dirt behind them. We still haven't shipped any water, and the lake music is a tune we are dancing to, a little grimly, but dancing still.

When I glance up, I see that Craig and Dorcas have gone over. Their canoe is a dull yellow log with waves breaking over it, and the two of them are flailing nearby.

"Shit, they're over!"

Kris and I have both stopped paddling. The waves heave under our rudderless weight. A small splash, the first, breaks over the gunwale, and we start up again. I think that if I blink, the picture will change and order will be restored.

In a minute we are up to them. The capsized canoe is dead in the water. We bump against it and circle around, forced to backpaddle to hold our place. The wind shoves at us and the boat bucks in the waves. Craig and Dorcas are the more experienced paddling team by far; they have guided trips in the Far North. Kris and I are the neophytes, and this is our first real expedition to the northern wilds. It should be us in the water. I fight off the certainty that we will join them, that it is only a matter of time and the right wave.

Craig is swimming toward us, towing a waterlogged pack. "I don't know how long the packs will float," he says between breaths. "If we lose this stuff, we're in trouble."

I am looking at my brother's face in the cold, weltered water. The picture is all wrong. He is pale with the shock but oddly matter-of-fact, surprisingly composed. "What happened?" I ask.

"A rogue wave." He has one hand on our gunwale now and looks up at me soberly. We're having an analytical conversation. "We must have leaned wrong. The downslope gunwale caught in the water, and we were over."

He muscles the pack a bit out of the water and I catch a corner of canvas. "Careful!" Kris warns, as I strain and Craig kicks under the weight. The pack streams water and slaps heavily into our boat. We have to paddle constantly, circling the stranded canoe and our two comrades. Dorcas is herding another pack toward us through the water.

"We can't tip," Kris says, her voice strident with fear. She is saying what everyone knows. If she and I go over, we will all die together in the frigid lake.

The second pack is heavier yet, more full of water. It takes both Craig and Dorcas pushing from underneath, me tugging hard, and Kris bracing with her paddle off the far side to lever it over the gunwale. It rides on top of our own load, leaking water into the canoe and raising our center of gravity. We are so deep in the water now that every wave slurps past the brink of the gunwales.

Craig is busy with the equipment pack, the heaviest one by far, full of frying pan and ax and tarp and blocks of cheese. We can't even get it a foot out of the water.

"It'll sink us!" I am shouting into my brother's face, as if the wind has become monumentally loud, our struggle deafening. "Tie it to the stern line!"

"We have to get this stuff to shore." I am desperately working to keep our stern to the waves. "We'll unload and get back as quick as we can. You guys stay with the canoe. Haul yourselves as much out of the water as possible; conserve your strength."

The two of them stroke slowly toward their foundered boat. I have to quell the edge of panic that makes me want to flail at the water with my paddle. Pace yourself, pace yourself, I keep muttering, but within minutes I am huffing for air. The canoe is an absolute leaden pig. A pool several inches deep sloshes around my knees; once in a while a passing wave pours in a little more. The equipment pack is a two-hundred-pound anchor pulling the stern down.

I pick out a boulder onshore. We paddle till our arms ache and still the rock hasn't moved. It is taking too long. The two of us say nothing. Every so often I crane my neck for a glance back. Sometimes I see Craig and Dorcas, two dots of life-vest color draped across the yellow log. Sometimes they are out of sight in a wave trough, the lake a heart-stopping emptiness.

We've made a terrible mistake. We should have taken people first. They are dying in the water while we inch toward land. We could have tied off the packs somehow and come back for them later; so what if we lost some things. When Craig came over with the first pack, with that practical certainty on his face, it never occurred to me that if we took packs on board we would have to leave people behind for a second trip. Then, once we'd gotten the packs in, it was as if we couldn't undo our strategy, had to play it out.

It isn't at all certain that we will make it, either. Water is coming in regularly, sinking us deeper. My arms are numb with fatigue. The fatalistic shadow of defeat looms in my thoughts like an eclipse. How long has it been? Kris has her head down and is paddling mechanically. Maybe it's too demoralizing for her to watch the shore. Maybe she is making the same assessment I am.

Suddenly I can see the sandy bottom. The water is still over my head, but soon the equipment pack will be dragging. Riveted by the sight, I mutter incantations against the chance that it is only a sandbar and that the bottom will drop away again. It doesn't. I can feel the equipment pack bump and catch.

Without saying a thing, I vault over the side. Kris jerks around in alarm and sees me chest deep in the waves. But with me pushing the boat while Kris paddles, we go much faster. Closer in, Kris jumps out, too, and we haul together into the surf breaking against round boulders.

There is no time for talk and no energy for it anyway. We throw the packs a few yards up the shore, just out of the waves' reach, tip the boat over to empty it of water, and turn it back into the waves. I have to over-come a visceral moment that I am ashamed of: the impulse, now that we have found land, to stay there, to survive. But I see those distant dots of color rise and fall in the wild lake as we take the first strokes into the implacable wind.

The boat is light now, buoyant, almost dangerously so. With the packs, even if we rode low, we were solid and steady in the water. Now the wind shoves us around; there are precarious moments. Still, com-pared with the trip in, and despite the strong wind, we make good headway.

The exertion of getting to shore and the overwhelming urgency to return for our partners have been so consuming that I haven't given a thought to how we'll execute the rescue, what aid we might need to administer. It is enough to do this simple task—get to shore and come back, quickly. It is enough, for now, to aim the bow for the two of them out there. I wonder if they see us coming, if they are talking, or if, like us, they are conserving strength and realizing that there isn't much worth saying.

The world has focused down to this tableau, this small bay on a remote northern lake that has been free of ice for less than a month. This wind-lashed sunny afternoon with four people, two canoes, and things gone irrevocably wrong. There is nothing else—no wider world, no families, no plans, none of the passions that seemed, minutes ago, to drive our lives. Only the next wave, the target of color, the scream-ing wind, our labored breathing.

When we finally get close, I see Craig's head up, watching our approach. It is as if we are seeing each other again after an extended separation, as if, say, we'd spent an isolated winter apart and, at this first meeting of spring, we need to take each other's measure again.

"We're in bad shape," he says, and he sounds as if he's just downed a pint of Jack Daniels. Dorcas barely lifts her head. They are dying right now, the cold lake sapping their life, chilling their blood, drugging them.

"Can you bring Dorcas to the side of our boat?" I ask him.

He starts to move, almost languidly, toward her. They have been sweethearts, but their romance is over. The recent months have been a bitter and painful trial. That relationship is over, and they have come on this trip out of loyalty to the adventure and commitment to us, not to be together. But if we can't do this next thing, they will die with each other.

The activity seems to rouse Craig. He pulls Dorcas off the boat, embracing her, he swims toward us. She manages to kick feebly. He latches her white fingers over our gunwale.

"Craig!" I am trying to haul him up from the cold depths with my voice. "Get around the canoe to the other side. Steady us when we pull her in.

"Dorcas! You have to help us." She nods, but it is dreamlike, and I feel as if I'm shouting across a great distance to someone who's walking away.

"Try to keep our bow into the waves," I say to Kris. We are both kneeling, hunkered as low in the boat as we can get. She looks back and I fix on her brown eyes. They are saying that we, too, will be dying if this doesn't work.

I count to three, and Dorcas barely gets her chin to the gunwale. I clutch at her life vest and wrestle her up. Craig steadies the boat. I grab her clothes, a belt loop. She is stiff, nearly unconscious, and seems to be mouthing words. When she slithers into the hull I have to manually bend her at the knees to get her under a thwart. She lies on the bottom, pale and distant.

But it is only half done. There is no one to hold a gunwale when Craig comes over the side, and he is half again Dorcas's weight. This is when we live or die. Right now. The world is in the space between our eyes, here in this canoe, in this charged moment.

Kris perches her weight on the gunwale and leans out on her paddle. I press my knees against the sides of the hull. My face is a foot from Craig's. "Help me," I say, and his eyes hold mine.

We count again; Craig tenses, kicks, and struggles upward. The canoe tips heavily. Kris shouts something incoherent, but I have Craig's belt in my hand, and I pull hard. He dives in face first and twists up along the bottom of the boat next to Dorcas.

"Jesus! Jesus! Jesus!" I hear myself saying. It seems as if I've been breathing hard for hours. I start fishing in the water for the bow line of their canoe.

"Forget the goddamn boat!" Kris screams.

"No way. I'm not coming back out here!" The thought of another trip terrifies me. When I finally get the rope, I tie it to our stern, and then we are paddling again, towing another anchor, listing heavily to the left.

It isn't until later that I marvel at the fact that we accomplished the rescue, at the daunting physics of dragging a waterlogged, half-dead, 170-pound human being over the side of a canoe in three- and four-foot waves. It isn't until later because we are still fighting for life, still battling wind and water, and two of us are past any hope of saving themselves.

"Talk to her!" I shout to Craig. "Make her respond."

My brother fumbles at Dorcas's face. He says something slurred and unintelligible. Confused, desperate, cold to the core himself, he tries to give her mouth-to-mouth breathing.

"Craig! Stop. She's breathing okay." Kris has turned around. "Dorcas! Look at me!"

Her face twitches. Sounds come out of her mouth, but that is all. Kris starts paddling again.

Craig hugs Dorcas to him in the bottom of the canoe. The lake pitches us forward, and the wind is finally our ally, hurrying us in. I can't imagine anything but this frenzied exertion, this grim panic that has been with us ever since I glanced up and saw their capsized boat an age ago. I have lost my capacity to adjust the pace. When we get to shore, we ram full speed into the rocks, leap into the water, and slide the boat with one heave into the boulders.

Supporting Craig and Dorcas one at a time, we stumble up a steep bank and into the dense, swampy forest. Kris rips packs apart in search of sleeping bags while I retrieve the second canoe from the waves. It takes both of us to work the two of them out of their wet, heavy clothes; their canvas pants fight back, catching on knees and shoes. We strip ourselves, too, and clamber naked into sleeping bags with them. Then we lie there, suddenly exhausted, hugging the blue-cold bodies of our friends.

The moss is soft and deep beneath us; the air is oddly still, the sound of wind diminished in the trees. I can still feel the lake bucking beneath me, but it is a sunny afternoon again and I refuse to think that our efforts will not be enough.

Dorcas mumbles something and begins to sob. Kris soothes her and holds her tighter, but she is far off, wrapped in a cold cocoon.

When Craig finally begins to shiver, it wakes me out of a timeless stupor. I have no idea how long we've been lying in the moss, but now his body is burning fuel, exercising to make heat. Soon he's shaking so hard I can barely hold on; his shivers are almost like convulsions.

"Maybe I could eat something," he stammers.

I nurse him with globs of honey on the end of my finger. His muscles work harder. He is grinning with warmth.

But it is a long wait for Dorcas. She lapses into bouts of sobbing, slips away from us, surfaces briefly. Kris talks to her, coaxes her back, and embraces her unresponsive body. And when she does revive, it is a slow, halting process. Finally she is able to swallow some honey. She begins to shiver. Her eyes kindle with first heat.

Craig rises on his elbow and reaches for her shoulder. "Dorcas! We're going to live!" His voice is hoarse with emotion, and the image of the two of them draped over the canoe comes stabbing back into my mind. I wonder how far down the path toward reckoning with death they traveled, out there on the relentless lake.

Consequences, Part II
by Dorcas S. Miller

Four years ago Alan Kesselheim sent me a draft of the story that begins on page 155. I'd never discussed the events of that day with anyone involved. I was stunned by his view of what happened—it was so different than my own. I went to the basement and pulled out a narration that I'd written shortly after the rescue. Here it is.

Craig and I should not be canoe partners, now that we are no longer together. I still feel the searing pain from the phone call, not too many weeks ago, when he informed me of the change in his intentions. He'd found someone else.

I had insisted on doing the trip. I loved the wilderness as much as I loved him. I couldn't give up both.

So we are a foursome. Craig's brother, Al, and his friend, Kris, are joining us for their first big canoe trip in the Canadian north woods. I am glad for another woman on the trip, but feel the pinch of loneliness. They are his friends.

We are an uncomfortable pair in his canoe, where every stroke is done in tandem, where we will have to follow each other's lead across windy lakes and through churning whitewater. Trust is essential and my stock of trust is low just now.

The third day of the trip signals trouble. In the afternoon we cross to a lee shore in a strong wind. The canoe handles poorly, wallowing in the waves. The wind keeps pushing the boat broadside, and I can't hold the course by myself in the stern. "Draw," I yell at Craig. "And keep drawing."

He stops paddling and turns around to look for the other boat. "I'm worried about Al and Kris," he says. Our boat swings broadside. "We've got to worry about ourselves first," I hiss. I lean out over the left gunnel and draw hard to correct the angle. "Keep paddling! We have to get into the lee."

He doesn't know what can happen on a windy lake. I do. I'd once seen a boat go over and realized that I couldn't rescue the swimmers without endangering my own canoe. I don't want to be a casualty in the wilderness of Quebec. I don't trust Craig's judgment, yet because Kris and Al paddle together, I am paired with Craig for the trip.

That night, after dinner, I walk along the beach and find a quiet place far from our tents. I leave my clothes in a rumpled pile and bath in the icy water. The air is still and clean and warm after the coldness of my swim. I walk back up the beach, dust the sand from my feet, and slip into my sleeping bag.

I wake once during the night. Northern lights ripple across the horizon. The Big Dipper hangs low and a nearly full moon illuminates the beach. The air is chill and sharp and I am utterly alone. I drink from a cup of water by the side of the tent. Tiny ice crystals have begun to grow around the edge.

The next morning we paddle a winding stream, lining some sections, to reach Opacopa Lake. A stiff breeze there greets us. The wind and waves will hit us broadside until we reach a point about a mile away; then, we will get some protection. I snug up my life jacket, as much for the warmth as the floatation.

In the bow, I move to my knees, bracing against the seat and pulling hard against the water. We keep up a steady pace, with Craig in the stern making adjustments in direction. The waves batter the right side of the canoe; the keelless boat pivots at the top of each wave. We paddle without rest, hard against the waves. We want to get to the point, to safety.

A cresting wave catches us dead broadside and turns us over in one smooth roll. I grab the gunwale in one hand and hold on to my paddle with the other as I slide into the icy water. I blink to keep out the cold. The three packs and the spare paddle bob around the boat. Kris and Al come up behind, wrestling with the wind. The cold squeezes me like a vice.

We have to do something quickly. No time for a leisurely discussion. We can't reload our canoe. We can't put everything in their canoe. We have to get to shore. We have to get our gear to shore. What should go first, gear or us? It is as if the decision makes itself. Will the gear still be there if we leave it behind?

We have to save the gear. I unclip my camera box and swim it over to Al. My pack goes next, then Craig's. Their canoe is full, so we tie the equipment pack to the stern line. Kris and Al head to shore.

They are thirty feet away when I shout, "No, wait." We are making the wrong decision. We shouldn't stay out while our packs go in.

Kris and Al stop. "What do you want us to do?"

"I don't know." We need those packs. "Go ahead."

Craig and I swim to opposite ends of the overturned canoe. We try to right it, but it has too little floatation. We turn it back over and try to sit on it, but the waves roll us off.

My fingers are stiff and useless with cold. I want to tie the bow line to the stern line to give us something other than the smooth hull to grab. I make the square knot with grotesque, wooden movements of my arms.

We talk to each other, our words starting to slur. "Put up hoood," I tell him. He puts up his windshell hood to conserve heat, then puts up mine because I can't. We shiver violently. The cold has pierced my muscles and bones.

"We should swim for shore," he says. So tempting—but it's too far away. Better to stay together, with the canoe. I don't want to be out here alone. We cling to the line, side by side, his numb hand over my numb hand, watching between cresting waves the slow progress of our rescuers. We say little, checking occasionally.

"OK?"

"Fiiine."

My heat drains away. I am beyond shivering. I see death standing by. All that is left is wanting to stay alive.

In the distance, the yellow canoe lands. I hold on. "They're coming," Craig says. I hold on.

They come to us at last. Somehow I get to the side of their boat. One clenched hand holds a red baseball cap and a bandanna. I try to put them in the canoe but the arm belongs to someone else. I can't lift it. The hand lets go of the hat and the bandanna and they drift off into the waves. I reach for the gunwale but the arm won't respond. Al takes hold of me and heaves me in. Craig comes in after me. We both lay in the bottom of the canoe.

I feel the sunlight on my face.

If I close my eyes, I am warm. It is so nice there, warm and dark and soft. I want to stay. It is easy to stay. I drift into the darkness.

Something tugs me back to the light. The sun hurts my eyes. The brazen blue sky is so bright.

Better back there, in the dark.

"She's not breathing," Craig says. He leans close and blows air into my lungs. Again, and again.

"I'm fine. I can breath on my own. There is nothing wrong. My mind is perfectly clear." I try to tell them, but they can't hear me. I can't reach them. I hover between the light and the dark. I have to choose which way to go.

The sunlight burns into my eyelids. I am sorry to leave the dark. It is so warm there. I pull myself into the light.

The canoe grinds against the rocky shore. I crawl over moss and lichen. Al strips off my clothes. Kris puts me into her purple sweatshirt and into a sleeping bag and climbs in with me, pressing her body against my own.

She holds me and talks to me. She hugs me and pulls the sleeping bag up around my shoulders and brushes dirt off my forehead.

Can I hear her? That's good. Can I move my toes? That's fine.

Tears brim onto my cheeks and low wail comes from my mouth. "Go ahead, you need to cry," she says.

Later, when I can sit up, Kris puts a cup to my mouth. The sweet liquid spills onto my chin and dribbles onto the clean sweatshirt.

Eventually Kris leaves to help Al set up tents and string line for wet clothes. I lay in the sleeping bag for a long time.

At last, I get up and move slowly around the impromptu camp. My sleeping bag is dry. My journal is dry. My camera and binoculars are dry. The tarp, the ax, and the frying pan are gone. Who cares. I'm alive.

We make an early supper and talk about the rescue. I say to Al and Kris, "I know this sounds corny but I want to thank you for saving my life."

We adjourn to the tents even though it is still light. Craig and I talk for a while. "I couldn't have stayed in the water much longer," I confess. "Me neither," he says.

Suddenly, I am on fire, as if I have some strange fever that comes on all at once. I am bathed in sweat. I want to get out of the sleeping bag, out into the open air, but am petrified by the thought of getting cold again.

When I close my eyes to sleep, I see the canoe looming over me as I slide into the frigid water. I hear my moans as I lay in the bottom of the boat.

"I'm afraid. Will you hold my hand?" He takes it. After a time the images dissolve. I let go of his hand and fall into a deep sleep empty of dreams.

We break camp before breakfast. A light breeze blows from the north. The wind will come up. We have to get across the exposed water before the lake gets rough.

We paddle out from the campsite and I realize how far the shallow, sandy shelf extends offshore. The northwest wind that swamped us had also put salvation close. If we had chosen to swim to shore, with the wind at our backs, perhaps we would have hit that shelf in time.

We easily reach the point that we had struggled toward the day before. We forego the comfort of tea and coffee, eating a cold breakfast of granola and talking once again about the capsize.

"It's my fault. I was in the stern," says Craig.

"I just can't believe that you two went over instead of us," says Kris.

"Should we abandon the trip?" someone says, giving voice to the question we all feel. The query sits among us like an unwanted guest. We can, after all, turn around, paddle back to the train tracks, and catch the next train south.

A pair of common loons surfaces just off the rocks. Their sleek features and beautifully etched plumage remind me why I want so much to be here. But it is hard to negotiate the silence. "We made a mistake and we can learn from it," I say. "We're just as skilled as we were two days ago. Only our confidence has changed."

We talk about our fears, our hopes. The loons come and go. When we're through we pack our cereal bowls and get in the canoes. Craig and I, without comment, distance ourselves once more. I cannot live with the power of knowing that our lives were twinned so closely. I push away: It's as if it all happened to someone else. We are once more strangers. We pick up our paddles, round the point, and go on to the Moisie, our backs to the bay where we spent a sunny afternoon under death's shadow.

from The Wind in the Willows

by Kenneth Grahame

Sometimes we fall into danger quite by accident. This selection by Kenneth Grahame (1859-1932) follows Mole as he sets out to find Badger, not knowing the dangers that lurk in the Wild Wood. When the sun goes down and the snow starts to fall, Mole finds out who his friends are.

The Mole had long wanted to make the acquaintance of the Badger. He seemed, by all accounts, to be such an important personage and, though rarely visible, to make his unseen influence felt by everybody about the place. But whenever the Mole mentioned his wish to the Water Rat he always found himself put off. 'It's all right,' the Rat would say, 'Badger'll turn up some day or other—he's always turning up—and then I'll introduce you. The best of fellows! But you must not only take him as you find him, but when you find him.'

'Couldn't you ask him here—dinner or something?' said the Mole.

'He wouldn't come,' replied the Rat simply. 'Badger hates Society, and invitations, and dinner, and all that sort of thing.'

'Well, then, supposing we go and call on *him*?' suggested the Mole.

'O, I'm sure he wouldn't like that at *all*,' said the Rat, quite alarmed. 'He's so very shy, he'd be sure to be offended. I've never even ventured to call on him at his home myself, though I know him so well. Besides, we can't. It's quite out of the question, because he lives in the very middle of the Wild Wood.'

'Well, supposing he does,' said the Mole. 'You told me the Wild Wood was all right, you know.'

'O, I know, I know, so it is,' replied the Rat evasively. 'But I think we won't go there just now. Not *just* yet. It's a long way, and he wouldn't be at home at this time of year anyhow, and he'll be coming along some day, if you'll wait quietly.'

The Mole had to be content with this. But the Badger never came along, and every day brought its amusements, and it was not till summer was long over, and cold and frost and miry ways kept them much indoors, and the swollen river raced past outside their windows with a speed that mocked at boating of any sort or kind, that he found his thoughts dwelling again with much persistence on the solitary grey Badger, who lived his own life by himself, in his hole in the middle of the Wild Wood.

In the winter time the Rat slept a great deal, retiring early and rising late. During his short day he sometimes scribbled poetry or did other small domestic jobs about the house; and, of course, there were always animals dropping in for a chat, and consequently there was a good deal of story-telling and comparing notes on the past summer and all its doings.

Such a rich chapter it had been, when one came to look back on it all! With illustrations so numerous and so very highly coloured! The pageant of the river bank had marched steadily along, unfolding itself in scene-pictures that succeeded each other in stately procession. Purple loosestrife arrived early, shaking luxuriant tangled locks along the edge of the mirror whence its own face laughed back at it. Willow-herb, tender and wistful, like a pink sunset cloud, was not slow to follow. Comfrey, the purple hand-in-hand with the white, crept forth to take its place in the line; and at last one morning the diffident and delaying dog-rose stepped delicately on the stage, and one knew, as if string-music had announced it in stately chords that strayed into a gavotte, that June at last was here. One member of the company was still awaited; the shepherd-boy for the nymphs to woo, the knight for whom the ladies waited at the window, the prince that was to kiss the sleeping summer back to life and love. But when meadow-sweet, debonair and odorous in amber jerkin, moved graciously to his place in the group, then the play was ready to begin.

And what a play it had been! Drowsy animals, snug in their holes while wind and rain were battering at their doors recalled still keen mornings, an hour before sunrise, when the white mist, as yet undispersed, clung closely along the surface of the water; then the shock of the early plunge, the scamper along the bank, and the radiant transformation of earth, air, and water, when suddenly the sun was with them again, and grey was gold and colour was born and sprang out of the earth once more. They recalled the languorous siesta of hot midday, deep in green undergrowth, the sun striking through in tiny golden shafts and spots; the boating and bathing of the afternoon, the rambles along dusty lanes and through yellow cornfields; and the long, cool evening at last, when so many threads were gathered up, so many friendships rounded, and so many adventures planned for the morrow. There was plenty to talk about on those short winter days when the animals found themselves round the fire; still, the Mole had a good deal of spare time on his hands, and so one afternoon, when the Rat in his arm-chair before the blaze was alternately dozing and trying over rhymes that wouldn't fit, he formed the resolution to go out by himself and explore the Wild Wood, and perhaps strike up an acquaintance with Mr. Badger.

It was a cold still afternoon with a hard steely sky overhead, when he slipped out of the warm parlour into the open air. The country lay bare and entirely leafless around him, and he thought that he had never seen so far and so intimately into the insides of things as on that winter day when Nature was deep in her annual slumber and seemed to have kicked the clothes off. Copses, dells, quarries and all hidden places, which had been mysterious mines for exploration in leafy summer, now exposed themselves and their secrets pathetically, and seemed to ask him to overlook their shabby poverty for a while, till they could riot in rich masquerade as before, and trick and entice him with the old deceptions. It was pitiful in a way, and yet cheering—even exhilarating. He was glad that he liked the country undecorated, hard, and stripped of its finery. He had got down to the bare bones of it, and they were fine and strong and simple. He did not want the warm clover and the play of seeding grasses; the screens of quickset, the billowy drapery of beech and elm seemed best away; and with great cheerfulness of spirit he pushed on towards the Wild Wood, which lay before him low and threatening, like a black reef in some still southern sea.

There was nothing to alarm him at first entry. Twigs crackled under his feet, logs tripped him, funguses on stumps resembled caricatures, and startled him for the moment by their likeness to something familiar and far away; but that was all fun, and exciting. It led him on, and he penetrated to where the light was less, and trees crouched nearer and nearer, and holes made ugly mouths at him on either side.

Everything was very still now. The dusk advanced on him steadily, rapidly, gathering in behind and before; and the light seemed to be draining away like flood-water.

Then the faces began.

It was over his shoulder, and indistinctly, that he first thought he saw a face: a little evil wedge-shaped face, looking out at him from a hole. When he turned and confronted it, the thing had vanished.

He quickened his pace, telling himself cheerfully not to begin imagining things, or there would be simply no end to it. He passed another hole, and another, and another; and then—yes!—no!—yes! certainly a little narrow face, with hard eyes, had flashed up for an instant from a hole, and was gone. He hesitated—braced himself up for an effort and strode on. Then suddenly, as if it had been so all the time, every hole, far and near, and there were hundreds of them, seemed to possess its face, coming and going rapidly, all fixing on him glances of malice and hatred: all hard-eyed and evil and sharp.

If he could only get away from the holes in the banks, he thought, there would be no more faces. He swung off the path and plunged into the untrodden places of the wood.

Then the whistling began.

Very faint and shrill it was, and far behind him, when first he heard it; but somehow it made him hurry forward. Then, still very faint and shrill, it sounded far ahead of him, and made him hesitate and want to go back. As he halted in indecision it broke out on either side, and seemed to be caught up and passed on throughout the whole length of the wood to its farthest limit. They were up and alert and ready, evidently, whoever they were! And he—he was alone, and unarmed, and far from any help; and the night was closing in.

Then the pattering began.

He thought it was only falling leaves at first, so slight and delicate was the sound of it. Then as it grew it took a regular rhythm, and he knew it for nothing else but the pat-pat-pat of little feet, still a very long way off. Was it in front or behind? It seemed to be first one, then the other, then both. It grew and it multiplied, till from every quarter as he listened anxiously, leaning this way and that, it seemed to be closing in on him. As he stood still to hearken, a rabbit came running hard towards him through the trees. He waited, expecting it to slacken pace, or to swerve from him into a different course. Instead, the animal almost brushed him as it dashed past, his face set and hard, his eyes staring. 'Get out of this, you fool, get out!' the Mole heard him mutter as he swung round a stump and disappeared down a friendly burrow.

The pattering increased till it sounded like sudden hail on the dry-leaf carpet spread around him. The whole wood seemed running now, running hard, hunting, chasing, closing in round something or—somebody? In panic, he began to run too, aimlessly, he knew not whither. He ran up against things, he fell over things and into things, he darted under things and dodged round things. At last he took refuge in the deep dark hollow of an old beech tree, which offered shelter, concealment—perhaps even safety, but who could tell? Anyhow, he was too tired to run any further and could only snuggle down into the dry leaves which had drifted into the hollow and hope he was safe for the time. And as he lay there panting and trembling, and listened to the whistlings and the patterings outside, he knew it at last, in all its fullness, that dread thing which other little dwellers in field and hedgerow had encountered here, and known as their darkest moment—that thing which the Rat had vainly tried to shield him from—the Terror of the Wild Wood!

Meantime the Rat, warm and comfortable, dozed by his fireside. His paper of half-finished verses slipped from his knee, his head fell back, his mouth opened, and he wandered by the verdant banks of dream-rivers. Then a coal slipped, the fire crackled and sent up a spurt of flame, and he woke with a start. Remembering what he had been engaged upon, he reached down to the floor for his verses, pored over them for a minute, and then looked round for the Mole to ask him if he knew a good rhyme for something or other.

But the Mole was not there.

He listened for a time. The house seemed very quiet.

Then he called 'Moly!' several times, and, receiving no answer, got up and went out into the hall.

The Mole's cap was missing from its accustomed peg. His goloshes, which always lay by the umbrella-stand, were also gone.

The Rat left the house and carefully examined the muddy surface of the ground outside, hoping to find the Mole's tracks. There they were, sure enough. The goloshes were new, just bought for the winter, and the pimples on their soles were fresh and sharp. He could see the imprints of them in the mud, running along straight and purposeful, leading direct to the Wild Wood.

The Rat looked very grave, and stood in deep thought for a minute or two. Then he re-entered the house, strapped a belt around his waist, shoved a brace of pistols into it, took up a stout cudgel that stood in a corner of the hall, and set off for the Wild Wood at a smart pace.

It was already getting towards dusk when he reached the first fringe of trees and plunged without hesitation into the wood, looking anxiously on either side for any sign of his friend. Here and there wicked little faces popped out of holes, but vanished immediately at sight of the valorous animal, his pistols, and the great ugly cudgel in his grasp; and the whistling and pattering, which he had heard quite plainly on his first entry, died away and ceased, and all was very still. He made his way manfully through the length of the wood, to its furthest edge; then, forsaking all paths, he set himself to traverse it, laboriously working over the whole ground, and all the time calling out cheerfully, 'Moly, Moly, Moly! Where are you? It's me—it's old Rat!'

He had patiently hunted through the wood for an hour or more, when at last to his joy he heard a little answering cry. Guiding himself by the sound, he made his way through the gathering darkness to the foot of an old beech tree, with a hole in it, and from out of the hole came a feeble voice, saying, 'Ratty! Is that really you?'

The Rat crept into the hollow, and there he found the Mole, exhausted and still trembling. 'O, Rat!' he cried, 'I've been so frightened, you can't think!'

'O, I quite understand,' said the Rat soothingly. 'You shouldn't really have gone and done it, Mole. I did my best to keep you from it. We river-bankers, we hardly ever come here by ourselves. If we have to come, we come in couples, at least; then we're generally all right. Besides, there are a hundred things one has to know, which we understand all about and you don't, as yet. I mean passwords, and signs, and sayings which have power and effect, and plants you carry in your pocket, and verses you repeat, and dodges and tricks you practise; all simple enough when you know them, but they've got to be known if you're small, or you'll find yourself in trouble. Of course if you were Badger or Otter, it would be quite another matter.'

'Surely the brave Mr. Toad wouldn't mind coming here by himself, would he?' inquired the Mole.

'Old Toad?' said the Rat, laughing heartily. 'He wouldn't show his face here alone, not for a whole hatful of golden guineas, Toad wouldn't.'

The Mole was greatly cheered by the sound of the Rat's careless laughter, as well as by the sight of his stick and his gleaming pistols, and he stopped shivering and began to feel bolder and more himself again.

'Now then,' said the Rat presently, 'we really must pull ourselves together and make a start for home while there's still a little light left.

It will never do to spend the night here, you understand. Too cold, for one thing.'

'Dear Ratty,' said the poor Mole, 'I'm dreadfully sorry, but I'm simply dead beat and that's a solid fact. You must let me rest here a while longer, and get my strength back, if I'm to get home at all.'

'O, all right,' said the good-natured Rat, 'rest away. It's pretty nearly pitch dark now, anyhow; and there ought to be a bit of a moon later.'

So the Mole got well into the dry leaves and stretched himself out, and presently dropped off into sleep, though of a broken and troubled sort; while the Rat covered himself up, too, as best he might, for warmth, and lay patiently waiting, with a pistol in his paw.

When at last the Mole woke up, much refreshed and in his usual spirits, the Rat said, 'Now then! I'll just take a look outside and see if everything's quiet, and then we really must be off.'

He went to the entrance of their retreat and put his head out. Then the Mole heard him saying quietly to himself, 'Hullo! hullo! here— *is*—a—go!'

'What's up, Ratty?" asked the Mole.

'*Snow* is up,' replied the Rat briefly; 'or rather, *down*. It's snowing hard!'

The Mole came and crouched beside him, and, looking out, saw the wood that had been so dreadful to him in quite a changed aspect. Holes, hollows, pools, pitfalls, and other black menaces to the wayfarer were vanishing fast, and a gleaming carpet of faery was springing up everywhere, that looked too delicate to be trodden upon by rough feet. A fine powder filled the air and caressed the cheek with a tingle in its touch, and the black boles of the trees showed up in a light that seemed to come from below.

'Well, well, it can't be helped,' said the Rat, after pondering. 'We must make a start, and take our chance, I suppose. The worst of it is, I don't exactly know where we are. And now this snow makes everything look so very different.'

It did indeed. The Mole would not have known that it was the same wood. However, they set out bravely, and took the line that seemed most promising, holding on to each other and pretending with invincible cheerfulness that they recognized an old friend in every fresh tree that grimly and silently greeted them, or saw openings, gaps, or paths with a familiar turn in them, in the monotony of white space and black tree-trunks that refused to vary.

An hour or two later—they had lost all count of time—they pulled up, dispirited, weary, and hopelessly at sea, and sat down on a fallen tree-trunk to recover their breath and consider what was to be done. They were aching with fatigue and bruised with tumbles; they had fallen into several holes and got wet through; the snow was getting so deep that they could hardly drag their little legs through it, and the trees were thicker and more like each other than ever. There seemed to be no end to this wood, and no beginning, and no difference in it, and, worst of all, no way out.

'We can't sit here very long,' said the Rat. 'We shall have to make another push for it, and do something or other. The cold is too awful for anything, and the snow will soon be too deep for us to wade through.' He peered about him and considered. 'Look here,' he went on, 'this is what occurs to me. There's a sort of dell down there in front of us, where the ground seems all hilly and humpy and hummocky. We'll make our way down into that, and try and find some sort of shelter, a cave or hole with a dry floor to it, out of the snow and the wind, and there we'll have a good rest before we try again, for we're both of us pretty dead beat. Besides, the snow may leave off, or something may turn up.'

So once more they got on their feet, and struggled down into the dell, where they hunted about for a cave or some corner that as dry and a protection from the keen wind and the whirling snow. They were investigating one of the hummocky bits the Rat had spoken of, when suddenly the Mole tripped up and fell forward on his face with a squeal.

'O, my leg!' he cried. 'O, my poor shin!' and he sat up on the snow and nursed his leg in both his front paws.

'Poor old Mole!' said the Rat kindly. 'You don't seem to be having much luck to-day, do you? Let's have a look at the leg. Yes,' he went on, going down on his knees to look, 'you've cut your shin, sure enough. Wait till I get at my handkerchief, and I'll tie it up for you.'

'I must have tripped over a hidden branch or a stump,' said the Mole miserably. 'O my! O my!'

'It's a very clear cut,' said the Rat, examining it again attentively. 'That was never done by a branch or a stump. Looks as if it was made by a sharp edge of something in metal. Funny!' He pondered awhile, and examined the humps and slopes that surrounded them.

'Well, never mind what done it,' said the Mole, forgetting his grammar in his pain. 'It hurts just the same, whatever done it.'

But the Rat, after carefully tying up the leg with his handkerchief, had left him and was busy scraping in the snow. He scratched and shovelled and explored, all four legs working busily, while the Mole waited impatiently, remarking at intervals, 'O, *come* on, Rat!'

Suddenly the Rat cried 'Hooray!' and then 'Hooray-oo-ray-oo-ray-oo-ray!' and fell to executing a feeble jig in the snow.

'What *have* you found, Ratty?' asked the Mole, still nursing his leg.

'Come and see!' said the delighted Rat, as he jigged on.

The Mole hobbled up to the spot and had a good look.

'Well,' he said at last, slowly, 'I *see* it right enough. Seen the same sort of thing before, lots of times. Familiar object, I call it. A door-scraper! Well, what of it? Why dance jigs round a door-scraper?'

'But don't you see what it *means*, you—you dull-witted animal?' cried the Rat impatiently.

'Of course I see what it means,' replied the Mole. 'It simply means that some very careless and forgetful person has left his door-scraper lying about in the middle of the Wild Wood, *just* where it's *sure* to trip *everybody* up. Very thoughtless of him, I call it. When I get home I shall go and complain about it to—to somebody or other, see if I don't!'

'O dear! O dear!' cried the Rat, in despair at his obtuseness. 'Here, stop arguing and come and scrape!' And he set to work again and made the snow fly in all directions around him.

After some further toil his efforts were rewarded, and a very shabby door-mat lay exposed to view.

'There, what did I tell you?' exclaimed the Rat, in great triumph.

'Absolutely nothing whatever,' replied the Mole, with perfect truthfulness. 'Well now,' he went on, 'you seem to have found another piece of domestic litter, done for and thrown away, and I suppose you're perfectly happy. Better go ahead and dance your jig round that if you've got to, and get it over, and then perhaps we can go on and not waste any more time over rubbish-heaps. Can we *eat* a door-mat? Or sleep under the door-mat? Or sit on a door-mat and sledge home over the snow on it, you exasperating rodent?'

'Do-you-mean-to-say,' cried the excited Rat, 'that this door-mat doesn't *tell* you anything?'

'Really, Rat,' said the Mole quite pettishly, 'I think we'd had enough of this folly. Who ever heard of a door-mat *telling* any one anything? They simply don't do it. They are not that sort at all. Door-mats know their place.'

'Now look here, you—you thick-headed beast,' replied the Rat, really angry, 'this must stop. Not another word, but scrape—scrape and scratch and dig and hunt around . . . especially on the sides of the hummocks, if you want to sleep dry and warm to-night, for it's our last chance!'

The Rat attacked a snow-bank beside them with ardour, probing with his cudgel everywhere and then digging with fury; and the Mole scraped busily too, more to oblige the Rat than for any other reason, for his opinion was that his friend was getting light-headed.

Some ten minutes' hard work, and the point of the Rat's cudgel struck something that sounded hollow. He worked till he could get a paw through and feel; then called the Mole to come and help him. Hard at it went the two animals, till at last the result of their labours stood full in view of the astonished and hitherto incredulous Mole.

In the side of what had seemed to be a snow-bank stood a solid-looking little door, painted a dark green. An iron bell-pull hung by the side, and below it, on a small brass plate, neatly engraved in square capital letters, they could read by the aid of moonlight:—

MR. BADGER

The Mole fell backwards on the snow from sheer surprise and delight. 'Rat!' he cried in penitence, 'you're a wonder! A real wonder, that's what you are. I see it all now! You argued it out, step by step, in that wise head of yours, from the very moment that I fell and cut my shin, and you looked at the cut, and at once your majestic mind said to itself, "Door-scraper!" And then you turned to and found the very door-scraper that done it! Did you stop there? No. Some people would have been quite satisfied; but not you. Your intellect went on working. "Let me only just find a door-mat," says you to yourself, "and my theory is proved!" And of course you found your door-mat. You're so clever, I believe you could find anything you liked. "Now," says you, "that door exists, as plain as if I saw it. There's nothing else that remains to be done but to find it!" Well, I've read about that sort of thing in books, but I've, never come across it before in real life. You ought to go where you'll be properly appreciated. You're simply wasted here, among us fellows. If I only had your head, Ratty—"

'But as you haven't,' interrupted the Rat rather unkindly, 'I suppose you're going to sit on the snow all night and *talk*? Get up at once and hang on to that bell-pull you see there, and ring hard, as hard as you can, while I hammer!'

While the Rat attacked the door with his stick, the Mole sprang up at the bell-pull, clutched it and swung there, both feet well off the ground, and from quite a long way off they could faintly hear a deep-toned bell respond.

They waited patiently for what seemed a very long time, stamping in the snow to keep their feet warm. At last they heard the sound of slow shuffling footsteps approaching the door from the inside. It seemed, as the Mole remarked to the Rat, like someone walking in carpet slippers that were too large for him and down-at-heel; which was intelligent of Mole, because that was exactly what it was.

There was the noise of a bolt shot back, and the door opened a few inches, enough to show a long snout and a pair of sleepy blinking eyes.

'Now, the *very* next time this happens,' said a gruff and suspicious voice, 'I shall be exceedingly angry. Who is it *this* time, disturbing people on such a night? Speak up!'

'O, Badger,' cried the Rat, 'let us in, please. It's me, Rat, and my friend Mole, and we've lost our way in the snow.'

'What, Ratty, my dear little man!' exclaimed the Badger, in quite a different voice. 'Come along in, both of you, at once. Why, you must be perished. Well I never! Lost in the snow, And in the Wild Wood, too, and at this time of night! But come in with you.'

The two animals tumbled over each other in their eagerness to get inside, and heard the door shut behind them with great joy and relief.

The Badger, who wore a long dressing-gown, and whose slippers were indeed very down-at-heel, carried a flat candlestick in his paw and had probably been on his way to bed when their summons sounded. He looked kindly down on them and patted both their heads. 'This is not the sort of night for small animals to be out,' he said paternally. 'I'm afraid you've been up to some of your pranks again, Ratty. But come along; come into the kitchen. There's a first-rate fire there, and supper and everything.'

He shuffled on in front of them, carrying the light, and they followed him, nudging each other in an anticipating sort of way, down a long, gloomy, and, to tell the truth, decidedly shabby passage, into a sort of a central hall, out of which they could dimly see other long tunnel-like passages branching, passages mysterious and without apparent end. But there were doors in the hall as well—stout oaken comfortable-looking doors. One of these the Badger flung open, and at once they found themselves in all the glow and warmth of a large fire-lit kitchen.

The floor was well-worn red brick, and on the wide hearth burnt a fire of logs, between two attractive chimney-corners tucked away in the wall, well out of any suspicion of draught. A couple of high-backed settles, facing each other on either side of the fire, gave further sitting accommodation for the sociably disposed. In the middle of the room stood a long table of plain boards placed on trestles, with benches down each side. At one end of it, where an arm-chair stood pushed back, were spread the remains of the Badger's plain but ample supper. Rows of spotless plates winked from the shelves of the dresser at the far end of the room, and from the rafters overhead hung hams, bundles of dried herbs, nets of onions, and baskets of eggs. It seemed a place where heroes could fitly feast after victory, where weary harvesters could line up in scores along the table and keep their Harvest Home with mirth and song, or where two or three friends of simple tastes could sit about as they pleased and eat and smoke and talk in comfort and contentment. The ruddy brick floor smiled up at the smoky ceiling; the oaken settles, shiny with long wear, exchanged cheerful glances with each other; plates on the dresser grinned at pots on the shelf, and the merry firelight flickered and played over everything without distinction.

The kindly Badger thrust them down on a settle to toast themselves at the fire, and bade them remove their wet coats and boots. Then he fetched them dressing-gowns and slippers, and himself bathed the Mole's shin with warm water and mended the cut with sticking-plaster till the whole thing was just as good as new, if not better. In the embracing light and warmth, warm and dry at last, with weary legs propped up in front of them, and a suggestive clink of plates being arranged on the table behind, it seemed to the storm-driven animals, now in safe anchorage, that the cold and trackless Wild Wood just left outside was miles and miles away, and all that they had suffered in it a half-forgotten dream.

When at last they were thoroughly toasted, the Badger summoned them to the table, where he had been busy laying a repast. They had felt pretty hungry before, but when they actually saw at last the supper that was spread for them, really it seemed only a question of what they should attack first where all was so attractive, and whether the other things would obligingly wait for them till they had time to give them attention. Conversation was impossible for a long time; and when it was slowly resumed, it was that regrettable sort of conversation that results from talking with your mouth full. The Badger did not mind that sort of thing at all, nor did he take any notice of elbows on the table, or everybody speaking at once. As he did not go into Society himself, he had got an idea that these things belonged to the things that didn't really matter. (We know of course that he was wrong, and took too narrow a view; because they do matter very much, though it would take too long to explain why.) He sat in his arm-chair at the head of the table, and nodded gravely at intervals as the animals told their story; and he did not seem surprised or shocked at anything, and he never said, 'I told you so,' or, 'Just what I always said,' or remarked that they ought to have done so-and-so, or ought not to have done something else. The Mole began to feel very friendly towards him.

When supper was really finished at last, and each animal felt that his skin was now as tight as was decently safe, and that by this time he didn't care a hang for anybody or anything, they gathered round the glowing embers of the great wood fire, and thought how jolly it was to be sitting up so late, and so independent, and so full; and after they had chatted for a time about things in general, the Badger said heartily, 'Now then! Tell us the news from your part of the world. How's old Toad going on?'

'O, from bad to worse,' said the Rat gravely, while the Mole, cocked up on a settle and basking in the firelight, his heels higher than his head, tried to look properly mournful. 'Another smash-up only last week, and a bad one. You see, he will insist on driving himself, and he's hopelessly incapable. If he'd only employ a decent, steady, well-trained animal, pay him good wages, and leave everything to him, he'd get on all right. But no; he's convinced he's a heaven-born driver, and nobody can teach him anything; and all the rest follows.'

'How many has he had?' inquired the Badger gloomily.

'Smashes, or machines?' asked the Rat. 'O, well, after all, it's the same thing—with Toad. This is the seventh. As for the others—you know that coach-house of his? Well, it's piled up—literally piled up to the roof—with fragments of motor-cars none of them bigger than your hat! That accounts for the other six—so far as they can be accounted for.'

'He's been in hospital three times,' put in the Mole; 'and as for the fines he's had to pay, it's simply awful to think of.'

'Yes, and that's part of the trouble,' continued the Rat. 'Toad's rich, we all know; but he's not a millionaire. And he's a hopelessly bad driver, and quite regardless of law and order. Killed or ruined—it's got to be one of the two things, sooner or later. Badger! We're his friends—oughtn't we to do something?'

The Badger went through a bit of hard thinking. 'Now look here!' he said at last, rather severely; 'of course you know I can't do anything *now*?'

His two friends assented, quite understanding his point. No animal, according to the rules of animal etiquette, is ever expected to do anything strenuous, or heroic, or even moderately active during the off-season of winter. All are sleepy—some actually asleep. All are weather-bound, more or less; and all are resting from arduous days and nights, during which every muscle in them has been severely tested, and every energy kept at full stretch.

'Very well then!' continued the Badger. '*But*, when once the year has really turned, and the nights are shorter, and half-way through them one rouses and feels fidgety and wanting to be up and doing by sunrise, if not before—*you* know!—'

Both animals nodded gravely. *They* knew!

'Well, *then*,' went on the Badger, 'we—that is, you and me and our friend the Mole here—we'll take Toad seriously in hand. We'll stand no nonsense whatever. We'll bring him back to reason, by force if need be. We'll *make* him be a sensible Toad. We'll—you're asleep, Rat!'

'Not me!' said the Rat, waking up with a jerk.

'He's been asleep two or three times since supper,' said the Mole, laughing. He himself was feeling quite wakeful and even lively, though he didn't know why. The reason was, of course, that he being naturally an underground animal by birth and breeding, the situation of Badger's house exactly suited him and made him feel at home; while the Rat, who slept every night in a bedroom the windows of which opened on a breezy river, naturally felt the atmosphere still and oppressive.

'Well, it's time we were all in bed,' said the Badger, getting up and fetching flat candlesticks. 'Come along, you two, and I'll show you your quarters. And take your time to-morrow morning—breakfast at any hour you please!'

He conducted the two animals to a long room that seemed half bed-chamber and half loft. The Badger's winter stores, which indeed were visible everywhere, took up half the room—piles of apples, turnips, and potatoes, baskets full of nuts, and jars of honey; but the two little white beds on the remainder of the floor looked soft and inviting, and the linen on them, though coarse, was clean and smelt beautifully of lavender; and the Mole and the Water Rat, shaking off their garments in some thirty seconds, tumbled in between the sheets in great joy and contentment.

In accordance with the kindly Badger's injunctions, the two tired animals came down to breakfast very late next morning, and found a bright fire burning in the kitchen, and two young hedgehogs sitting on a bench at the table, eating oatmeal porridge out of wooden bowls. The hedgehogs dropped their spoons, rose to their feet, and ducked their heads respectfully as the two entered.

'There, sit down, sit down,' said the Rat pleasantly, 'and go on with your porridge. Where have you youngsters come from? Lost your way in the snow, I suppose?'

'Yes, please, sir,' said the elder of the two hedgehogs respectfully. 'Me and little Billy here, we was trying to find our way to school—mother *would* have us go, was the weather ever so—and of course we lost our-selves, sir, and Billy he got frightened and took and cried, being young and faint-hearted. And at last we happened up against Mr. Badger's back door, and made so bold as to knock, sir, for Mr. Badger he's a kind-hearted gentleman, as every one knows—'

'I understand,' said the Rat, cutting himself some rashers from a side of bacon, while the Mole dropped some eggs into a saucepan. 'And what's the weather like outside? You needn't "sir" me quite so much,' he added.

'O, terrible bad, sir, terrible deep the snow is,' said the hedgehog. 'No getting out for the likes of you gentlemen to-day.'

'Where's Mr. Badger?' inquired the Mole, as he warmed the coffee-pot before the fire.

'The master's gone into his study, sir,' replied the hedgehog, 'and he said as how he was going to be particular busy this morning, and on no account was he to be disturbed.'

This explanation, of course, was thoroughly understood by every one present. The fact is, as already set forth, when you live a life of intense activity for six months in the year, and of comparative or actual somnolence for the other six, during the latter period you cannot be continually pleading sleepiness when there are people about or things to be done. The excuse gets monotonous. The animals well knew that Badger, having eaten a hearty breakfast, had retired to his study and settled himself in an arm-chair with his legs up on another and a red cotton handkerchief over his face, and was being 'busy' in the usual way at this time of the year.

The front-door bell clanged loudly, and the Rat, who was very greasy with buttered toast, sent Billy, the smaller hedgehog, to see who it might be. There was a sound of much stamping in the ball, and presently Billy returned in front of the Otter, who threw himself on the Rat with an embrace and a shout of affectionate greeting.

'Get off!' spluttered the Rat, with his mouth full.

'Thought I should find you here all right,' said the Otter cheerfully. 'They were all in a great state of alarm along River Bank when I arrived this morning. Rat never been home all night—nor Mole either—something dreadful must have happened, they said; and the snow had covered up all your tracks, of course. But I knew that when people were in any fix they mostly went to Badger, or else Badger got to know of it somehow, so I came straight off here, through the Wild Wood and the snow! My! it was fine, coming through the snow as the red sun was rising and showing against the black tree-trunks! As you went along in the stillness, every now and then masses of snow slid off the branches suddenly with a flop! making you jump and run for cover. Snow-castles and snow-caverns had sprung up out of nowhere in the night—and snow bridges, terraces, ramparts—I could have stayed and played with them for hours. Here and there great branches had been torn away by the sheer weight of the snow, and robins perched and hopped on them in their perky conceited way, just as if they had done it themselves. A ragged string of wild geese passed overhead, high on the grey sky, and a few rooks whirled over the trees, inspected, and flapped off homewards with a disgusted expression but I met no sensible being to ask the news of. About halfway across I came on a rabbit sitting on a stump, cleaning his silly face with his paws. He was a pretty scared animal when I crept up behind him and placed a heavy fore-paw on his shoulder. I had to cuff his head once or twice to get any sense out of it at all. At last I managed to extract from him that Mole had been seen in the Wild Wood last night by one of them. It was the talk of the burrows, he said, how Mole, Mr. Rat's particular friend, was in a bad fix; how he had lost his way, and "They" were up and out hunting, and were chivvying him round and round. "Then why didn't any of you *do* something?" I asked. "You mayn't be blest with brains, but there are hundreds and hundreds of you, big stout fellows, as fat as butter, and your burrows running in all directions, and you could have taken him in and made him safe and comfortable, or tried to, at all events." "What, *us*?" he merely said: "*Do* something? Us rabbits?" So I cuffed him again and left him. There was nothing else to be done. At any rate, I had learnt something; and if I had had the luck to meet any of "Them" I'd have learnt something more—or *they* would.'

'Weren't you at all—er—nervous?' asked the Mole, some of yesterday's terror coming back to him at the mention of the Wild Wood.

'Nervous?' The Otter showed a gleaming set of strong white teeth as he laughed. 'I'd give 'em nerves if any of them tried anything on with me. Here, Mole, fry me some slices of ham, like the good little chap you are. I'm frightfully hungry, and I've got any amount to say to Ratty here. Haven't seen him for an age.'

So the good-natured Mole, having cut some slices of ham, set the hedgehogs to fry it, and returned to his own breakfast, while the Otter and the Rat, their heads together, eagerly talked river-shop, which is long shop and talk that is endless, running on like the babbling river itself.

A plate of fried ham had just been cleared and sent back for more, when the Badger entered, yawning, and rubbing his eyes, and greeted them all in his quiet, simple way, with kind inquiries for every one. 'It must be getting on for luncheon time,' he remarked to the Otter. 'Better stop and have it with us. You must be hungry, this cold morning.'

'Rather!' replied the Otter, winking at the Mole. 'The sight of these greedy young hedgehogs stuffing themselves with fried ham makes me feel positively famished.'

The hedgehogs, who were just beginning to feel hungry again after their porridge, and after working so hard at their frying, looked timidly up at Mr. Badger, but were too shy to say anything.

'Here, you two youngsters be off home to your mother,' said the Badger kindly. 'I'll send someone with you to show you the way. You won't want any dinner to-day, I'll be bound.'

He gave them sixpence apiece and a pat on the head, and they went off with much respectful swinging of caps and touching of forelocks.

Presently they all sat down to luncheon together. The Mole found himself placed next to Mr. Badger, and, as the other two were still deep in river-gossip from which nothing could divert them, he took the opportunity to tell Badger how comfortable and home-like it all felt to him. 'Once well underground,' he said, 'you know exactly where you are. Nothing can happen to you, and nothing can get at you. You're entirely your own master, and you don't have to consult anybody or mind what they say. Things go on all the same overhead, and you let 'em, and don't bother about 'em. When you want to, up you go, and there the things are, waiting for you.'

The Badger simply beamed on him. 'That's exactly what I say,' he replied. 'There's no security, or peace and tranquillity, except underground. And then, if your ideas get larger and you want to expand— why, a dig and a scrape, and there you are! If you feel your house is a bit too big, you stop up a hole or two, and there you are again! No builders, no tradesmen, no remarks passed on you by fellows looking over your wall, and, above all, no *weather*. Look at Rat, now. A couple of feet of floodwater, and he's got to move into hired lodgings; uncomfortable, inconveniently situated, and horribly expensive. Take Toad. I say nothing against Toad Hall; quite the best house in these parts, *as a house*. But supposing a fire breaks out—where's Toad? Supposing tiles are blown off, or walls sink or crack, or windows get broken—where's Toad? Supposing the rooms are draughty—I *hate* a draught myself—where's Toad? No, up and out of doors is good enough to roam about and get one's living in; but underground to come back to at last—that's my idea of *home!'*

The Mole assented heartily; and the Badger in consequence got very friendly with him. 'When lunch is over,' he said, 'I'll take you all round this little place of mine. I can see you'll appreciate it. You understand what domestic architecture ought to be, you do.'

After luncheon, accordingly, when the other two had settled themselves into the chimney-corner and had started a heated argument on the subject of *eels*, the Badger lighted a lantern and bade the Mole follow him. Crossing the hall, they passed down one of the principal tunnels, and the wavering light of the lantern gave glimpses on either side of rooms both large and small, some mere cupboards, others nearly as broad and imposing as Toad's dining-ball. A narrow passage at right angles led them into another corridor, and here the same thing was repeated. The Mole was staggered at the size, the extent, the ramifications of it all; at the length of the dim passages, the solid vaultings of the crammed store-chambers, the masonry everywhere, the pillars, the arches, the pavements. 'How on earth, Badger,' he said at last, 'did you ever find time and strength to do all this? It's astonishing!'

'It *would* be astonishing indeed,' said the Badger simply, 'if I *had* done it. But as a matter of fact I did none of it—only cleaned out the passages and chambers, as far as I had need of them. There's lots more of it, all round about. I see you don't understand, and I must explain it to you. Well, very long ago, on the spot where the Wild Wood waves now, before ever it had planted itself and grown up to what it now is, there was a city—a city of people, you know. Here, where we are standing, they lived, and walked, and talked, and slept, and carried on their business. Here they stabled their horses and feasted, from here they rode out to fight or drove out to trade. They were a powerful people, and rich, and great builders. They built to last, for they thought their city would last for ever.'

'But what has become of them all?' asked the Mole.

'Who can tell?' said the Badger. 'People come—they stay for a while, they flourish, they build—and they go. It is their way. But we remain. There were badgers here, I've been told, long before that same city ever came to be. And now there are badgers here again. We are an enduring lot, and we may move out for a time, but we wait, and are patient, and back we come. And so it will ever be.'

'Well, and when they went at last, those people?' said the Mole.

'When they went,' continued the Badger, 'the strong winds and persistent rains took the matter in hand, patiently, ceaselessly, year after year. Perhaps we badgers too, in our small way, helped a little—who knows? It was all down, down, down, gradually—ruin and levelling and disappearance. Then it was all up, up, up, gradually, as seeds grew to saplings, and saplings to forest trees, and bramble and fern came creeping in to help. Leaf-mould rose and obliterated, streams in their winter freshets brought sand and soil to clog and to cover, and in course of time our home was ready for us again, and we moved in. Up above us, on the surface, the same thing happened. Animals arrived, liked the look of the place, took up their quarters, settled down, spread, and flourished. They didn't bother themselves about the past—they never do; they're too busy. The place was a bit humpy and hillocky, naturally, and full of holes; but that was rather an advantage. And they don't bother about the future, either—the future when perhaps the people will move in again—for a time—as may very well be. The Wild Wood is pretty well populated by now; with all the usual lot, good, bad, and indifferent— I name no names. It takes all sorts to make a world. But I fancy you know something about them yourself by this time.'

'I do indeed,' said the Mole, with a slight shiver.

'Well, well,' said the Badger, patting him on the shoulder, 'it was your first experience of them, you see. They're not so bad really; and we must all live and let live. But I'll pass the word round to-morrow, and I think you'll have no further trouble. Any friend of *mine* walks where he likes in this country, or I'll know the reason why!'

When they got back to the kitchen again, they found the Rat walking up and down, very restless. The underground atmosphere was oppressing him and getting on his nerves, and he seemed really to be afraid that the river would run away if he wasn't there to look after it. So he had his overcoat on, and his pistols thrust into his belt again. 'Come along, Mole,' he said anxiously, as soon as he caught sight of them. 'We must get off while its daylight. Don't want to spend another night in the Wild Wood again.'

'It'll be all right, my fine fellow,' said the Otter. 'I'm coming along with you, and I know every path blindfold; and if there's a head that needs to be punched, you can confidently rely upon me to punch it.'

'You really needn't fret, Ratty,' added the Badger placidly. 'My passages run further than you think, and I've bolt-holes to the edge of the wood in several directions, though I don't care for everybody to know about them. When you really have to go, you shall leave by one of my short cuts. Meantime, make yourself easy, and sit down again.'

The Rat was nevertheless still anxious to be off and attend to his river, so the Badger, taking up his lantern again, led the way along a damp and airless tunnel that wound and dipped, part vaulted, part hewn through solid rock, for a weary distance that seemed to be miles. At last daylight began to show itself confusedly through tangled growth overhanging the mouth of the passage; and the Badger, bidding them a hasty good-bye, pushed them hurriedly through the opening, made everything look as natural as possible again, with creepers, brushwood, and dead leaves, and retreated.

They found themselves standing on the very edge of the Wild Wood. Rocks and brambles and tree-roots behind them, confusedly heaped and tangled; in front, a great space of quiet fields, hemmed by lines of hedges black on the snow, and, far ahead, a glint of the familiar old river, while the wintry sun hung red and low on the horizon. The Otter, as knowing all the paths, took charge of the party, and they trailed out on a bee-line for a distant stile. Pausing there a moment and looking back, they saw the whole mass of the Wild Wood, dense, menacing, compact, grimly set in vast white surroundings; simultaneously they turned and made swiftly for home, for firelight and the familiar things it played on, for the voice, sounding cheerily outside their window, of the river that they knew and trusted in all its moods, that never made them afraid with any amazement.

As he hurried along, eagerly anticipating the moment when he would be at home again among the things he knew and liked, the Mole saw clearly that he was an animal of tilled field and hedgerow; linked to the ploughed furrow, the frequented pasture, the lane of evening lingerings, the cultivated, garden-plot. For others the asperities, the stubborn endurance, or the clash of actual conflict, that went with Nature in the rough; he must be wise, must keep to the pleasant places in which his lines were laid and which held adventure enough, in their way, to last for a lifetime.

from The Climb Up to Hell
by Jack Olsen

To keep people from attempting the dangerous North Face of the Eiger, the local guides had decreed that they would not rescue people who became stranded there. The strategy didn't work. Climbers were still drawn to the face, including— in 1959—Claudio Corti, his partner Stefano Longhi, and two Germans. When they ran into trouble, noted mountaineers and crack rescue teams from around Europe converged to mount a rescue. Jack Olsen (born 1925) described the events in his book written shortly thereafter.

Slowly, very slowly, as he sat on the little ledge Friday, reason had returned to Claudio Corti. He did not know how long he had been sitting, but it was still daylight, perhaps late in the afternoon, to judge by the sun which had now dropped down the back of the mountain. His head ached dully; he reached up and touched a muslin bandage which swathed it. As he made this motion, he felt a pain in his hands; he pulled off his gloves and saw the long, bloody serrations in his palms. And then he remembered. Stefano, poor Stefano, was on another ledge down the mountain. And the Germans? Where were they? Painfully, he turned his head and looked up the exit cracks where he had seen them a few hours before, smiling wanly down at him. A light rain was falling, and the crack disappeared in the mists. They must be beating their way to the top. They would send help, and he and Stefano would be saved.

He looked over his perch, and saw that it was almost the same as Stefano's: a yard or so wide, four or five feet long. But it was more sheltered than the other, if any place on this mountain could be described as sheltered. The ledge was indented in the mountain, back from the wall, and protected at one end by a shattered pillar covered with rock rubble. At least he would not be troubled with avalanche and rockfall. He saw them now and then in the rain; they would roar down the mountain and arc out over his head. He shuddered for Stefano below.

When the clouds parted, he could see the Kleine Scheidegg hotels and once he caught a glimpse of Grindelwald and the little meadow-village of Alpiglen. But he could not see down to Stefano; bulging shields of rock cut off the view. And he could see neither to right nor left across the precipice. The ridges which marked the east and west edges of the north face were shut off to him by the pillar on one side and the wall on the other. He felt a complete isolation.

"Stefano!" he called down the face. "Stefano!" But there was no answer. He spotted the rucksack left by the Germans. There was no food inside; all of their food had long since been roped down to Longhi. But inside the rucksack was the red plastic tent. Moving slowly on the ledge, he pitched it and secured it firmly to the wall with an ice hammer and a few pitons the Germans had left him. Then he crawled inside. His clothes were drenched through, but at least he would get no wetter. He took off the red wool shirt which clung stickily to his skin, put his jacket back on, and gingerly adjusted the skiing hat and wool hood over the muslin of his bandage. Hardly had he finished the simple but laborious task of rearranging his clothing when a metallic drone came to his ears. He groped his way out of the tent and saw an airplane buzzing the face, not more than two hundred feet away. He waved the shirt with all his strength, and shouted, "Help! Help me!" But the plane moved off into the clouds. He did not know whether the pilot had spotted him in his depressed bivouac.

He could feel the blood from his head wound dripping down over his face. He removed the bandage, picked up a handful of snow and packed it on the gash to relieve the hemorrhaging. And then it was night.

Sitting inside the tent, he began to feel cold; the winds and rain were getting worse, and lightning was crackling around the face. He kept himself sternly immobile to keep the lightning from finding him. Through the long hours of the storm, he sat rigidly, afraid to move. Then the lightning stopped; the rain changed to snow, and finally stopped altogether. But the winds whined more violently than ever, and he could feel the temperature dropping hour by hour. He tried to move his fingers and his toes and found he could not. Pounding his hands against the ice for several hours, he brought the circulation back to his fingers. Painstakingly, he took off his climbing boots to massage his feet and ankles; the cold was so intense that he felt a humming in his wound, under the muslin and the ski cap and the hood. He became aware of a terrible thirst. He knew that eating ice was an act of desperation on a mountain. Ice was devoid of minerals; it merely chilled the stomach and carried off the minerals already in the body. Sometimes it was contaminated with glacier dust, and this could tie knots in a man's stomach. Still he shoved handfuls of ice into his mouth, breaking his teeth against it, until the area around him in the tent had been scraped down to bare rock. He wanted to sleep, but, in his delirium, he said to himself that the cold water inside him would freeze, and he would die slowly, freezing from the inside out. He rubbed snow across his face every five or ten minutes; the air was so cold, and his face was so chilled, that the snow felt warm and comforting, and the simple task of applying it kept him awake for many hours. But then he dozed off, sheltered by the red tent, and dreamed that he was a child again, lying in his mother's arms in Olginate.

When he awoke, it was already late in the morning. A red glow suffused the roof of the tent; the sun must be shining. For a long time, he rubbed his arms and legs to restore the circulation. He did a sort of cramped calisthenics on the ledge, sliding his legs back and forth until they began to feel warmer. He washed his face with snow, and crawled out of the tent. There was the sun, big and warming; he laid his red wool shirt on the tent to dry, and then he heard the airplane again. This time the sky was clear, and he could make out two figures in the plane as it flitted past his ledge. He waved the red shirt again, and shouted,

"Here! Here! Help me!" He was sure that they had seen him, but in his jumbled state of mind, he felt annoyed that they had merely flown away. A few minutes later more planes came by, crossing and recrossing the face. He could see the pilots looking in his direction, and he cried with all his strength, "Here! Here! Can't you see me?" Then he became enraged and cursed the pilots for leaving him all alone. "Fools!" he shouted. "Idiots! Why do you not come for me?" They were so close; his life was being taken from him, and those stupid fliers were doing nothing about it. Below he could see Grindelwald, the Kleine Scheidegg, the miniature tracks of the Jungfraujoch Railway. It seemed he could reach out and touch them all. People were living and walking around down there. Could they not see that his life was being taken away?

The planes came by all day long, and soon he merely sat and watched them, no longer flapping the red shirt, no longer calling or even acknowledging their waves. Darkness was coming on; the lights began to twinkle from the valleys below. When the last flicker of daylight passed, he looked down into the valley and said aloud: "They don't come any more." He pronounced his last good-byes to everybody: to his mother and father, to Fulvia Losa, to Zucchi and Bigio and all his old comrades, and to poor Stefano, trapped down below. "I do not see them again," he said. "Not even once again." He rapped his ice hammer against the wall and shook loose some chips. Piece by piece he took the bits of ice into the tent and made a mound of them. Then he slowly pulled the tent-flap closed and lay down with his head on the ice. "Now," he said, "this is my tomb." He could feel his heartbeat only faintly; his breathing was slow and irregular. His body was numbed with fatigue and cold, and life seemed so far away that it was as if he had never lived at all. He closed his eyes and said in a low voice: "*Muoio qui.* I die here."

Even under ideal conditions, the summit ridge of the Eiger was no place for a bivouac. It sliced into the sky almost like a giant ax-blade, tilted slightly downward from west to east. It was possible to walk for several hundred yards along the ridge with one foot stepping on the north wall and the other on the south; it was also possible to misstep and fall all the way down either wall. To worsen matters, the whole ridge was covered by an ill-fitting icecap of varying thickness. In places, snow and ice had slid out from underneath, cutting away the underpinning fixing the cap to the ridge. A few raps of the ice ax over spots like these and the climber would plummet through to his death. It was all but impossible to tell the good surface from the bad; one hacked away and hoped for the best.

As darkness fell on the ridge that Saturday night, and fifty climbers from six nations laid their plans in a farrago of tongues and accents, it was decided to remain overnight on the mountaintop despite the dangers. Work must resume promptly at dawn; already the men trapped below had endured seven or eight enervating bivouacs on the face, more than anyone in Eiger's macabre history. They must be saved—if, indeed, they still survived—with no more delay than absolutely necessary. Some few rescuers made the decision to go back down the west flank for a night's sleep in the Eigergletscher Hotel, and to return in the morning; but most of them stayed and began hacking caverns into the treacherous icecap. The unimpeded winds from the north swirled the chips of ice back into their faces as they dug carefully, probing for thin spots and making sure they did not cut an inch deeper than they had to.

After a few hours, all the rescuers were encamped in their recessed igloos for the night. Those who spoke Latin tongues stayed together in one hole; the Swiss split into a few groups; Gramminger dug a one-man shelter for himself and his equipment, and the other members of the Mountain Guard lay close together for warmth, thirty feet away. The Poles were the best off; they had brought complete bivouac equipment and at least enough food to make a meal. For the rest, there was almost nothing to eat or drink. Terray and de Booy, sheltered now with Eiselin, Cassin, and Mauri, had blitzed up the west wall without even eating breakfast. The other three had nothing. They had not expected an overnight bivouac on this chill summit.

Huddled together, the five men carried on their conversations with difficulty. Terray could speak French, English and Spanish; so he could communicate with Eiselin, who spoke French, English, German and a little Italian, and with Mauri, who spoke Italian and Spanish. Mauri would pass the conversation along to Cassin, who spoke only Italian. The polyglot de Booy, who understood all the languages ricocheting about the bivouac, acted as a sort of senior interpreter for the group. On the whole, it seemed to Terray, he had seen many worse bivouacs, and many with less of an atmosphere of fellowship. Eiselin proved to be an amiable young man; Cassin and Mauri were experienced Alpinists who knew how to live with the situation, and de Booy, the companionable teacher from Amsterdam, brought a glow of warmth and solidarity to the group.

Further down the icecap, the Germans were having a less satisfactory time of it. Gramminger had intended to buy food in Grindelwald, but they had entrained for the summit before the first stores opened up in the morning. He had brought a little salami and bread from Munich, barely enough to provide a few snacks on the drive to the Oberland, but it was impossible to eat the leftover food without something to drink. His Mountain Guard comrades had a gasoline cooker with which to thaw snow for tea, but in the confusion at the Grindelwald station in the morning, the Poles had promised to bring extra fuel for the cooker, and then had forgotten. Now they were limited to the few drops in the tank of the cooker, barely enough to start the device, but certainly not enough to melt snow to provide liquid for any substantial number of men.

"Well," Gramminger said to himself as he snuggled into his ice-walled lodging for the night, "I shall not have my evening cup of tea after all." He pulled the heavy bivouac sacks over himself, arranged the pieces of the stripped-down winch, which the heat of his body would keep thawed through the night, and prepared to sleep. He had not yet begun to doze, his head swarming with the logistic problems of the day to come, when he saw a familiar face peering owlishly into his cavern. "Yes, Alfred," said Gramminger. "What is it that has taken you out of your shelter on such a night?"

"It is like this, Wiggerl," the burly Hellepart said against the moaning of the wind. "We are together in a nice hole, and we even have a candle for light and a little warmth for our hands. But we do not have an extra bivouac sack to cover over the entrance to the hole, and the wind keeps blowing our candle out. We thought perhaps—"

"I will strike you a trade, Alfred. You have the spirit cooker?"

"Yes, but there are only a few drops of fuel left in it."

"If there are a few drops of fuel left, you can brew me some tea. And if the tea is enjoyable, I will give you an extra bivouac sack."

It was an odd bargain, Hellepart thought as he struggled back to his cavern. But it would be worth a try. He fired up the cooker and began thawing some snow. The fuel sputtered and fumed and produced mostly smoke, and while a few crystals of unmelted snow still swirled around in the cup, the flame went out altogether. Hellepart dropped a tea bag in the chilly mixture and kneaded it until the water took on a vaguely rusty color. "It is tea," Hellepart told his comrades. "But is it *enjoyable* tea?" He carried the cup of liquid back to Gramminger's hole and passed it inside with a grandiose gesture. "Here," said Hellepart. "We have lived up to our part of the bargain."

There was a long silence from within, and then a bivouac sack came hurtling out at Hellepart's feet. "You do not brew a very good tea, Alfred," the leader's voice came from inside. "But I would have given you the sack anyway."

"I always knew that, Wiggerl," Hellepart answered. He went back to the others and rigged the extra sack over the hole to shut out the wind. The men of the Mountain Guard went slowly off to sleep.

At dawn the icy Tower of Babel on top of the Eiger summit sprang quickly to life. Gramminger was first up, and began the complex operation of laying out the cable system for new descents. The main problem was to anchor the large, drum-type winch on the shifting icecap. He made it with ice-pitons, then tied it to the porous rock of the cornice with several other cables. Another cable was wound around a big block of ice and connected to the winch, and several loose ropes were added on; as a final safety measure, some of the rescuers would grip these ropes tightly, scratch secure stances into the ice with their crampons, and hold on. Gramminger stepped back and surveyed his work. It was an insecure arrangement; he would have given anything for one solid outcropping of firm rock as a cornerstone for the rig. But the top of this mountain offered no concessions to the mechanical needs of the rescue party. They would have to make do.

Friedli watched the Germans set up their equipment and recognized that they were doing a skilled job under the adverse conditions. Still, he was not going to abdicate his own responsibilities in the operation. For all his deep respect for Gramminger and the Mountain Guard, he had serious misgivings about the winch. Under stress, it might tear loose and hurtle down the cliff, impartially taking rescuers and rescued to their deaths below. And even if the winch remained in place, he doubted that it was geared low enough to enable its operators to haul up the men below. At best, it would be an inch-by-inch struggle, taking long hours. And at this stage of the rescue, the life expectancies of the four men down below had to be measured in minutes.

Weighing all these factors, the skilled technician of Thun ordered a backstopping operation of his own. While Gramminger and the Mountain Guard struggled to anchor the winch, Friedli called together a work gang of Swiss and ordered them to extend the length of the level path which had been cut parallel to the ridge on the south side of the peak. Soon Friedli's men had hacked a path almost two hundred feet long, and had even rigged a sort of rope fence on its outer edge. Now men could walk along the trench in comparative safety. If the winch failed to work, the cable could be passed through pulleys over the top and back to crews in the trench, and old-fashioned, dependable manpower could take over the pulling operation. Friedli's move, taken with his usual taciturnity and strictly on the basis of his own forebodings, was a brilliant stroke of planning, even though it seemed to the digging crews in the trench that their leader had simply found a way to keep them busy and uncomfortable.

Overnight, the master plan for this Sunday morning had been

worked out. It was known that Longhi was alone on a ledge about one thousand feet down, and it was assumed that the other three were in the tent several hundred feet above Longhi's perch. Reconnaissance pilots, toward the end of Saturday, had noticed Longhi slumping on his ledge. Probably he was in the worst condition of the four. Therefore the tentative plan was to lower a man past the red tent and down to Longhi, give him first aid and a stimulant, and haul him up to the tent. Then other rescuers would go down on the cable and bring the four men, one by one, to safety on the ridge. The only remaining question was whom to send down on the first trip. An Italian-speaking rescuer would have good verbal communication with Longhi and his comrade. But he would not be able to talk to the Germans. A German-speaking rescuer would have the opposite problem. Gramminger and Friedli talked the situation over, and the deciding factor was that the Italian members of the rescue party had had no experience with the Gramminger equipment, but the men of the Mountain Guard knew their gear like firemen. Gramminger and Friedli selected Alfred Hellepart, an old hand at mountain rescues, and a man of tremendous strength and courage. At two hundred pounds, he was the heaviest of the Mountain Guard crew, but the quarter-inch cable had a tensile strength of nearly two tons, and Hellepart's bull-like power would be needed below. Gramminger fixed his friend to the end of the cable, strapped on the short-wave radio, covered Hellepart's head with a white plastic helmet, attached a rucksack to his back, and sent him over the side. Friedli took over the radio for the over-all direction of the operation, and Gramminger scurried to the anchorage of the winch, there to stand ultimate guard over the life of his friend in case the equipment began to rip loose. Despite the insecurity of the anchorage, Gramminger felt fairly confident that it would stay in place. And if it did not, the other members of the rescue team would hold tightly, and somehow they would work Hellepart back up to the top. They had had to improvise before, and they had never lost a man. Neither, however, had they attempted a rescue one thousand feet down, or from such a treacherous perch. "Well," Gramminger said to himself, "we shall merely do our best." What worried him most was the weather. In good weather, the Mountain Guard could accomplish almost anything. But on this unprotected summit, the slightest break in the weather could mean the end of the whole operation. Even a minor electrical storm could be fatal; the steel cable was also a long lightning rod, and the man dangling at its end would risk electrocution. If clouds came, the important radio liaison with the spotters below at the Kleine Scheidegg would be useless, and the descents would have to be made on a hit-or-miss basis. And if there were high winds, the rescuers would be in danger of losing their delicate stances on the knife-edge of the summit. The weather simply had to remain clear. But a glance at the sky gave Gramminger a chill of apprehension. The sun hung between bilious clouds in a dirty-gray rectangle of visibility. To Gramminger, it seemed a poisonous yellow, a certain harbinger of storm. High black clouds could be seen coming down from the north. He was sure that they would reach the Eiger within hours and begin to discharge their loads of snow and rain and electricity against the face. If they did, the rescuers would have no choice but to beat a hurried retreat down the west flank. There could be no question of risking dozens of lives by trying to remain on the summit during a storm.

It was exactly eight o'clock on Sunday morning when Alfred Hellepart began moving down the mountain into aloneness. As he walked slowly backward on the fifty-degree angle of the summit ice field, watching his friends operate the winch above him, he set about preparing himself psychologically. From long experience, he knew that one had to purge one's mind of all outside thoughts; the entire concentration had to be on the job at hand, and on the men to be rescued. One could not think at all of oneself; the slightest glimmer of fear could be deadly. Nor could he allow his thoughts to drift back to Munich, to his wife and his eleven-year-old son. From this minute on, they must be forgotten, until he had succeeded or failed in his rescue mission.

Certainly, there was no need to worry about the cable. The experienced Gramminger was up at the anchorage, protecting him as he had so many times before. The men of the Mountain Guard had an almost childlike faith in their leader; they acted on his orders without question or hesitation. In practice exercises, Hellepart had carried two men on his back up the side of a mountain, and the cable had held. He would press a button in his mind and give the matter no further thought.

Now he was halfway down the summit ice field, and he tested the portable radio. The contact was excellent; he could hear Friedli loud and clear, and Friedli could hear him. When he had gone 250 feet, almost to the end of the field, he heard Friedli telling him to make himself secure on his crampons; the cable had to be disconnected from the winch and joined to the next three-hundred-foot length by a frog coupling. Hellepart waited until the go-ahead came from the top, backed over the last few feet of the snow field, and found himself looking down the vast sweep of the north wall. For a moment, despite all his psychological preparations, he felt wild panic. An indescribable feeling of abandonment came over him; be could no longer see the men on the top, and instinctively he looked up at the quarter-inch cable spinning up into the mists, like a thin strand of cotton thread. Below him the north wall fell endlessly away, down and down and down, black and menacing, broken only by a few insignificant snow ledges. Dangling from the cable, he gulped for air, and almost forgot what he had come for. Just then the voice of Gramminger broke in on the radio. "You are doing fine, Alfred," the calm voice said. "Everything is secure for you. Keep control of yourself, and remember that there are men on the wall depending on you for their lives." The soothing words brought composure back to Hellepart; he was no longer alone; he felt the strong ties to the men above, all their concentration fixed on him and his task, and he gave the order to continue letting the cable down. Off to his right, he could see a black rift coming up, one of the gaping exit cracks leading to the White Spider. He made a short traverse to the crack, and began wriggling his way obliquely downward. He did not know if this was the right route, but at the moment it was the only one. Two thousand feet below him, he could see the morning mists walking up the wall. For brief seconds, he glimpsed the village of Alpiglen, but then the mists closed together again and blanketed the valley. All around him the wind probed the holes and cracks on the mountain, and the low, hollow "whoo" gave him an uncomfortable feeling.

Now he had to find a secure stance again, to hold himself against the wall while another three-hundred-foot roll of cable was attached above. Friedli's voice crackled down to him from above: "All is well. You will be on your way in a few minutes." The signal came, and he continued his descent. After a hundred more feet, he went on the air to tell Friedli that he was coming in sight of the Spider. Against the low howl of the wind, he talked to the summit, and during that brief conversation he heard another human voice, barely audible at first, then growing louder and coming from the east. He traversed toward the voice and came to a shattered pillar bulging out across the face. He stepped onto the pillar and sent rocks and rubble clattering down the face with his crampons. Still he went on, only partially supported by the cable which now had assumed a sort of J-shape as it followed him on the level course across the pillar. About sixty feet away, he spotted a man in a half-sitting, half-lying position on a narrow ledge pitched with a small red tent. Nervously, he pushed the transmitting button and signaled the summit: "I have found a man."

Across the litter-covered pillar, Hellepart shouted: "Who are you? Are you Mayer, or Nothdurft?" The voice came back: "*Italiano.*"

Slowly, still sending tons of rubble down the mountain, Hellepart continued the difficult traverse. Now he was within six or seven feet of the Italian, and he could hear the man calling, "*Mangiare!* Something to eat!" Hellepart fumbled in his pocket, found a frozen half-bar of black, hard Cailler chocolate, and tossed it across the edge to the hungry man. The Italian did not even pause to remove the wrapper. He rammed the chocolate into his mouth and began to chew. His mouth full of paper and chocolate, the man called to Hellepart: "*Sigaretta?*" But Hellepart had none. He paused for a moment and considered the situation. He could traverse the remaining few feet of the pillar, but only at increasing risk to himself, since he no longer dangled straight down from the cable. And if he reached the Italian in this manner, he would be unable to make the rescue. The two men, no matter what their condition, could not have effected the traverse back across the rubble without undue danger. Hellepart decided to retreat to the exit crack and ask the summit to pull him up to another position. From there he would try to make a straight perpendicular descent to the Italian. "Take me up," Hellepart called to the summit. "I am going to look for another route." A hard jerk on the cable yanked him off the pillar and out into space. Spinning in mid-air, he fought to turn himself toward the wall so that he could take up the shock of the return impact with his legs. He had barely succeeded in twisting around when he crashed into the wall feet first. "All right," said Hellepart to the summit, "haul me straight up. I will tell you when to stop."

Up he went, inches at a time, for 150 feet, and then set himself into a slow swing until he was able to grab a jutting rock straight above the Italian. "Now let me down," he instructed. As he descended a sheer gully, stones began to shake loose again, and he shouted to the Italian to take cover. Finally he dropped the last few feet and onto the ledge. While the marooned man mumbled *"Grazie! Grazie!"* and put his arms around Hellepart, the German called triumphantly to the summit: "I am with the Italian!" It was nine-fifteen, and he had been on the wall for more than an hour. The Italian gave his name, and Hellepart reported it to the summit. Friedli asked where the others were. Hellepart said to Corti: "Where is Longhi? Where is Mayer? Where is Nothdurft?"

Corti pointed down the mountain. The two men leaned over the edge and called, but there was no response. Hellepart asked Corti in German, "Your condition?" Corti understood—the phrase is similar in both languages—and answered, *"Buona."* But Hellepart, seeing that the man's knees were trembling, ordered him to sit down, and gave him coffee from a thermos which had been provided by the Poles. Corti was talking in Italian, and Hellepart got the impression from the torrent of words in the peculiar dialect that Nothdurft and Mayer had tried to force through to the top and that Corti had not seen them for several days. He looked at Corti's scarred hand and his bloodied head and decided that the Italian's condition was too poor to permit him to attempt a climb up to the top on a separate cable. Hellepart would have to make the carry on his back. He radioed to the summit for an Italian-speaking man to take the radio and explain the situation to Corti. Cassin's voice came on, and Hellepart handed the speaking mechanism to Corti, who seemed befuddled by it and nervously pushed the wrong buttons. Finally the contact was established, and Cassin could talk to his friend from the Ragni. *"Rispondi,* Claudio," Cassin's voice said. "This is Cassin. Now listen to me: you have not the strength to go up by yourself. Watch how he shows you how to get up on his shoulders! Try everything to make it easy for your rescuer! Drink something when he gives you to drink. Remember, you are safe. Do not lose your spirit!" Hellepart took back the radio as the last words of Cassin crackled through the earphones: *"Coraggio, Claudio, coraggio!"*

Hellepart took a final look at Corti's tiny resting place. It was totally cleared of ice and snow, gobbled up by Corti in his terrible hunger and thirst. Some of his teeth were broken and splintered, shattered against the hard, cold ice for a last few useless "meals." Hellepart packed the rucksack, strapped it on the sitting Corti's back, and began lacing him into the webbing of a Gramminger-Sitz. He sat down with his back to Corti's front and pulled the harnesses of the human back-pack around his own chest and up over his shoulders. This left no place for the radio; using snap links to lengthen the girth, he fixed the apparatus so that it dangled across his chest. Bearing the uncomfortable weight, he struggled to his feet and snapped the cable in place. All these preparations had taken nearly an hour. "We are ready," he said to the summit. It was ten o'clock.

Back came Friedli's voice: "We have been rearranging the equipment. It will take us a few minutes more."

Hellepart sat down with his heavy load and waited for the signal. Finally it came. "We bring you up now," Friedli called. "Prepare yourself!"

Hellepart wrenched himself into a standing position, but still the cable hung slack above him. "What is the matter?" he called to the summit.

"We are having a little trouble," Friedli answered. Long minutes went by, and then the cable began to tense. Hellepart pressed his feet against the wall and pushed outward with all his strength so that he would keep the cable from rubbing against the wall and prevent it from fouling. Now the wind began to hum across the tightening thread of steel. It sounded to Hellepart like a giant violin string, starting on a low note and gradually whining higher as it tensed, until it had reached a screaming, piercing pitch. And still they did not move up from the ledge. He looked above him at the delicate strand and wondered, for the first time, if it would hold.

On top, Friedli's fears about the winch had only increased as it had become necessary to haul Hellepart back up 150 feet to find a better route down to the Italian. By now there were eight hundred feet of cable reaching down the mountain. Where it made contact with the rock, it had abraded fissures of its own, increasing the friction and multiplying the force required for the upward pull. The men cranking the winch had barely been able to lift Hellepart up to his new stance, and after lowering him back down to the ledge, Friedli discussed the situation with Gramminger. "I do not think we can use the winch to pull the weight of two men," Friedli said. Gramminger agreed. While Hellepart went about his tedious task of readying Corti for the ascent, the crew on top discarded the winch and prepared to shift over to raw manpower. It was a quick improvisation, made possible only by Friedli's foresight in ordering the pulling path dug into the south ridge. Now the cable would go up to the ridge and through a direction-changing roller placed on top of the rotten cornice. The roller would steer the cable back along the path, where thirty men were scrambling into position. At intervals of twenty feet, pulling ropes were attached to the cable by clamps which could be loosened and moved along to a new position.

Now teams of five were in place at each pulling rope, waiting for the signal from Friedli to begin the haul. A last-minute check was made of the three security brakes on the cable; they were so constructed that the cable could be pulled upward through them, but at the slightest accidental downward movement they would clamp tightly shut. As a final security, Gramminger remained at the big block of ice on the far end of the pulling path to anchor each new length of slack cable to the block as it was hauled in. Now they were ready.

With the voice of a Swiss drill sergeant, Friedli shouted to the men to haul away. They strained backward against the pulling ropes. But nothing moved. More hands were added to the ropes, and the order was repeated. Still the cable did not budge. Fearful that the combined strength of all the rescuers would snap the tensing lifeline to the two men below, Friedli frantically waved the operation to a halt. He did not think it possible that the cable had become wedged into the rock below; the soft limestone on the upper part of the Eiger might increase the friction, but it would not have been solid enough to imprison the cable against all this pressure. He decided that the mechanical equipment must have jammed. If his diagnosis was incorrect, if indeed the cable *was* fouled tightly on the mountain, they would have to abandon Corti and try to find some way to bring Hellepart back up. Nervously, Friedli went from device to device and finally came to one which had fouled. He cleared the jam and ordered the crews to begin pulling again. The cable tensed and whined in the wind, after a few long seconds, the men could feel it begin to move.

Now, at last, the long violin string had hit a pitch and held it, and Hellepart was coming up the mountain, his human cargo heavy on his back, the radio dangling clumsily in front of him. At first, the ascent was not on a true perpendicular line. They swayed from side to side as the cable whipped them about; Hellepart shoved his crampons into the icy patina on the wall, seeking to steady himself, and sent slabs of ice and rock crashing down the wall. Every fifty feet, he had to cling to the wall, leaning as far forward as he could, while the men on the summit secured the cable and moved up to new pulling positions. These were agonizing delays to the strong man of Munich; sometimes he would have to kneel against a tiny ledge, gripping an outcropping of rock with his knees the way a jockey grips a horse, the harsh metal edges of the radio digging into his chest. Sometimes he had to stand upright on scallops of snow, with all the weight of Corti on his shoulders. Once he said aloud, in a slightly annoyed, slightly quizzical voice: "Well, he's quite heavy, this fellow." But Corti seemed not to have heard. He was mumbling, *"Fame! Fame!"* and whenever Hellepart kneeled against the wall, Corti would push his own face into the snow and bite off big mouthfuls.

"Don't gobble so much snow!" Hellepart hollered. "It is bad for the stomach." But the famished Corti took his cold snacks anyway.

After about forty minutes of the torturous rise, the cable rasped over the last foot of the exit cracks and swung the two men onto the summit ice field. Out of the shadow of the overhang, they now could feel the rays of the sun, and Corti reacted peculiarly. *"Que bello e il sole,"* he said in a strangely loud voice. "How beautiful the sun is." Then he slumped forward into a coma. Hellepart recognized this as a shock reaction, and he knew that men in a seriously weakened condition could die from it. He would have to force the final 250 feet of the field. Up he came, staggering like a drunk under his heavy load, while Friedli shouted encouragement from the top. Now Hellepart was taking almost all of Corti's weight, receiving little assistance from the cable which no longer hung straight down to hold them in firm suspension. The men on top knew he was forcing, and increased their own pace, once pulling too far too fast and nearly wrenching Hellepart and Corti face forward into the wet snow of the ice field. Hellepart merely regained his balance, kicked up through the sticky snow, and finally, fifty-nine minutes after the ascent had begun, stumbled with his cargo across the ridge. "Help me out of this!" he shouted to Friedli and pitched forward into the snow. Gasping for breath, while the others wrenched at the harnesses holding Corti and the radio to him, Hellepart felt a slap on the shoulder and heard an unfamiliar voice say, "Good! You have done well!" Relieved of his

load, he was lifted to his feet and congratulated all around. "A cigarette!" he said. "I would like a cigarette!" Weak, and afraid he would
slip off the summit, he wobbled to the safety of a bivouac hole for a
smoke and a rest.

from Raft of Despair

by Ensio Tiira

Ensio Tiira (born 1929) signed up for the French
Foreign Legion in a moment of desperation. As
his troop carrier steamed toward Indo-China,
however, he could not face his future as a merce-
nary. He and his friend, Fred Ericsson, laid hands
on a tiny raft and used it to escape the ship.
Expecting to reach land that day, they took only a
small amount of food, but the current didn't
cooperate. Ericsson died on the eighteenth day in
the raft, and matters soon grew worse for Tiira.

Clouds saved me from the sun on the morning of the twenty-third day. I couldn't escape the horror of the raft, but otherwise it was the coolest and best morning I'd had since leaving the *Skaubryn*. There was no need for a shelter above the raft and for most of the day I lay along the lifejackets, trying to forget where I was and what was happening to me. Three big sharks remained as my permanent escort and the four or five smaller ones; but this day there were no more attacks against the raft, not even occasional bumpings and nudgings.

Ericsson's body had suffered much during the night, but as far as I could tell there was no great increase in the number of fish in and around the raft.

Rain fell again in the afternoon, just a few hours after I'd emptied the bottle. I got a fresh supply of perhaps half a bottle and drank the equivalent of several cups while I was gathering it. The rains seemed to get colder as I became weaker and for several hours after the storm had gone by I lay shivering on the ropes. I was very weak and thought that I would get a fever.

I wanted to eat, but the sight of the fish and crabs and the knowledge of what they were doing and had done in the raft only brought on another attack of nausea.

To warm myself I put on my shoes and socks which I'd discarded several days earlier. With these on I could sleep better. I had a fear of waking up to find that my feet had been attacked by fish. Each time now that I lay down I pulled my socks over my trouser ends and covered my head with the tattered remains of Ericsson's blue shirt.

My clothes were rapidly falling to bits. Even Ericsson's blue shirt, which once served so proudly and stoutly as a sail, was full of holes. My under shirt had gone at the seams and my trousers had fallen victim to the sun and the sea and were in rags.

I'll be a fine-looking figure, I thought, as I go up the gangway of a passenger ship. It was a good, morale-building thought, for now I got the safety-pins out of the bandages and pinned up the worst gaps in my shirts and trousers and felt very much better for it. The bandages themselves were now pushed firmly underneath the remaining coil of rope in the corner of the raft. Many times I tried to untie this rope, thinking to improve the rope-work across the raft, but always I was unsuccessful. Now it came in useful as a safe for my bits of broken mirror and the bandages.

The plastic bag and water-bottle I put in a fold of one of the life-jackets. My shirt was no longer a good place to keep them. I'd lost so much weight that my belt wouldn't hold up my trousers. Before putting on my boots I tucked them around my waist and fastened the belt over the top; it was still too loose to pin firmly on the last hole. I had to hold on to my trousers every time I moved and I was afraid that in my sleep my shirts might come untucked and the precious bag and bottle would come out.

I thought of cutting an extra hole in my belt, but decided that it was better, with my flesh so ulcerated, to keep my trousers loose at the waist. I got more air around my stomach that way, and air, I believed, would help to heal up the sores. I estimated that I'd lost twelve inches from my waist-line—and I'm not a big man under the best of circumstances.

Seven days had passed without sight of a ship and I began to worry that I'd either missed Ceylon or was making only the poorest progress to the west. With the water supply now fairly constant, my physical condition improved somewhat, but this day I lost all hope of rescue and didn't care whether I lived or died. I had surprisingly few regrets. I looked back over my life and thought I'd been very happy for the first twenty years. The last four had been unpleasant and there was not much point in going on with a life that offered so little.

During the afternoon, when the rain had gone, I lay on the ropes on the far side of the raft from Ericsson and fell asleep. The fish were still in the raft, but I was past caring and no longer drove them away. I dreamt that we were in a storm and that the raft was pitching and tossing. But when I awoke all was calm. I noticed with surprise that two of the ropes near Ericsson had been cut through but thought no more about it at this time. When we stretched the ropes across the raft we knotted them at each turn and a break in one or two didn't prejudice the network.

The cut ropes were immediately above the old holes in the canvas at the bottom of the raft, and, much later, when I began to repair the damage, this worried me. My dreams about the pitching of the raft might have been caused by one of the sharks that cruised so smoothly around us. The rope was not thick but of good quality linen and it couldn't have broken of its own accord.

Many times during the night I awoke and had some water. Once I tried to whistle, but the sound wouldn't come through my lips. They were too cracked and broken to assume whistling shape.

It had become difficult to drink water. My throat appeared to be shrinking and tightening and I couldn't swallow well. Even a small sip took some seconds to make the passage through my throat. And it brought no relief to the pain there, only stirring up the hurts.

My mouth was vile and I tried to wash its smell away with salt water, and in this I was at least more successful than I had been with the bathe I once gave my ulcers.

Despite my resignation about the future, hope never abandoned me for long and many times after I'd had a sip or two of water during the night I sat high up on the lifejackets and looked for lights.

When I saw none all my horror of the situation returned. The raft was putrid and I felt often that death would be preferable to this unspeakable foulness in which I was living. The prolonged absence of ships convinced me that I was off the sea lane and again I half hoped that my own end wouldn't be delayed.

But the fight for life persists to the end. Man can't give up the struggle. Almost against my will I went on with the tasks I had to do to stay alive.

I swore at daylight the next day to keep my quarter bottle of water until it rained again. I had a sip, no more, and covered the bottle with the lifejacket, hoping to keep it away from the sun and cool.

I took the flashlight from my pocket and tied it to the ropes in the corner of the raft. Its cover was rubber and the sea would do it no harm. During the night I'd flashed it on the sharks as they cruised around me, and now I chided myself with this waste. The batteries wouldn't last long with foolish behaviour like this.

Through the ropes I saw that two new types of fish had joined the raft. They were about eighteen inches long, brown and with round mouths that always stayed open. They were savage attackers of the smaller fish and made a strange "poomph" noise as they seized them. Several times they sucked against the lifejackets and their noise, when I first heard it, was very disturbing.

Once, when there were about thirty tiny fish in the raft, the "poomph" fish came in for a quick raid and scattered the smaller ones.

About noon on the twenty-fourth day I got renewed heart. I'd been lying down for a long time when I looked up and saw a freighter about three or four miles away. I hoisted my white shirt on one of the paddles and waved to the ship. I couldn't trust myself on my feet but kneeled near the edge and in this position waved for as long as I had strength.

When my knees buckled under me I sat and waved. Many times

before we'd waved to ships that came much closer, and my disappointment when this one went down on the horizon was less than it might have been. Rather than down-hearted, I was reassured by the thought that I'd come back to the sea lane and that where there was one ship there would almost certainly be others.

No wind this day, but I'd run into a big swell and often, when I was deep in the depressions, two or three minutes went by and I didn't see the ship. It was infuriating that my time on the crests seemed so much shorter than my time in the deeps, and I felt cheated by the sea which for so long had been so calm and still.

All the afternoon I looked for other ships; but none came. Once again overcome with detestation I tried to rid the raft of the corpse. I couldn't endure it any longer, but though I heaved and struggled with Ericsson's belt I achieved nothing but my own exhaustion.

I worked at it on my knees at first and then, with a tremendous effort, got to my feet and pulled and heaved. But I fell down and could do no more and began to think that it was better that I hadn't succeeded, for more ships would come and Ericsson could be buried and I wouldn't have broken my agreement with him. He was the best friend I'd ever had. It was just bad luck that we'd missed Sumatra. If only the *Skaubryn* hadn't come back at the wrong time and caused us to row west when we should have been going east. . . . If that hadn't happened both of us would have been safely in Indonesia.

Now all the ropes holding Ericsson were foul and there was nothing I could do for him. I straightened his legs and covered his eyes again; there was nothing else I might do.

Suddenly after this I had a craving for a cigarette. The only crushed and battered packet that survived was in one of my pockets. I brought it out and tipped some of the tobacco into my hand. The cigarettes had long ceased to be cigarettes, but the tobacco hadn't lost its aroma and as I crushed it between my fingers and held it to my nose the air became sweet and pleasant.

I took a sip of water and renewed my pledge to myself to hold out against another drink until the next rain.

The sun went down that night in a blaze of glory among the clouds in the west and came up on the morning of the twenty-fifth day in a thunderstorm. Lightning and thunder were all around the raft and the rain came down in streams. A strong wind tossed the raft too much for my weak hands and often, as I cradled my plastic bag with a brimming consignment of water for the bottle between my knees, a sudden lurch would send it all splashing into the bottom of the raft. But I had a good drink and filled about half the bottle and was not dissatisfied with myself when the storm passed.

In the half light of the passing storm a ship went by. I broke off my water-gathering to flash at it with the torch and to wave the shirt; but in the poor half light of early morning my chances of rescue, I knew, were poor.

The sea later in the morning was back to a glassy calm, clear and smooth and bright. I could see deep underneath the raft, where the "pilot" lay, and beyond to the attendant sharks, now seven in all, three of them big, four small.

The day was uneventful and hot and uncomfortable until about noon. I spent the morning lying on the lifejackets with my head wrapped in the blue shirt. I toyed with the idea of lying in the water at the bottom of the raft, but there were too many fish aboard now and I didn't want to lose such flesh as I had to the "poomph" fish or any of their companions.

To get myself a drink of water I threw off the blue shirt. I tilted the bottle and had a long, painful draught of water. I didn't care to look about the sea in this glare, but I did so now, hoping, as ever, that I might see a ship. There were no ships, but around the raft now were not seven but ten sharks and the three newcomers were the biggest I'd ever seen. Their dorsal fins, brown at the base and white at the top, stood a clear foot above the water. Their heads looked about two feet across and chunky like shovels. They were three times as long as the raft and as they swam past, not more than a yard or two away, I recoiled in terror at the sight of these creatures. I'd been taking the sharks for granted. But not now. I cringed back in the raft in unholy fear.

• • •

The sharks had the scent. They'd marked down their target and were preparing to attack. They swam against the sides of the raft and underneath, coming up immediately under me in long sweeping runs that left trails of bubbles behind.

They weren't in a hurry. Their target was here and they were looking simply for the best way to get at it. This time it was not the fish they were after. Those other times—they seemed months ago—when the sharks came they wanted the fish that then swarmed beneath the raft. It was our bad luck that the raft happened to be in the way, a concentration point for the fish that foolishly sought in its shadow a sanctuary that didn't exist.

Now even the "pilot" had left us and the sprats and the four-inchers and quarter-pounders which for seven days had been with me in the raft. There was nothing here but the sharks and the raft, Ericsson's body and I. They were not after fish.

I wondered how long this preparation had taken. How many times they had negotiated the raft and gone by, striking it, perhaps, as I slept? I had little hope against ten sharks. I waited with my right hand on one of the paddles, my left clutching one of the rope cross-pieces. Underneath me, in a fold of the lifejackets, were the plastic bag and water-bottle, my only links with hope and life. Without them I should die as surely as if the sharks got me.

They circled the raft like soldiers moving cautiously against a fort. For a minute, maybe five, the sea was quiet. The sun, high overhead, burnt down from the cloudless blue sky. No breeze touched the water and there was no swell and only the slightest movement beyond the raft for as far as I could see.

The sharks were very quiet, waiting. Close by were three of the largest, and I knew they would start the attack. There were four others, barely moving as they cruised in a wide circle well beyond the raft. Deep below, through the raft, were the others.

I didn't see the first blow, only the big shark as it flashed white past the side of the raft, leaving the metal floats ringing. In all the awful moments before when Ericsson and I had staved off the sharks there was never such a blow as this. It was staggering and I don't know now how I saved myself.

It was an experiment in force against the main defences of the raft, an effort to break in one blow my little stronghold that for three weeks and four days had defied the seas and the storms and the sharks. Now it was meeting its most serious challenge.

The reconnaissance was over. I'd just recovered from the first blow when another shark attacked. He came along the top of the water, going very fast, with his fin cutting a wide wake. He struck under the float with his head and the raft cleared the water and I had a blurred vision of the beastly square head, brown going into white. Another rushed from below and turned to savage the metal.

He hit a glancing blow and the speed with which he came carried him forward and into the air and I could see two feet of his glistening carcase above water.

A torrent of spray fell over me and I shut my eyes when the water came and opened them slowly, expecting to find the shark had landed inside the raft. Now all around the water was torn and threshed. I counted the blows as they hit and lost count and closed my eyes again to shut out the despair and horror of it all.

A fin was coming nearer and nearer in a wide circling motion. All the time I watched the fin, every second. It disappeared and now it was a shape coming up at the raft, brown and fast and white. I heard the canvas strips at the bottom give way and the tearing of the ropes. A shark was in the raft. Its ugly head stuck up above the level of the floats and I hit it with frenzied terror. I struck it with the blade of the paddle, jabbing for its eye, its brown eye that was so close to mine. Four times I hit it as it struggled in the mesh of ropes, caught by its shovel head. It was like hitting solid bone and my hands and arms jarred. The paddle would break but I didn't care. I hit again and again and the ropes snapped and flew apart like bands of rubber. I hit with hate and horror and anger. For this moment I was beyond fear. I found a strength I hadn't known for weeks. But I wasn't hurting the shark. Even when I hit its eye the shark wasn't hurt. But it went down through the broken ropes and into the sea and back again against the side.

Now I was spent and horribly afraid. What more could I do? A dying man can't fight sharks. I got back into the corner of the raft, clutching my lifejacket and my bottle and the bag. There was too much upheaval about me to see the sharks now. The water boiled and foamed and I couldn't tell what was happening. Only now and then I glimpsed a brown shape in the white foam as one came through the water and smashed against the raft. The floats quivered with the blows and I knew that even the stoutest raft could not survive this battering. It would fall apart and I would be with the sharks in the churning water.

Once I saw a shark go way up out of the water, off beyond the raft. A leap like that ending in the raft itself will end it all, I thought. That is how it will end.

But the sharks had different plans and while some went for the sides, others came up from the bottom against the canvas. This was even more terrifying than the side attacks. They shot up against me into the four feet square of canvas and water that was my home, jostling Ericsson's body and sometimes taking some of it before they fell back into the sea. They were getting more expert.

I saw them begin their dives with tails up and watched them as they shot back. Sometimes they hit the sides as they came but now more and more they were coming through the bottom of the raft. I couldn't move or call out. I was paralysed.

Sometimes there were two heads in the raft at the same time, angry heads, trying to get free. The raft jumped and tossed and I couldn't move. I couldn't pray. I could think of nothing but the unspeakable horror, the madness that went on around me. The heads went down through the raft into the water and I forced myself to think. I couldn't survive unless I did something. By now the canvas bottom was ripped to shreds. Nothing remained but a strip, four inches wide, going one way and two of a similar width going the opposite way. Half the ropes in the raft had gone and soon there would be a square of metal and nothing in between.

The sharks were after Ericsson, not me. I knew that I couldn't keep him any longer. I was surprised that he had stayed on the raft so long. The sharks had hit him many times as they came through the raft. The ropes were broken and full of holes where he lay; in my corner they were almost intact. I had to get the body out of the raft. I had to. It was the only hope I had. The sharks were circling when I decided to make another effort to push the body overboard. And the raft was steady, so that I could crawl on my hands and knees across the ropes to Ericsson. I was fearful that I might slip through the broken ropes into the sea.

I knelt over the body with one knee close to the side of the raft, the other resting on two sound pieces of rope. I tried to move the body by the belt, but though the middle came up I hadn't the strength to raise the head and feet. Urged on by the desperation of my fear I took the head by the hair and it came away in my hand. I wanted to cry with frustration. Any minute, any second, the sharks would be back.

Before they returned I had to have the body overboard and then they wouldn't worry me any more. I pushed and tugged, took hold of the feet and jerked them over the edge of the raft. Now they stuck out over the water and the sharks began to gather again. I thought they would come and take the legs, which were just above the water, and that, when I pushed, together we would get the body from the raft.

But they seemed determined to get into the raft and came back underneath and I heard the ropes go and saw more sharks come in. One had a little sucker fish clinging to its neck.

If I could get the body through the holes in the ropes the sharks would go away. But though the damage to the ropes was a constant danger to me there were still enough cross-pieces under the body to prevent me from getting it through. The sharks had broken Ericsson's flesh where it sagged in the water but they couldn't take him away and it made them mad. They attacked time after time and I pushed and struggled, clinging to the sides of the raft as they hit around me. Their jaws were up close to me in the raft itself, or just beyond the thin metal of the floats close to which I was now lying. I'd survived miraculously so far. But I couldn't expect my luck to hold much longer. The sharks were going for everything now, ripping and tearing at the rope-grips along the outside of the raft, lashing at the ropes inside. Soon there would be nothing but the ring of floats. When that happened they would get the body and it would be impossible for me to stay in the raft when they took it.

Desperately I struggled with the body, one moment trying to get it through the bottom of the raft, the next pushing to roll it over the side. Rolling was the best method. Kneeling on three of the surviving strands of knotted rope I got my hands under the side of the body and slowly levered it nearer the edge. To get it up and over was beyond me, but by holding on tight I managed to stop it rolling back again. I was in this position when the sharks hit us again. They would take me from underneath before I could get the body over. There were so few ropes left now and when they all went I would be unable to perch on the floats. Then it would be all over. I heaved and lifted, just a few inches up and I would have it over.

The sharks came underneath the raft. I felt it tilting high in the air, up and over. Here was my chance. As we poised at this awful angle I gave a final despairing heave and the body of my friend balanced on the edge and rolled into the sea.

Though many weeks have passed the nightmare of the next few minutes is with me still in all its horror. They got Ericsson within a yard of the raft as he floated on the top of the water, and fighting among themselves, lashing and churning, they took him away. I couldn't move. I sat on the side of the raft, worn out and horrified, and clasped my hands.

"Our Father, Which art in Heaven, hallowed be Thy Name . . . Thy Will be done . . ."

I remembered a prayer I had heard long ago in Poland, and as the sharks took my friend away I whispered what I knew of it to him:

"Dust thou art, and unto dust return.

The Lord Jesus Christ raise you up . . .
In the Name of the Father, and of the Son, and of The Holy
Ghost. Amen."

And now there was peace on the raft. Ericsson had gone and I tried not
to look at the sea where it boiled and flashed. Pieces of clothing were
scattered over a wide area. I was safe on my broken raft. The sharks
were all with my friend.

Farther and farther I drifted and soon there was nothing left, just a
small agitation on the water far away. And then it was all smooth, no
movement, as though it had never happened. There was nothing any
more. Everything had gone. Nothing but me and the raft and the endless sea. For a long time I sat there, spent and full of sorrow and
despair. I didn't want to move. I sat and saw the broken raft, trailing
streamers of rope and canvas.

Then the thoughts of self-preservation came rushing back.
Feverishly I felt for the water-bottle and the plastic bag. They were there
and I didn't want to die. I felt for the torch and the bits of mirror
pushed in under the one hard knob of rope in the corner.

I surveyed my sorrowful craft. Frayed wisps of rope dangled in the
water. Where Ericsson had been the strands of rope had almost all disappeared. Huge holes showed down to the sea beneath me. All that
was left of the canvas meshing, the original bottom of the raft, was one
solitary strip. Two other torn strips dragged in the water; all the rest
had gone.

On one side of the raft there was enough of the rope framework to
sit on, but that was all. I was practically sitting on the sea. Alone in a
bottomless raft.

Before nightfall, I decided, I had to make a place to lie down. I
couldn't sit up all night and if I moved in my sleep with the raft in its
present shape I would certainly roll into the sea.

The rest of the raft was in a frightful state. Scraps of Ericsson's white shirt stuck to the ropes and the sides of the floats. Pieces of flesh were all over the ropes.

I knew what had to be done, even before I started to get the ropes fixed. But I don't know how I did it. Something drove me on, something stronger than the shaking, half-dead wreck, crouching and crawling around the floats. All I wanted to do was to lie down and be away from it all, but if I didn't make the repairs there would be no place to lie down. It was all very simple.

Clean it up first. Holding on to the sides of the floats with one hand, I used the other as a scoop, splashing the sea-water over the horrible things on the raft, scrubbing with my hand to get the pieces off. I washed and scrubbed for half an hour, then rested for another half-hour.

It must have been about four o'clock in the afternoon now, a cloudless sky, unchanging flat calm water. I had some fresh water and there was about a quarter of the bottle left when I'd satisfied my thirst. With Ericsson's blue shirt around my head I started again, working with a slow, painful energy, removing the broken wisps of rope, untying the knots we'd put in so long ago when there'd been hope for us both. The knots were easy to undo and I was thankful.

The big coil of rope in the corner which we hadn't used before was just what I needed. I crawled carefully over the ropes to it, wishing I had a knife to loosen the tight coils. With my fingers I made no progress at all. And the broken mirror was no good for such a job. My teeth would have to do it. I put my mouth to the rope but the hurt on my lips was too much for me. I couldn't bear the pain and gave it up as a bad job, deciding, after all, to use the old pieces of rope again.

From side to side, side to side, I crawled around the edges of the raft, making the rope firm on the outside. I rested a lot, one rope across the raft then a rest, resting and taking the ropes over for hour after hour. My hands and knees were sore and my whole body ached. But I worked and worked with the force inside me making me go on. I think the work kept me sane.

After a while I sat back and looked at the work. It was a firmer and better job than before. There was no sagging and I'd be higher out of the water, safer from underneath attacks from sharks. Before there had been two men, now I was the only occupant and not a very heavy one at that; the ropes hardly gave at all when I tested them with my weight.

I was very pleased with my work. Pleasure gave me hope and I worked harder, tightening ropes here and there, testing and tying and putting a few more strands across to make a tighter central platform. I worked at it until I couldn't do any more. Tomorrow I'd do the last little bit. The canvas was beyond all hope and would have to stay as it was, but my ropes were fine and strong.

I set to making my bed. Now that I was alone I could really stretch out for the first time. The paddles diagonally across the raft gave me a longer bed and I threw the two lifejackets on top of them. One jacket was badly broken. It had burst in the heat and water and with all the wear and tear on the raft. As I picked it up corks dropped out and through the new mesh and floated away under me. I didn't care. The jacket was softer without the corks.

Getting ready for bed was a long business. I took a sip of water, rolling it on my parched-up tongue and letting it slip painfully down my throat. I put back the stopper and folded the bottle into the lifejacket with my other possessions—the plastic bag and the torch that now was mine.

I stretched my aching body over the lifejackets. My head was inside the raft. No fear of getting wet. My feet were inside, too. I was safe from the sharks and the sea in my rope basket.

A new moon shone in the sky that night and many stars. Looking at them I thought of what had happened during the day, trying to forget the horrors of Ericsson's end. It was my first night alone at sea. Even after his death Ericsson had been there to keep me company. I mustn't think of Ericsson, but about the work I'd done on the raft. I was foolishly proud of my efficiency. I fell asleep with my mind still making crisscross patterns across the raft.

Once I woke in the night and felt the raft going along very fast. The wind was strong and I vaguely thought of putting up the blue shirt-sail to catch the wind. I sat up and looked into the darkness and felt the aches and pains all over my body. My left side was the worst and I tried to think of some way to ease the pain and to take the strain off the bad parts.

The wind blew ever stronger. Going along like this, snug in my own raft with my own good, new ropes, I felt suddenly strong, in spite of the ills and tiredness of my body. I felt the wind must take me some-where. Tomorrow would be different. Tomorrow what would happen? Perhaps tomorrow I would be dead. Maybe a man felt strong just before he died. The thought didn't worry me. Death wouldn't hurt.

Now I could sleep. I'd done a good job with my ropes. They would last for a long time. I felt quite comfortable apart from the pain in my side. Turning over I felt the bottle beneath me and dragged it out from the lifejacket. I fell asleep, contented in the tearing cold, with the rub-ber bottle, like a soft cushion, pressed against my sore side.

I finished the rope-work first thing the next morning. With some loose ends I made an even stronger patchwork in the centre of the raft where I would lie. Since Ericsson had gone the raft floated higher in the water and the ropes gave four or five inches of freeboard. I should now be able to keep dry and be out of the way of the sharks. They came for Ericsson because he was in the water. My handiwork had removed that danger.

The "pilot" rejoined the raft during the morning, also three small sharks and the "poomph" fish. All the crabs, I was thankful, had gone. About ten o'clock a ship passed about a mile from the raft. Kneeling on the ropes, I waved to it until it went away. My spirits went with the ship and after it had gone I finished the rest of my water, despairing of ever being able to attract a ship.

I made an inverted V of the paddles and tied the blue shirt around them and lay in the shelter for most of the rest of the day. The sun was brutally hot. During the afternoon the sky clouded over and I saw a most remarkable cloud. It was much darker than the generally blue-black overcast, but it seemed to be only a yard or so across. I was about a mile from this tiny black balloon of a cloud when rain suddenly began to fall heavily from it. It wasn't a water-spout: I'm certain of that. But there seemed to be no explanation of this downpour which dropped in a thin column into the sea and went on for about half an hour. Later, rain fell on the raft and I replenished my supply of water.

The rain continued very lightly until after dark. I was soaking wet and after the heat of the early morning the cold hit me again. All night I shivered on the lifejackets.

It was not until just before daybreak that I fell into an uneasy sleep, which lasted until the sun was high in the sky on the morning of my twenty-seventh day at sea. I still had most painful dreams of food, but I couldn't face the thought of seizing any of the fish around the raft. The events of the previous days were heavily and horribly in my thoughts. I swore I'd never eat fish again.

That morning another ship went by. It was about three or four miles from the raft and I waved without hope. Later I conserved my strength by resting as much as possible and for the rest of the day I dozed in the sun.

About ten or eleven o'clock that night the sharp splashing of water over the raft and the whistle of a high wind awakened me from a deep sleep. I moved my bed more into the centre of the raft and curled up to keep away from the edges. The waves were sharp and hard. Though not of great height, they were sufficient to keep me from sleeping for the rest of the night. The raft leapt alarmingly and the waves which followed in quick succession dashed over me and surged up through the ropes.

The next morning I decided against wearing boots any more. The skin on my feet hung in unwholesome pouches and was sore to touch. The leather merely aggravated the ulcers which were spreading to all parts of my body.

Ericsson had discarded his shoes some days before he died. They were still tied to the ropes in the corner of the raft, and now I put my boots there, too.

The morning of the twenty-eighth day was bright and clear but the wind was heavier. I wasn't strong enough to sit up against it. The raft moved along quite quickly, but not, I discovered from the sun, to the west. I was now being driven back towards Sumatra, over our old tracks, by one of the stiffest breezes we'd had since leaving the *Skaubryn*.

I'd pinned such hopes as I still had on Ceylon and now it was a heavy blow to find that I was going in the wrong direction. To buck up my spirits I looked for my comb to do my hair. Always when we saw a ship Ericsson and I used to take out our combs to tidy our hair. We were a fearful-looking pair of pirates with long hair hanging down, bedraggled beards and clothes that were only shreds with no patches. By brushing up our moustaches and combing our hair we thought we looked a bit better. Mine is that fine, undisciplined hair that needs lots of oil, but I did my best with a comb and salt water. But now my comb had gone. So I did the next best thing, and cleaned my finger-nails with the broken mirror.

I turned to my ulcers and cleaned up these foul, expanding sores. Nothing I could do improved them much. Salt water was too rough and painful. My mouth was awful with foul sores along my gums and between my teeth. It hurt like the devil, but I rinsed out my mouth with salt water and afterwards felt better for it.

During the day my right arm began to ache. I had several big and especially painful ulcers in my arm-pit and the poison from these gradually spread down my arm until I could no longer use it. I was getting weaker every day. And I knew it. I thought I mightn't live for even another day. But such thoughts were with me many times and always my depressions were followed by surges of confidence and optimism. My mind was clear. I was sorry for Ericsson, but not greatly concerned for myself. It'd been a good effort and if I failed, well, then, I might have lived only to die even more unpleasantly with the Legion.

In the evening another tired seagull arrived and sat on the edge of the raft. I made a tentative move towards it, but it flew off, returning when I settled down. I had no strength to grab it and it stayed for some hours. It was there when I fell asleep at night but was gone in the morning.

The twenty-ninth day. My mouth was much worse. It was now six-teen days since I'd eaten my few fragments of turtle, my last food of any kind. And I was still drifting to the east, away from Ceylon.

The heat was worse than ever before. I bent the ropes, hoping that I might be able to lie in the water, but I'd done the repairs too well. I gave up lying on the lifejackets because they stopped the water when it welled up through the raft; and I needed the water to keep me cool. I put my feet through the ropes and let them dangle in the water, a slight relief. I hated the heat more than I dreaded the prospect of death.

I knew I had to save my water supply, but the agony of burning hour after hour in the sun, my body crying out for water every second, was torture. I tossed endlessly. No part of my body was unaffected by the spreading ulcers and there was no position in which I could hope for even momentary comfort.

One of the big sharks returned this day, and a treacherous-looking skate, with broad yellow bands across its back, took up position under the raft and angrily drove away the small fish that sought the shade there.

The shark's arrival meant that I couldn't risk my feet in the water even under the raft. After a passing feeling of repugnance that the shark was back and a similar pang of fear, I reflected that the raft had never been in better shape. Even if I died the sharks would find it difficult to get at me.

Before I died I planned to scratch a message on the side of the raft, so that one day when a ship found it they would learn our fate. Using the broken mirror I would scratch our names, home towns and the date we left the *Skaubryn* and when Ericsson died.

I still had some water, but about noon rain fell again. Despite my bad right arm I got about half a bottle and drank all I could.

After the rain I tried to sing and was shocked to discover that I had no voice left. "Is my voice gone for good?" I asked myself, and just a whispered croak came out of my mouth. "Hullo," I shouted, and only parts of the word came.

My throat had become so sore I couldn't swallow any more. Water had to find its way down by itself and in the smallest quantities. I took a little in my mouth and held my head back to let the drops go down one by one. I'll never be able to talk again, I thought and lay down on the ropes, sick and miserable and all hope gone.

The sun was worse after the rain. Blinding, terrible heat. I felt that I was being grilled and that the ropes were the bars of the griller. No sweat came out of my pores, no moisture. I was dried up and cooking in the sun. I had no hope of living until the evening. I wanted to die. I couldn't endure the pain. The ropes bit into my side and back.

I burnt and ached and wanted it all over. The blue shirt flapped uselessly on one of the paddles. My tattered white shirt covered my head. But nothing stopped the sun burning through it all. I was only half conscious and maybe a trifle mad.

Night brought a cool breeze and deep, wonderful relief. I felt the heat until the sun went down. I could see it going, big and red, towards the horizon, slowly, so slowly. I felt it was a race between us. If I lived until it went down I'd be all right. But would I live so long?

The west wind blew me farther from Ceylon all night. What was the use of it all? Wouldn't it be better to die this night than to race another day of purgatory in the sun.

The thirtieth day. No ships. No rain. No clouds. No hope. No will to live. Only the heat again, worse than ever before. I could no longer even try to make a shelter. I could sit up only by holding to the ropes with one hand, or by propping myself with my elbow. I had the water close by but the effort of getting at the bottle and the pain and difficulty of drinking. . . . It must be noon, I thought, and it was no more than early morning. Hour after hour, gasping and twisting in pain. The hurt from the ulcers was one great hurt that went all through my body and was multiplied a thousand times by the sun.

I was in a semi-coma and saw myself walking out of the raft and into the sea and up a sandy, tropical shore. I came to and found myself with my feet over the edge of the raft in the water. Twice this happened. And I didn't care. Sharks, the sea, nothing mattered.

All the water went a long time before sunset, most of it spilled over my shirt. All the water gone and no strength, I felt sure, ever to get more.

If I have ever been certain of anything in my life it was that on March 25, 1953, my thirty-first day at sea, I was about to die. Sometimes I thought that I had died. The thread between life and death had now become so slender, the transition from one state to another almost a matter of degree.

I lay on my stomach in the sun, waiting for death, expecting it at any moment. The pain had gone from my body, or, if it hadn't gone, it was all one pain and I couldn't tell where it was that I hurt.

The day began well with rain early in the morning. It started to fall before daybreak and went on for more than an hour, heavy and drenching, forcing me into action. Not knowing why I did it I worked my way painfully into a half-lying, half-sitting position on one of the lifejackets. I fumbled to bring out the plastic bag and the water-bottle. I cradled the bag on my stomach, making a sort of funnel with it that led down into the bottle.

Sometimes I slept while I was gathering the water and sometimes the bottle fell over and all I had collected spilled out over my legs and went down into the raft. But somehow I got half a bottle. My fingers were so weak I couldn't put the stopper back in the bottle. They shook and couldn't find the opening. I took it quietly and rested and tried again, holding the top of the bag between my knees and using both hands until I got the stopper in the hole and turned it tight.

When I had finished I wondered why I bothered. I was utterly without hope. I had no will to do these things that helped to keep me alive a little longer. I didn't want to live. I remembered the prayers I had said for Ericsson when he went out of the raft to the sharks and now I wanted to say them for myself. I couldn't speak them but my lips moved and formed the shape of the words:

• • •

"The Lord bless thee and keep thee,
The Lord make His face to shine upon thee. . ."

These were my better moments. During one I thought I should try to scratch the names on the side of the raft. But there was no power left in my arms and legs, nor any in my heart, that could move me to this labour. Though I was often unconscious I moved constantly in the raft, turning from side to side, rolling and struggling. When I came to my senses for a few fleeting minutes I would see that I had moved again, sometimes perilously towards the edge. Lapsing into unconsciousness, I felt drawn all the time from the raft, and once more awoke to find my feet in the water.

In a moment of terrifying reality I saw more sharks than I had seen all the time on the raft. A long procession of them came past the raft. Again I thought they were porpoises until they came close and I saw them for what they were, a parade, a very convocation of the brutes. Coming for me. It didn't matter. Nothing mattered.

The sharks went on their way and the skeleton on the raft drifted back into delirium. During the dreadful heat of this thirty-first day I don't remember having any water. I am sure I didn't. In the evening when a cool breeze brought me back to life I found the bottle still rolled in the lifejacket. The stopper was in hard and I would never have had the strength to unfasten it and close it up again. I took a little water now but it had no effect on my throat if it ever got that far. I felt my lips wet with the water and took a long time getting the stopper back into the bottle. There was little relief in the water now.

I'd lost all sense of a second person being in the raft. The guardian angel who kept me company after Ericsson's death left the raft with my own loss of hope.

Though the cool of the evening brought a little strength back to me I still could not sit up. I fixed my bed for the night, pushing the paddles together with the lifejackets over them. The torch batteries had expired at last and I smiled with a foolish pride that I'd lasted the longer.

The night was a repetition of the day, some real sleep and a good deal of delirium. I believed I was dead and that I had been rescued and that I was having a great dinner. Again I was leaving the raft and awoke to find myself draped half over the edge.

The thirty-second day blends into the thirty-first. I don't know where one ended and the other began. I have no recollection of the sunrise or anything that happened until the morning was well advanced. There was nothing by which I could measure the passing of time.

Life returned and the day began when despair changed into hope and I came slowly out of the gloom into reality. The change was spiritual, but the body responded. My nerves produced a final effort, my muscles worked and my mind coordinated. It was about mid-afternoon, very hot, no wind. A fair swell sluggishly moved the raft on the sea. I lay on my right side, completely conscious now, staring out across the water with only half-seeing eyes, when I saw a ship. It was a tanker going west, about three miles off. I forced myself on to my elbows and took the shirt lying by my side and waved. The paddle was beyond my capacity. I couldn't lift it. But I must get higher. Up on the lifejackets and they would be able to see me better. I pushed one paddle against the side of the raft and inched forward until I was sitting on it. I waved more successfully now, but there was little strength in my back and repeatedly my head fell forward and my back slumped after it. To straighten my back and get my head up took another great effort, but I managed it and waved until the ship had gone down and there was nothing left to wave to.

Before despair could settle in me I saw another ship, another tanker of about 8,000 tons. This one was going east and was not more than a mile away. It was on the far side of the raft and to signal to it I had to turn about. I found my body heavier than the shirt. Much heavier. First I got one leg around, then the other, and with it my body. I seemed to have no backbone and several times I fell forward and had to heave up with all my strength, pulling on the ropes for additional support.

The ship came very close. Though my eyes were weak and I couldn't focus properly, the seconds of proper vision were rewarding. There were people on deck and I waited for someone to see me, for the ship to signal and turn towards me. But like the many others that had gone before it, this one also sailed on its way. I was too weak to wave for more than a few seconds at a time. My arm wouldn't stay upright and the longer I sat up the more tired and uncontrollable my back became.

This second ship had not disappeared, however, before another came on the scene. This, like the second, was going east, though farther off. Two, perhaps three, miles. I had no hope of attracting attention aboard this ship. If I'd missed out on the ship that came so close to me it was unlikely that I could hope to make myself seen aboard one three times the distance off.

But I wasn't disappointed. Three ships in an hour. How could I be disappointed? The ships had been on both sides of me and I felt that I was back in the sea lane. If there were three ships, there would be more.

Now I wanted to live. If I could last another day I still had a chance. I was determined to stay alive. I willed myself to live. For two days I'd expected death, welcomed death. A lot of the time I was more dead than alive. I was dying and I wanted to die.

Everything had changed now. Another day, if only I could live just one more day. I hadn't touched the water-bottle all day but now the exertion and the hope filled me with thirst and I got the bottle from the lifejacket. I held the water in my mouth and tried to swallow it, but my throat was bound up. The muscles had ceased to work. I got a little water down and I thought of babies and how they had to learn to drink and to swallow. When I got away—if I got away—I would have to learn all over again.

In the twilight of the thirty-second day, a fourth ship appeared. It was on the far horizon as the sun went down and by the time it came opposite the raft my shirt-waving was a pitiful, hopeless effort. But I waved, nevertheless. With the dark the ships would not see me and this one was my last hope. The swell which had been running in the morning was still fairly heavy and I rested when the raft was in the deep with my head and shoulders bent forward. But when the raft came briefly to the top of the swell I forced myself upright again, as high as I could, and waved and waved.

The ship was close. Perhaps just over a mile away. It was too dark already and I cursed that the torch had given out. This was flashlight time and I had no means of signalling. One S–O–S, I was convinced, would have brought a boat to my side.

I flicked the torch again with fumbling fingers but there was no life in it. In the exasperation of despair I hit it against the side of the raft. No glimmer of light came. But the lights of the ship went on to the east.

Now there was no point in looking for ships. If I saw them they wouldn't see me. I had no hope of attracting their attention. Just at the time when I needed to use every minute of every hour left to me in this world I had half of my day and all my chances snatched away from me.

I pulled at the lifejackets and paddles to make myself a bed. I was frightened to lose control of my much-improved senses. I was living on my spirit, and sleep, I was afraid, might lead me to death. I desperately wanted to live. I wanted to wake up alive the next morning more than I have ever wanted anything in my life before. "I must stay alive, I must stay alive," I repeated over and over to myself. And to stay alive I had also to stay awake.

I didn't wrap my head in the shirt this night because I didn't want to do anything that would help me to sleep. If water splashed over the raft and woke me by falling on my head, well and good. If the moon was too bright in my eyes, so much the better. I dreaded the early hours of the morning most. Those were the hours when the night was darkest and the spirit lowest. I wanted to get through the crisis hours. I was on the sea lane and when the sun came up there would be ships. I had to stay awake until sunrise if I wanted to live for another day.

The moon was very bright. The evening of our escape had been a night like this. The brightness might help to keep me awake. I looked at the stars and for mental exercise tried to place the planets. I wanted to keep my mind active and this was the only way. But the more I looked the more difficult it was to keep my eyes open. The stars twinkled and merged and disappeared. I fought against the darkness when my eyes closed. I forced them open by will-power and saw the stars again. But my eyes could not stay open and, hating myself for my weakness and afraid that I wouldn't live to see the sunrise, I fell asleep.

Sleep . . . and now the great noise of a ship going fast through the water came to me. It cut into my troubled dreams and registered in my subconscious mind. My body didn't react even when I awoke. The night was full of sound. Suddenly all the importance of the noise hit me.

I moved as I hadn't moved in days. Not twenty yards from me, going east, was the bow of a ship. A light. If only I had a light I could make myself seen. I tried to shout but it was a tiny sound, no voice to carry even the few yards across the water to the ship. What I shouted was, "Hello, ship," in English. But no one could have heard me.

I saw some men on deck, but whether they were looking at me or far out across the sea I couldn't say. I took the white shirt and waved it, but who would see a shirt even on a moonlit night like this?

The black sides of the ship slid along beside me; high above my head were lights and the sound of shouting voices. It was right on top of me. Instead of saving me the ship was going to run me down. I cursed myself for sleeping. I screamed a great shout to tell them and no sound came out. Even to me my shout was soundless. How could I expect the ship to hear?

It missed me and I grabbed for a paddle, slipping and clawing over the ropes until I reached it. It couldn't go without seeing me. With my two hands I lifted the paddle and banged with all my might on the floats, mouthing shouts at the ship. As I brought the paddle down I heard the ringing sound on the metal. The ship had to hear it, too.

I banged again and again and, exhausted, went down with my head in my shaking hands. As I sat there I heard a man's voice, very loud. There was no form in his words, just the sound of a human voice. The most wonderful sound in the world. At once I heard a bell, the engine-room bell, and I took the paddle again and brought it banging down on the floats. My shouting voice was silent but the noise of the paddle on the floats was loud and I was sure it would be heard on the ship.

The ship went away. I willed it to return and it got farther and farther away. I've never felt so futile. I had no light to flash. No voice to call. My mouth made the right movements but no sound reached me. "Please, please, come back," to the ship. Lying on the ropes, I watched it leave me. There was no more I could do.

At least on the ship they had thought there was something on the water. Out from its deck came a light which fell on the sea about a hundred yards from my raft. It lit up a great patch of water and the light went in and out, in and out.

But the ship went slowly back into the darkness. I couldn't get it back. If only I had the torch—just the flicker of a light and it wouldn't go away. Someone had been curious but his curiosity had died. I would die, too. There'd been no answer to the voice and no answer to their light. I had no voice and no light. But surely someone would have heard the noise as I banged on the floats.

I sat, not daring to hope, and was surprised a long time later to see the lights coming nearer again. There was no mistaking it. This time the ship came in a large circle and I knew it looked for me. I didn't try to shout. I waited for the right moment when I could start banging again.

When the lights were very close I lifted the paddle and let it fall on the metal sides of the raft to guide them to me. And suddenly it was all right. They found me. A great beam of light came straight on my face and I sank down on my knees to save my eyes from the glare, and knew it was all over.

The good light stayed on me and suddenly I was ashamed of my appearance, tattered and torn, straw-like hair sticking up all over my head, bristling, matted beard, a barefooted derelict.

But I still wasn't prepared for the voice that came from the ship as someone saw me, caught in the beam of light.

"It's a Russian," I thought I heard the voice say.

Perhaps it was the colour of my hair or perhaps the wildness of my appearance that made me look like a Russian. Maybe it wasn't

"Russian," but that's how it sounded to me. My lips formed the words: "I'm not a Russian," and nothing came out. It didn't matter.

For five minutes the light was on me and then the ship turned again. She was too far away to pick me up. But I knew she wouldn't leave me now. This ship was going to save me.

As it turned and the beam left my face I looked up again and saw the ship and the lights and movement along the decks. The whole ship was alive. Lights from cigarettes were all along the rails and the sound of men's voices—a pleasant sound to a man who hadn't heard another voice for so long. Not even his own.

I felt sure they would throw me a rope now and waited anxiously, trying to catch the words that came to me over the sea. I wished they didn't have to go away. I didn't want to be alone again. If they lost me this time they would give up. They couldn't be expected to search all night.

Out into the dark the ship went again. It made another great circle and a flare went out on the water a long way from me. The ship went away and with it the lights. I was exhausted and wanted to lie down and to sleep, to be away from the anxiety and doubts.

They were trying hard and there must be something I could do to help. I was so helpless, so useless. They might lose me even now if I fell asleep. And I wanted to sleep so badly. If I slept they would never find me. Keep my eyes open. My eyes were all I had. I had no voice to call, no light to shine. What else? I racked my slow mind and saw the shirt and tied it to a paddle. It was the biggest effort of my life. I'd achieved something miraculous. I'd saved my own life. So long as I could keep the shirt upright on the paddle I would live.

Hold it up. Hold it up straight. Don't let the paddle wobble. But the paddle was a drunken man, falling to the raft and wavering all the time in my unsteady hands. Still, it was most important to keep the paddle in the air. Even as my eyes dropped, when I had to lie right down, I forced myself to keep the paddle up. I fell into sleep or unconsciousness and woke to find the paddle beside me, its tattered white shirt lifeless on the ropes. Angry, I stuck it into the ropes and it stood quite well and easily without my help. Trying to hold on I fainted and fell into darkness. I stopped existing and left it to the ship and to the paddle, standing crookedly in its place, to save me.

I couldn't have been out for long. Now there were two ships, one close by with lots of lights, the other away over the water. My paddle still stood, but the shirt had fallen down and I let it stay there.

My boots. I must get my boots on; this was important. I put them on as the ship came closer. My feet were so thin and the boots felt enormous. Struggling with the laces, being very clever about tying them to keep them on my wasted ankles.

There was a lot to do and I did nothing well. My feet were falling out of the boots. I felt for the paddle and put the shirt back on it. I was full of a great effort, a frenzy of painfully slow activity. I'd fallen down on what I should have done. I must hang on hard to consciousness. Try to do something, try to keep alive until they get me. I clutched with my hands and legs to the paddle with its shirt waving and let it drop again and took up the paddle and rowed, or tried to row, into the light that couldn't find me.

I did things in spasms. In the middle of something I would go out and find myself lying on my back, my feet in the water. I picked up the paddle again, lifted my body from the ropes and banged and the ship came very slowly, its bow pointed straight at the raft. There were many voices, so many men against the rails.

A rope came down over the raft, over my body and I caught it in the air as the end fell into the water. I was happy to be doing things well. I nearly forgot the plastic bag and the bottle. My precious bottle. I needed the bottle. There was still some water in it. I put the bottle with the bag against my stomach and put the rope around them, around my waist. I knew it would hold.

They would want a signal. I lifted my hands and made a circle in the air and people shouted while the ship slid by, all its long side. Then the stern came nearer. And now I was in the air. The raft fell behind me and I was in the water up to my waist. The thought of sharks came to me then, only once and I didn't care any more.

It was as well for my peace of mind in this moment of rescue that I didn't see what the officers and men waiting above could see. For the water was boiling with sharks and the rope that pulled me high and free against the steel hull of the ship moved only just in time. As I swung out of the water the men above saw the upheaval of an attack that came too late, the white belly and the fin of the shark that had missed its prey.

I knew nothing now until hands had me by the shoulders. There were faces all around me. Indian faces and white faces and the faces were tender and kind. Hands put me on a blanket and hands gave me water.

"Thank you," said my mouth, and they took away the water. Only a mouthful.

"More, please, oh, please."

They cut away my clothes and my flesh came, too, in long strange pieces. Tenderly the hands stripped my shirt and wrapped me in a blanket.

Lying on my back I looked up and saw an officer, standing high on another deck. He was looking at his watch. They told me later it was twenty-past three in the morning of March 27, thirty-two days almost to the minute since Ericsson and I jumped off the *Skaubryn* and into the sea.

from West With the Night
by Beryl Markham

In the early days of flying in Africa, pilots who went down had to survive both the crash and the wild animals. So when a fellow flier disappeared into the void, Beryl Markham (1902-1986) didn't know whether to look for twisted metal or bones. At first she found neither, but her bush training helped her to ask the most important question: What's wrong with this picture?

I f you were to fly over the Russian steppes in the dead of winter after snow had fallen, and you saw beneath you a date palm green as spring against the white of the land, you might carry on for twenty miles or so before the incongruity of a tropical tree rooted in ice struck against your sense of harmony and made you swing round on your course to look again. You would find that the tree was not a date palm or, if it still persisted in being one, that insanity had claimed you for its own.

During the five or ten minutes I had watched the herd of game spread like a barbaric invasion across the plain, I had unconsciously observed, almost in their midst, a pool of water bright as a splinter from a glazier's table.

I knew that the country below, in spite of its drought-resistant grass, was dry during most of the year. I knew that whatever water holes one did find were opaque and brown, stirred by the feet of drinking game. But the water I saw was not brown; it was clear, and it received the sun and turned it back again in strong sharp gleams of light.

Like the date palm on the Russian steppes, this crystal pool in the arid roughness of the Serengetti was not only incongruous, it was impossible. And yet, without the slightest hesitation, I flew over it and beyond it until it was gone from sight and from my thoughts.

There is no twilight in East Africa. Night tramps on the heels of Day with little gallantry and takes the place she lately held, in severe and humourless silence. Sounds of the things that live in the sun are quickly gone—and with them the sounds of roving aeroplanes, if their pilots have learned the lessons there are to learn about night weather, distances that seem never to shrink, and the perfidy of landing fields that look like aerodromes by day, but vanish in darkness.

I watched small shadows creep from the rocks and saw birds in black flocks homeward bound to the scattered bush, and I began to consider my own home and a hot bath and food. Hope always persists beyond reason, and it seemed futile to nurse any longer the expectation of finding Woody with so much of the afternoon already gone. If he were not dead, he would of course light fires by night, but already my fuel was low, I had no emergency rations—and no sleep.

I had touched my starboard rudder, altering my course east for Nairobi, when the thought first struck me that the shining bit of water I had so calmly flown over was not water at all, but the silvered wings of a Klemm monoplane bright and motionless in the path of the slanting sun.

It was not really a thought, of course, nor even one of those blinding flashes of realization that come so providentially to the harried heroes of fiction. It was no more than a hunch. But where is there a pilot foolhardy enough to ignore his hunches? I am not one. I could never tell where inspiration begins and impulse leaves off. I suppose the answer is in the outcome. If your hunch proves a good one, you were inspired; if it proves bad, you are guilty of yielding to thoughtless impulse.

But before considering any of this, I had already reversed my direction, lost altitude, and opened the throttle again. It was a race with racing shadows, a friendly trial between the sun and me.

As I flew, my hunch became conviction. Nothing in the world, I thought, could have looked so much like reflecting water as the wings of Woody's plane. I remembered how bright those wings had been when last I saw them, freshly painted to shine like silver or stainless steel. Yet they were only of flimsy wood and cloth and hardened glue.

The deception had amused Woody. 'All metal,' he would say, jerking a thumb toward the Klemm; 'all metal, except just the wings and fuselage and prop and little things like that. Everything else is metal—even the engine.'

Even the engine!—as much of a joke to us as to the arrant winds of Equatorial Africa; a toy engine with bustling manner and frantic voice; an hysterical engine, guilty at last perhaps of what, in spite of Woody's jokes and our own, we all had feared.

Now almost certainly guilty, I thought, for there at last was what I hunted—not an incredible pool of water, but, unmistakable this time, the Klemm huddled to earth like a shot bird, not crushed, but lifeless and alone, beside it no fire, not even a stick with a fluttering rag.

I throttled down and banked the Avian in slow, descending circles.

I might have had a pious prayer for Woody on my lips at that moment, but I didn't have. I could only wonder if he had been hurt and taken into a manyatta by some of the Masai Murani, or if, idiotically, he had wandered into the pathless country in search of water and food. I even damned him slightly, I think, because, as I glided to within five hundred feet of the Klemm, I could see that it was unscathed.

There can be a strange confusion of emotions at such a moment. The sudden relief I felt in knowing that at least the craft had not been damaged was, at the same time, blended with a kind of angry disappointment at not finding Woody, perhaps hungry and thirsty, but anyhow alive beside it.

Rule one for forced landings ought to be, 'Don't give up the ship.' Woody of all people should have known this—did know it, of course, but where was he?

Circling again, I saw that in spite of a few pig-holes and scattered rocks, a landing would be possible. About thirty yards from the Klemm there was a natural clearing blanketed with short, tawny grass. From the air I judged the length of the space to be roughly a hundred and fifty yards—not really long enough for a plane without brakes, but long enough with such head wind as there was to check her glide.

I throttled down, allowing just enough revs to prevent the ship from stalling at the slow speed required to land in so small a space. Flattening out and swinging the tail from side to side in order to get what limited vision I could at the ground below and directly ahead, I flew in gently and brought the Avian to earth in a surprisingly smooth run. I made a mental note at the time that the take-off, especially if Woody were aboard, might be a good deal more difficult.

But there was no Woody.

I climbed out, got my dusty and dented water bottle from the locker, and walked over to the Klemm, motionless and still glittering in the late light. I stood in front of her wings and saw no sign of mishap, and heard nothing. There she rested, frail and feminine, against the rough, grey ground, her pretty wings unmarked, her propeller rakishly tilted, her cockpit empty.

There are all kinds of silences and each of them means a different thing. There is the silence that comes with morning in a forest, and this is different from the silence of a sleeping city. There is silence after a rainstorm, and before a rainstorm, and these are not the same. There is the silence of emptiness, the silence of fear, the silence of doubt. There is a certain silence that can emanate from a lifeless object as from a chair lately used, or from a piano with old dust upon its keys, or from anything that has answered to the need of a man, for pleasure or for work. This kind of silence can speak. Its voice may be melancholy, but it is not always so; for the chair may have been left by a laughing child or the last notes of the piano may have been raucous and gay. Whatever the mood or the circumstance, the essence of its quality may linger in the silence that follows. It is a soundless echo.

With the water bottle swinging from my hand on its long leather strap, like an erratic pendulum, I walked around Woody's plane. But even with shadows flooding the earth like slow-moving water and the grass whispering under the half-spent breath of the wind, there was no feeling of gloom or disaster.

The silence that belonged to the slender little craft was, I thought, filled with malice—a silence holding the spirit of wanton mischief, like the quiet smile of a vain woman exultant over a petty and vicious triumph.

I had expected little else of the Klemm, frivolous and inconstant as she was, but I knew suddenly that Woody was not dead. It was not that kind of silence.

I found a path with the grass bent down and little stones scuffed from their hollows, and I followed it past some larger stones into a tangle of thorn trees. I shouted for Woody and got nothing but my own voice for an answer, but when I turned my head to shout again, I saw two boulders leaning together, and in the cleft they made were a pair of legs clothed in grimy work slacks and, beyond the legs, the rest of Woody, face down with his head in the crook of his arm.

I went over to where he was, unscrewed the cap of the water bottle and leaned down and shook him.

'It's Beryl,' I called, and shook him harder. One of the legs moved and then the other. Life being hope, I got hold of his belt and tugged.

Woody began to back out of the cleft of the rocks with a motion irrelevantly reminiscent of the delectable crayfish of the South of France. He was mumbling, and I recalled that men dying of thirst are likely to mumble and that what they want is water. I poured a few drops on the back of his neck as it appeared and got, for my pains, a startled grunt. It was followed by a few of those exquisite words common to the vocabularies of sailors, airplane pilots, and stevedores—and then abruptly Woody was sitting upright on the ground, his face skinny beneath a dirty beard, his lips cinder-dry and split, his eyes red-rimmed and sunk in his cheeks. He was a sick man and he was grinning.

'I resent being treated like a corpse,' he said. 'It's insulting. Is there anything to eat?'

• • •

I once knew a man who, at each meeting with a friend, said, 'Well, well—it's a small world after all!' He must be very unhappy now, because, when I last saw him, friends were slipping from his orbit like bees from a jaded flower and his world was becoming lonely and large. But there was truth in his dreary platitude. I have the story of Bishon Singh to prove it and Woody to witness it.

Bishon Singh arrived in a little billow of dust when there was nothing left of the sun but its forehead, and Woody and I had made insincere adieus to the Klemm and were preparing to take off for Nairobi and a doctor—and a new magneto, if one could be had.

'There's a man on a horse,' said Woody.

But it wasn't a man on a horse.

I had helped Woody into the front cockpit of the Avian, and I stood alongside the craft ready to swing her propeller, when the little billow made its entrance into our quasi-heroic scene. Six wagging and tapered ears protruded from the crest of the billow, and they were the ears of three donkeys. Four faces appeared in four halos of prairie dust, and three of these were the faces of Kikuyu boys. The fourth was the face of Bishon Singh, dark, bearded, and sombre.

'You won't believe it,' I said to Woody, 'but that is an Indian I've known from childhood. He worked for years on my father's farm.'

'I'll believe anything you tell me,' said Woody, 'if only you get me out of here.'

'Beru! Beru!' said Bishon Singh, 'or do I dream?'

Bishon Singh is a Sikh and as such he wears his long black hair braided to his long black beard, and together they make a cowl, like a monk's.

His face is small and stern and it peers from the cowl with nimble black eyes. They can be kind, or angry, like other eyes, but I do not think they can be gay. I have never seen them gay.

'Beru!' he said again. 'I do not believe this. This is not Njoro. It is not the farm at Njoro, or the Rongai Valley. It is more than a hundred miles from there—but here you are, tall and grown up, and I am an old man on my way to my Duka with things to sell. But we meet. We meet with all these years behind us. I do not believe it! Walihie Mungu Yangu—I do not believe it. God has favoured me!'

'It's a small world,' groaned Woody from the plane.

'Na furie sana ku wanana na wewe,' I said to Bishon Singh in Swahili. 'I am very happy to see you again.'

He was dressed as I had always remembered him—thick army boots, blue puttees, khaki breeches, a ragged leather waistcoat, all of it surmounted by a great turban, wound, as I recalled it, from at least a thousand yards of the finest cotton cloth. As a child, that turban had always intrigued me; there was so much of it and so little of Bishon Singh.

We stood a few yards in front of his three nodding donkeys, each with a silent Kikuyu boy in attendance, and each with an immense load on its back—pots, tin pans, bales of cheap Bombay prints, copper wire to make Masai earrings and bracelets. There was even tobacco, and oil for the Murani to use in the braiding of their hair.

There were things made of leather, things of paper, things of celluloid and rubber, all bulging, dangling, and bursting from the great pendulous packs. Here was Commerce, four-footed and halting, slow and patient, unhurried, but sure as tomorrow, beating its way to a counter in the African hinterland.

Bishon Singh raised an arm and included both the Klemm and the Avian in its sweep,

'N'dege!' he said—'the white man's bird! You do not ride on them, Beru?'

'I fly one of them, Bishon Singh.'

I said it sadly, because the old man had pointed with his left arm and I saw that his right was withered and crippled and useless. It had not been like that when I had seen him last.

'So,' he scolded, 'now it has come to this. To walk is not enough. To ride on a horse is not enough. Now people must go from place to place through the air, like a *diki toora*. Nothing but trouble will come of it, Beru. God spits upon such blasphemy.'

'God has spat,' sighed Woody.

'My friend was stranded here,' I said to Bishon Singh, 'his n'dege—
the one that shines like a new rupee—is broken. We are going back to
Nairobi.'

'Walihie! Walihie! It is over a hundred miles, Beru, and the night is
near. I will unpack my donkeys and brew hot tea. It is a long way to
Nairobi—even for you who go with the wind.'

'We will be there in less than an hour, Bishon Singh. It would take
you as long to build a fire and make the tea.'

I put my hand out and the old Sikh grasped it and held it for a
moment very tightly, just as he had often held it some ten years ago
when he was still taller than I—even without his fantastic turban. Only
then he had used his right hand. He looked down at it now with a
smile on his thin lips.

'What was it?' I asked.

'Simba, Beru—lion.' He shrugged. 'One day on the way to Ikoma . . .
it makes us like brothers, you and me. Each has been torn by a lion. You
remember that time at Kabete when you were a little child?'

'I'll never forget it.'

'Nor I,' said Bishon Singh.

I turned and went forward to the propeller of the Avian and grasped
the highest blade with my right hand and nodded to Woody. He sat in
the front cockpit ready to switch on.

Bishon Singh moved backward a few steps, close to his Tom Thumb
cavalcade. The three donkeys left off their meagre feeding, raised their
heads and tilted their ears. The Kikuyu boys stood behind the donkeys
and waited. In the dead light the Klemm had lost her brilliance and
was only the sad and discredited figure of an aerial Jezebel.

'God will keep you,' said Bishon Singh.

'Good-bye and good fortune!' I called.

'Contact!' roared Woody and I swung the prop.

He lay, at last, on a bed in the small neat shack of the East African Aero
Club waiting for food, for a drink—and, I suspect, for sympathy.

'The Klemm is a bitch,' he said. 'No man in his right mind should ever fly a Klemm aeroplane, with a Pobjoy motor, in Africa. You treat her kindly, you nurse her engine, you put silver dope on her wings, and what happens?'

'The magneto goes wrong,' I said.

'It's like a woman with nerves,' said Woody, 'or no conscience, or even an imbecile!'

'Oh, much worse.'

'Why do we fly?' said Woody. 'We could do other things. We could work in offices, or have farms, or get into the Civil Service. We could. . . .'

'We could give up flying tomorrow. You could, anyhow. You could walk away from your plane and never put your feet on a rudder bar again. You could forget about weather and night flights and forced landings, and passengers who get airsick, and spare parts that you can't find, and wonderful new ships that you can't buy. You could forget all that and go off somewhere away from Africa and never look at an aerodrome again. You might be a very happy man, so why don't you?'

'I couldn't bear it,' said Woody. 'It would all be so dull.'

'It can be dull anyway.'

'Even with lions tearing you to bits at Kabete?'

'Oh, that was back in my childhood. Some day I'll write a book and you can read about it.'

'God forbid!' said Woody.

from The Last Blue Mountain
by Ralph Barker

Just as four climbers completed their frustrating reconnaissance of Haramosh I in the Himalayas, two of them—Bernard Jillott and John Emery—climbed a few steps higher for some last photographs. An avalanche swept them off the ridge, leaving Tony Streather and Rae Culbert to attempt a rescue. When Culbert lost a crampon on the climb down, the situation turned from bad to critical, as described in this moving account by Ralph Barker (born 1917).

J illott and Emery watched anxiously as Streather and Culbert began on the traverse. With any luck the others would join them in another two or three hours; and they began moving across to a position just below the crevasse, opposite the point where the ice-cliffs gave out. But as they watched, it became apparent that the surface on which the others were moving had changed.

Streather and Culbert seemed to have come almost completely to a stop. They didn't seem to be making any progress at all. Jillott and Emery watched them cutting a way along the top of the ice-cliffs, moving painfully slowly. The surface must be hard ice, desperately hard ice. They ran their eyes along the top of the cliffs to the point where the cliffs gave out and the slope plunged on down to the bergschrund. At their present rate they would be many, many hours on the traverse, probably all day.

Jillott and Emery completed their move across to the point at which the cliffs petered out and stood just short of the lower lip of the bergschrund. Ahead of them the slope still looked terribly steep. Even when Streather and Culbert had finished the traverse they had a very nasty climb of about three hundred feet down to the snow-basin to meet them.

Fortunately, providentially, the weather was holding good. There would be no chance for any of them if the weather changed now.

It was warm in the sun and Jillott and Emery felt their bodies slowly thawing out from the night in the basin. They felt drowsy and languid. There was nothing they could do but sit there and watch the others moving step by step across the slope towards them. It was horribly frustrating. They were still suffering from the effects of the fall, and the lack of food and drink was beginning to tell. They sat in a half stupor, unable to think much for themselves, conscious of their complete dependence on those two slowly moving figures silhouetted against the white slope. They were conscious, too, of the colossal feat of endurance that was being enacted up there: Streather and Culbert must have been climbing almost continuously since eleven o'clock yesterday.

Throughout the day Streather and Culbert took it in turns to lead. The ice was as hard as concrete; chipping at it hardly did more than splinter the surface—they had to hack at it with all their strength. Cutting steps across a steep ice-slope was one of the most awkward of all climbing movements. You could bring your outside leg forward fairly readily, although it was very difficult to keep in a straight line. But bringing your inside leg through, the leg against the slope, balancing your weight on it tentatively, and planting it firmly in front of you in a step you'd cut with great difficulty, was an almost unbearable strain on the muscles, besides being extremely precarious. Exhausted as they were from the night's climb, this traverse seemed brutally long. The whole body from the waist down, and indeed even the shoulders and neck, had to be held in a twisted and deformed position for hour after hour, when the instinct of every muscle was to relax and give in.

It was late afternoon before they realised that they were nearing the end of the traverse. They could see the others quite clearly now, huddled together beyond the bergschrun. Streather and Culbert hailed them again and again, and they answered, but neither could make out what the others were saying.

"Start climbing up the slope," called Streather. "Start climbing." And then when his words seemed to have no effect: "Start climbing, however difficult it is. It's a matter of life and death."

"We can't cross the crevasse," Jillott and Emery shouted. "We've lost our ice-axes." But Streather and Culbert couldn't hear.

They had almost reached the end of the ice-cliff now, and the slope was beginning to fall away down to the bergschrund. On the traverse the slope had eased to fifty-five degrees; but here it steepened to sixty as it plunged down the last three hundred feet to the basin. For a moment, as the ice-cliff petered out, it seemed to be even steeper, so that they had to carry on with the traverse, finding it impossible to start cutting their way down and losing height.

Reaching down with their ice-axes to cut steps down this last slope would be the hardest thing of all. It was almost impossible to cut steps going down as steeply as this. You simply couldn't get any weight into your ice-axe ahead of you down the slope without losing your balance.

Just before they left the traverse, Streather noticed a dark object in one of the steps that Culbert had just cut. It looked like a crampon—he was sure it was a crampon. He called to Culbert. "Rae! Hold on. You've left a crampon in that last step." Culbert, balancing on his right foot, bringing his left leg through against the slope and planting it in front of him, realised as he put it in the new step that something was wrong. He stopped, turned, and began the awkward business of moving a step back along the traverse to retrieve the crampon. As he moved, the climbing-rope, dangling in the snow, caught the crampon and lifted it out of the step, sending it hurtling down the steepest part of the slope into the bergschrund. For a brief moment the two men, now facing one another, caught each other's eye. Both realised how serious the loss of a crampon at this stage might be.

Culbert tried to go on, but he had to let Streather take over, and he had to take his left canvas overboot off in order to gain any foothold at all with his climbing-boot. Eventually they reached a point directly above where Jillott and Emery were sitting. Now they had to get safely down the steep slope to the bergschrund. Obviously it was going to be very nasty indeed. There was about a foot of snow covering the ice on the slope, much of the snow was rotten, and it was extremely difficult to get any sort of grip. Even so, the covering of snow meant that they were able to kick steps, which they had been unable to do on the traverse.

It was now late afternoon, the sun had gone down, and the cold of the evening was upon them. But the effect of this was to harden and bind the rotten snow on the slope and make the kicking of steps easier. Between them they kicked and cut a level platform in the slope where they finished the traverse, and Culbert stood on this platform and belayed Streather down. The method of descent was exactly the same as it had been on the upper slope—Streather went down backwards, kicking the steps beneath him, getting his foot firmly embedded in one step and then reaching down still further to kick a step with the other, his hands gripping the steps he had recently made. He felt like a spider crawling backwards down a wall, a thin strand of web stretched out above him in case he should fall.

When he reached the end of the climbing rope, Culbert came down in his steps and then passed him and began kicking and crawling down in the same way. Then, when the rope was exhausted again, Streather took over. It was extremely awkward to pass each other on the slope, but they managed it with care. At last they reached the bottom of the slope above the bergschrund. Here Streather advanced to the upper lip of the great crevasse and lowered a rope to Jillott and Emery. They tied on and crossed the crevasse one by one.

The reunion, a moment of great warmth, was strangely inarticulate. The gratitude felt by Jillott and Emery, was mostly unspoken. What did one say to men who had climbed without pause day and night under the most treacherous and exhausting conditions, climbing all the time towards danger rather than away from it? There were words enough in the English language to fit such an occasion, but it wasn't like the English to use them. The most that Jillott and Emery could manage was a muttered "Thanks, Tony," and "Thanks, Rae." Even that, charged with gratitude as it was, seemed almost too much.

Streather and Culbert, immensely relieved to find Jillott and Emery not seriously hurt and in good heart, gave them the two flasks of soup and some glucose tablets. Unfortunately one of the flasks had broken on the climb down the slope, and they were forced to pour the precious liquid, now thickened and rattling with silver glass, away. To Jillott and Emery the soup in the other flask seemed no more than a mouthful.

Although the light was already failing, none of them had any doubt that the right thing to do was to begin the climb out that night. They had no more food or liquid, the best way to keep warm was to keep moving, and they would gain absolutely nothing by spending the night in the basin and waiting for morning. Each man had already drawn heavily on his reserves of strength, but he was hardly likely to build them up again by snatching what rest he could in the open at this height.

As Jillott and Emery were without ice-axes, Streather joined the two ropes together so that in effect they were all climbing on one rope. He was confident that now the steps were made they would all succeed in getting out of the basin, and he felt that being roped together would add to their sense of assurance and comradeship. It would take them some hours to get to the top, but it wouldn't be anything like the tedious and precarious business it had been coming down.

Culbert led the way up the lower slope, followed by Streather, then Jillott and Emery. They seemed to be making height quickly, and it wasn't long before they were looking down some two hundred feet beneath them to the bergschrund. Another hundred feet and they would reach the platform at the beginning of the traverse. At this point there was a grunt from above and Culbert, who had been having considerable difficulty on only one crampon, slipped and fell down the slope on to Streather, knocking Streather off as well. The weight of these two falling together dislodged Jillott and Emery like ninepins, and all four climbers fell in a tangled mass down the slope and across the bergschrund back into the snow-basin.

Streather called the names of the climbers and they all answered cheerfully. Fortunately they had fallen in soft snow, and somehow they had managed to avoid spiking each other with their crampons. Streather had lost his ice-axe, but Culbert had retained his.

It was now nearly dark, but they knew there would be a moon later, and they decided to try again, this time with Streather leading, using Culbert's ice-axe, followed by Emery, who had found reserves of energy from somewhere and was now climbing confidently, then Culbert, with Jillott last. This time they made slow progress; but in spite of the darkness Streather could see above them the platform that he and Culbert had stamped out earlier in the day. That was the first landmark, the end of the first lap, and he kept going steadily to reach it. Their method of progression now was for Streather to climb fifty feet or so, take a belay, and then help the others up one at a time until they were all standing in the steps immediately below him. This was reasonably foolproof provided no one fell off while Streather was moving; and there was no reason why anyone should do this unless he collapsed or fell asleep. They made steady progress, and they had nearly reached the platform when Streather, moving up alone, felt a sustained heavy pull on the rope. The shaft of his ice-axe was dug into the slope just above him to assist his climb, and he tried to hold the weight on this. Suddenly the tug was too much, he lost his foothold, and found himself swinging in midair. Now he felt himself falling again; and all four men, hopelessly entangled, dropped the two hundred and fifty feet down to the far side of the bergschrund again and into the snow-basin. Jillott, utterly exhausted, had gone to sleep in his tracks and dragged them all off one by one.

Getting out of the snow-basin in their present state was obviously going to be a very much more difficult proposition than any of them had imagined. They were all tired and dispirited, they had lost the last ice-axe, and no one felt like attempting that slope again before daylight. Perhaps after all it might be best to try to get a few hours' sleep. If they huddled together in a crevasse, they would at least be protected from the biting wind.

They moved up to the bergschrund and found a point where there was a ledge in the crevasse and where both the crevasse edges had an overhang that would prevent snow falling in on them. They climbed down about ten feet into the crevasse and on to the ledge. At this depth they found the crevasse was almost full of frozen snow and ice, with only one small gap leading down into the crevasse proper. They were able to jam themselves between the crevasse walls, shoulders against the lower lip and feet against the upper, so that there was no danger of falling through the gap.

They huddled together in an attempt to keep warm. Culbert particularly was troubled by his left foot, which had not had sufficient protection against the intense cold since he was forced to remove the canvas overboot and had become frostbitten. At Streather's suggestion, Culbert took off his climbing-boot as well and pushed his foot under Streather's shirt against his stomach, where Streather nursed it. If they could get the foot warm, there was a good chance that the circulation would return. Streather and the American Pete Shoening had saved their feet in this way on K2.

Streather and Culbert, being without their eiderdown jackets, lay in the middle, with Jillott and Emery on the outside. Somehow they all managed to snatch a little sleep. But during the night they were awakened by several shouts from Jillott. "Will you go and get my tent for me?" he was saying. "Come on, chaps, stop fooling about." His voice sounded perfectly natural, but there was a note of strain in it, and now and again he would groan as though in pain. Streather roused Emery. "I brought some morphia and a syringe down with me, in case either of you were injured," he said. "It sounds as though Bernard may be in pain. Can you give him an injection?"

Emery took the phial of morphia and tried to cut the top off so as to draw up the fluid into the syringe, but his fingers were so numb that he could feel nothing. He had lost his gloves in the first fall; Streather and Culbert had brought some spare socks down with them and he had put a pair of these on his hands, but he had lost these as well in one of the later falls. His hands were in bad shape, probably frostbitten. He had to give the phial back to Streather, who was able to knock the top off and fill the syringe. Emery climbed over the others to Jillott, tugged at his clothes until he had freed a small patch of his buttock, and gave him a jab. Jillott, wondering what was going on, protested all the time. "It'll be all right, Bernard," coaxed Emery. "Just lie still." Almost immediately after the injection, Jillott quietened and fell into a deep sleep.

It was very cramped on the ledge, and comfort for one almost inevitably meant discomfort for another. They seemed to be stiff and sore all over. Sometimes gusts of powdery snow blew in on to them, but although the cold was intense they were protected from the wind. Somehow the night passed.

As soon as it started to get light, Streather began to climb up out of the crevasse. "I'm going down the slope to disentangle the rope and see if I can find either of the ice-axes," he told the others. "Will you help Rae on with his boot, John? We'd better get started as soon as we can."

Streather soon found the rope, which was very badly tangled from the second fall of the previous night; but he could see no sign of either of the missing ice-axes. He looked up at the lower slope straight above him and then along the top of the ice-cliff, as he worked on disentangling the rope. Being without an ice-axe would add to their difficulties, but along the dangerous traverse the steps were already cut. He still had good hopes that they would all get out of the basin, but the two abortive attempts of last night were a warning of how difficult it was going to be. The night's rest very probably hadn't done them any real good, but it would have been bad psychology to keep on struggling hopelessly in the darkness. Now they knew what they were up against, and there would be a determination to succeed first time today.

He still felt fairly strong himself, but he knew that the others had been less fortunate. Culbert's loss of a crampon had been cruel luck; it had not only reduced his climbing efficiency but had resulted in frostbite in the affected foot. Jillott was very probably suffering from concussion, and was obviously in an exhausted state. Emery had been climbing strongly last night, but his hands were frostbitten. Their minds and bodies would hardly withstand another day's frustration on the slope and another night out in the basin.

Streather looked up at the slope again grimly. They had a fateful day's climbing ahead of them. At the top of the slope, a thousand feet up, lay safety; but there was little hope for anyone who didn't get out of the basin today.

He knew it would be up to him to get them out, and the responsibility drained him of concern about himself. Nevertheless the thought of Sue, and of his young son Charles, now six months old, was always in his mind, sustaining him. Somehow he must keep going.

The sun was now up and the air was slightly warmer. The weather was still clear. In the crevasse, Emery was struggling with Culbert's boot. Culbert had three pairs of socks on, and his foot had swollen from frostbite. Emery kept trying to force the boot on, but it wouldn't go. He realised how painful it must be. Culbert, as ever, made not the slightest complaint. In the end Culbert had to take off two pairs of socks to get the boot on. Emery then climbed up to the lip of the crevasse and called down to Streather that the boot was on. Streather came across and joined them. They now began a search for the lost ice-axes and gloves. They found nothing.

Jillott thought he could see an axe sticking out at the bottom of the ice-cliff some four hundred yards to the left, one of the two that he and Emery had lost two days earlier. He decided to try to get it. He thought, too, that he might find an easier way back on to the ridge that way. Culbert, hampered by having only one crampon, decided to try this route as well. Streather and Emery, convinced that the only likely route lay to the right, moved off in that direction.

"We'll start remaking the steps up here," said Streather. "Then we shan't be wasting time. If you find anything, give us a shout." He and Emery crossed the bergschrund, which had been partly filled at this point with snow brought down by their falls the previous night, and began on the slope.

Jillott and Culbert traversed across the basin for some distance before crossing the bergschrund just below the point where they thought they could see the ice-axe. As they came up under the ice-cliff, Jillott was sure that he was right. Regaining his ice-axe would be a great start to the day. He stooped to pick it up, only to find that it was nothing more than a broken, useless shaft sticking out of the snow.

They had come some distance to the left and there was still no sign of a break in the ice-cliff. With an ice-axe they might have explored a little further, but now it was pointless. They decided to retrace their steps and catch up with the others.

Streather and Emery seemed to be gaining height very slowly indeed. All the steps they had kicked so laboriously in this slope had been broken or wiped away in last night's falls. Now, with no ice-axe, Streather began punching the hard snow with his clenched fists until he had enough depth for a purchase, pulling himself up, punching more cup-shaped holes, and then kicking the lower holes out into proper steps. At first he winced from the pain in his hands as he beat out the steps, but soon his knuckles went numb and he felt nothing. Emery behind him did the same, improving the steps all the way.

They looked down from time to time and watched Jillott and Culbert, first going away from them, then retracing their steps. Soon they were at the bottom of the slope. Streather and Emery had been climbing now for some hours, and they had thought they were doing well, but Jillott and Culbert seemed to catch them up very quickly. It was a measure of the very slow progress they had been making.

Emery took over the lead, followed closely by the others. Now that they were all without ice-axes, Streather decided not to use the climbing-rope. If one man fell, he only pulled all the others off; and while they must do all they could to stick together, they had to conserve what was left of their strength. The two falls last night had been terribly demoralising. Also it might not be psychologically bad for each man to know to what degree his survival depended on himself. They had to get out of the basin today. If one of them fell back into it, the others must go on, back to Camp IV for food and drink and rest, before coming back on another rescue attempt. Otherwise it would be certain death from exhaustion and exposure for all of them.

By now, any decisions and resolutions that Streather made were not arrived at by any process of conscious thought or reasoning. They had all lost the power of reasoning, and their actions were instinctive. The loss in terms of balanced judgment was less in Streather than it might be in some men. In these circumstances a formally trained mind might be a burden. The man who was accustomed to making his decisions and judgments untrammelled by lengthy thought processes and free of fixed principles or bias was at an immense advantage.

After they had climbed some three hundred feet and were about a hundred feet below the platform at the beginning of the traverse, Emery suddenly saw an ice-axe sticking out of the slope directly above his head. It was Culbert's, the axe Streather had been using in the second attempt to climb out last night. Emery shouted back to Streather, and Streather came through, lifted the axe out of the slope, and began cutting steps up the last hundred feet to the platform. "You hang on here," he told the others. "This last bit is the worst part. When I get to the platform, I'll drop the rope to you and bring you up one by one."

Finding Culbert's axe had been the most wonderful stroke of luck. The second of last night's falls had been in complete darkness, and in the confusion he had had no idea what had happened to the axe and had assumed it had been lost in the fall. He had been feeling very apprehensive about how they would manage on the traverse. Finding the axe would make all the difference.

The last hundred feet of the slope, too, was very rotten. It was much steeper here than lower down, the surface snow tended to flake or break away, and the hard ice was not far below. Now that he had the axe he could make much better steps and there was less danger of anyone slipping off. He reached the platform safely, helped Emery up on the rope, and then untied and started off on the traverse, leaving Emery to drop the rope for Jillott and Culbert in turn. The traverse would be the hardest part of all and there was no time to waste: this he knew although he had lost all real sense of time. Morning, afternoon and evening were all one, indistinguishable, like colours that had run. Somewhere ahead of them lay the night; and the darkness might be complete.

It was a world of extremes: there was no light or shade. It was snowing or it was fine. It was day or it was night, it was black or it was white. They were moving forwards or backwards, there was no standing still. There was danger and there was safety. There was life and there was death, and there was nothing in between.

Emery couldn't take a belay on the platform as he had no ice-axe, but he lowered the rope and took as firm a stance as he could. Then he hauled gently on the rope while Jillott and Culbert climbed up the last hundred feet. If either of them had come off the slope he couldn't have held them, but he could have checked a slip. In fact, both men were able with the steadying aid of the rope to reach the platform safely.

They unroped and followed Streather along the traverse. Snow had blown down the slope into the steps of the traverse during the night, and Streather was having difficulty in finding the steps and cleaning them out. The steps were slightly rising at first, where they had tried to lose height as they neared the end of the ice-cliff on the way down, and suddenly Streather realised that he had come too high and that he was off the traverse altogether. Looking down the slope, he thought he could see the faint line of the old steps some twenty feet below. Cutting new steps at this higher level would take them two or three times as long, and if they were going to make any sort of progress they must regain the old line.

Streather went down the slope first, cutting and kicking the steps until he reached the original line. Back on the traverse, he didn't stop to wait for the others, but kept on cutting and cleaning out the steps. Coming down the slope was every bit as difficult for those behind, since although the steps were made, the snow was rotten and the slope was steep. Suddenly Emery, following down immediately after Streather, felt his feet slipping. He knew that to come off the traverse meant to drop over the ice-cliffs again and down into the basin. He was unroped and he had no axe. He twisted his body frantically to face the slope, kept his legs rigid, and dug his crampons hard into the snow. His action served as a brake, the slide was arrested, and he went on gingerly down to the traverse. As each man came down, the steps got better, and at last they were all following Streather on the original line.

When Streather had first come down the upper slope two nights ago, he had come almost to the edge of the ice-cliff before realising that he had this sheer drop directly underneath him. To the left the top of the ice-cliff had risen slightly where the cliff reached its highest point above the bergschrund before falling away steadily towards the lower slope. Thus he had had to climb up slightly at the beginning of the traverse to keep above the ice-cliff. Coming in this direction, the last piece of the traverse went down.

It was very awkward indeed. The steps were packed with ice, and having been cut the other way there was nothing for the toe to slide into. Each man had to make a sort of twist from the knee downwards to get a foothold. Meanwhile there was nothing they could do with their hands except use them to aid balance. The whole weight of the body was virtually being held by the crampons.

Streather was still leading, with Emery behind him, then Culbert, then Jillott. Streather and Emery started down this last piece of traverse, moving with extreme care. Once they reached the final slope and this nightmare traverse was behind them, the worst was over. But Streather hadn't gone more than twenty feet when Jillott shouted from the rear.

"Rae's in trouble."

The difficulties under which all the climbers had been labouring had been magnified several times for Culbert throughout the day, being as he was minus a crampon and with his left foot badly frostbitten. Not once during that time had he made the smallest complaint or ever asked for help. But at this crucial point, as the traverse led obliquely down to the start of the upper slope, he stopped, unable to go further. The absolute dependence of each climber on his crampons over this last hundred feet or so of the traverse meant that Culbert, as he put his left leg forward and tried desperately hard to dig in with his right, knew for certain that he would come off.

"Do you think you could give me a belay over this bit?" he called to Streather.

"Stay where you are," answered Streather. "I'll give you a belay from the end of the traverse." Emery was carrying one rope, Streather himself had the other. He tied the two ropes together to make sure of having enough, and gave one end to Culbert. Then he and Emery continued on the traverse. Eventually they reached the point directly above the ice-cliff where Streather had stopped on the way down two nights ago. Above them the slope was steep, but the surface was infinitely better, there was no ice and the snow was packing beautifully. They would be able to climb up hand over hand, just as Streather and Culbert had climbed down.

Streather climbed a few feet up the slope to be sure of being on safe ground. Even now he remembered that progress of some kind was essential to their chances. "You go on up the slope," he told Emery. "We'll follow as soon as we've got Rae across the traverse."

Emery moved off up the slope and Streather turned to the business of the belay. The two hundred feet of rope had been only just enough. Even with the rope, that downhill traverse would mean an agonising few minutes for Culbert, and indeed for all of them. The rope would help to steady Culbert, give him something to hang on to, but only a remarkably good belay would hold if he came off.

As soon as Streather had his axe firmly embedded he shouted to Culbert to begin. Culbert managed the first step or two, but only as a man falling downstairs will feel the first few steps pass under him. Almost immediately he came off.

He swung through space in a wide pendulum, down the slope and over the edge of the ice-cliff, until he was directly below Streather. At this point his weight came on the rope. The jerk was terrific. Streather had seen and heard nothing, but he could feel himself losing his balance and slipping. Soon he was falling as in a dream, silently, a fall without an end, seemingly into nothingness. Then the illusion was shattered as a white blanket suddenly reached up and grabbed him roughly, rolling him on down the slope and finally bringing him to rest. He knew that Culbert was somewhere near him, but how he knew this was not clear.

Streather and Culbert had fallen the lower half of the avalanche fall suffered by Jillott and Emery, but the shock had been much greater because they hadn't had the great weight of snow falling with and around them that had helped to cushion Jillott and Emery. Both men were now back in the snow-basin, utterly exhausted and badly concussed.

Jillott, standing behind Culbert on the traverse, had watched it all happen. Now he began on the last few steps of the fatal traverse. When at last he reached the bottom of the upper slope, he peered down over the ice-cliffs towards the point where he knew Streather and Culbert must be. He was surprised to find he was peering into darkness. Another day had gone.

He began to shout down into the basin, down into the blackness. "We'll go on back to camp and get some food. We'll come back and help you as soon as we can."

Streather still dazed by the fall, heard a voice from the far end of a long tunnel, a voice yet so clear that he could feel the sibilance of it in his ear. He heard it subconsciously, and it registered subconsciously. It was like being sound asleep and yet hearing a voice in the room.

Streather, clung to the words and let them revolve in his mind until consciousness returned. After the shock of the fall the darkness seemed inevitable. He realised that they were just below the bergschrund. He dragged himself up the slope, and Culbert followed. They found a point where the crevasse was filled with snow, toppled themselves over the lip and into the crevasse for shelter, and huddled together.

"Are you all right?"

"Yes. And you?"

"I'm all right."

They had no strength to say more. They were past the stage of caring for their hands or their feet, and they sank at once into a merciful but uneasy sleep. They would wake for the morrow, but this would be their last night.

After Jillott had shouted down into the basin to Streather and Culbert, he began to follow Emery up the slope. Emery meanwhile was making good progress. As often seemed to happen to them during these days, he suddenly found a new lease of energy. It was partly because the snow surface on the upper slope was so much better, and partly the psychological effect of doing something constructive again. He was going well.

He was climbing up the slope in much the same way as Streather had climbed down. The steps Streather had made had mostly disappeared and he was forced to make new steps. He pulled himself up with a crawling movement and kicked the steps out with his feet as he went. The darkness didn't trouble him. On some places the snow was too brittle and it crumbled when he tried to fashion steps, but when he reached these points he moved out to the right or left and clawed and kicked new steps where the snow was firm. His progress was slow but fairly direct and he was gaining height steadily.

He had been climbing for quite a long time and had reached a point about a hundred feet above the ice-cliffs when he heard a shout from below. He waited for a few minutes, expecting to see Streather, and then to his surprise he was joined by Jillott, who told him what had happened.

The irony of this reversal of their situations, rescuers in the basin and rescued on the upper slope, was so unbearable that they couldn't discuss it. They continued silently up the sloping wall of snow that towered above them, deeply aware of the dependence of the two men in the basin on their efforts in the next few hours.

They climbed purposefully and well, concentrating only on the task in hand, until, as they neared the top of the slope, they remembered that there was one point of paramount importance—they must hit the ridge at the point where they had originally come through the cornice, otherwise they might stumble straight through the cornice in the darkness. This meant aiming for a point a little to the left of the Cardinal's hat below which they had been avalanched. It was now intensely dark and they weren't quite sure what line they were on.

"I think we ought to go slightly to the left or maintain our present line," said Emery. Jillott disagreed—he thought they had come too far to the left and ought to veer slightly right. "All right," said Emery, "we'll try your line." He was leading, and he began to swing a little to the right. In fact Jillott proved to be wrong and they came out exactly at the point of the avalanche.

Hitting the ridge at this point had one advantage in that at least they knew which way to turn. They couldn't be more than fifty or sixty feet from the break in the cornice, but in the intense darkness they could see nothing. Emery led off along the ridge. He had taken no more than three or four paces when he went straight through the cornice.

As he fell his mind rotated like a roulette wheel, feverishly trying to alight on the answer to the question—what had been on the other side of the cornice? What was he going to hit or fall into? It was infinitely worse than his fall into the crevasse that day below Camp IV, because every nerve in his body had been tensed for it then, he had been roped, and he had still had his ice-axe. It almost seemed worse than the fall in the avalanche. He might be falling to his death; and even that he felt he could bear if only he knew about it.

In fact he fell no more than thirty feet, and the shock of hitting the ground so soon caught him unprepared. He landed awkwardly, and found that he couldn't get up.

He called up to Jillott. "I'm O.K., but I think my hip's gone again." As before, it was extremely painful and he couldn't move for a minute or two, and again he happened to turn the right way and it jumped back into its socket.

"Keep going along the ridge," he called up to Jillott. "I'll meet you at the cut in the cornice." Emery climbed unsteadily through the gap, Jillott made his way gingerly along the ridge, and soon both men stood at the point where, two and a half days earlier, they had gazed for the first time on the elusive secrets of Haramosh.

Somewhere here, they knew, Streather and Culbert had left their rucksacks. They began to kick about in the snow, until at length they found them. In one of the rucksacks they knew there was a water-bottle. After all this time the water in it would be frozen solid. They knew this beyond doubt. And yet both men went straight for the water-bottle, hoping unreasonably that somehow the water might still be liquid. One wasn't satisfied with the evidence of the other. Both men tore frantically at the water-bottle just in case.

They began to search feverishly for food. In one of the rucksacks was a packet of glucose tablets. It was dark and their fingers were numb. In their haste and confusion they searched one rucksack several times but hardly disturbed the other. They were incapable of tackling the task sys-tematically and they both searched the same rucksack. They didn't find the glucose tablets.

Jillott picked up the rucksack they had searched so vainly and shouldered it. It wasn't worth burdening themselves with both ruck-sacks, but they would need one to carry food and drink back to Streather and Culbert, and there might not be one at Camp IV. There was also a rope with the rucksacks, and they took this, though they decided not to rope up. Having no ice-axes, if one of them fell he would simply pull the other with him and they would both be in trou-ble. They felt no compunction about being unroped. Going down unroped was something they had done many times when climbing together and they were perfectly used to it.

They climbed down through the cut in the cornice, felt their way down the slope, and jumped across the crevasse. At this point Emery's dysentery troubled him again and he had to stop. Then they began to look for the route on. To begin with they knew they had to go along the lower lip of the crevasse before branching off to the left. It was very difficult indeed, they could see absolutely nothing, and they felt their way along apprehensively for several minutes. Then Emery stopped.

"I think we ought to sit down here till the moon comes up," he sug-gested. "It can't be long before it does—two hours at the most." They'd sat through two nights now, they could easily manage another two hours. "When the moon comes up we shall be able to see fairly well."

"I think we ought to go on," said Jillott. He couldn't bear to waste time here when they might be making progress towards Camp IV, and he was obsessed with the urgent need to strengthen themselves with food and drink and get back as quickly as possible to Streather and Culbert. "I'm certain we ought not to wait. We've got to go on."

Emery was extremely weak physically now; and he found that in this state, at this height, faced by a man who seemed absolutely certain of what they ought to do, he couldn't hold out for long. Obviously they had to keep together at all costs. He gave in, and they started off.

Jillott could move very quickly downhill, and he soon went ahead. It was characteristic of Jillott to forge ahead; and Emery, less obsessed with the extreme urgency of getting back to Camp IV, and therefore more conscious of the difficulties of the route and the importance of sticking to it, went more slowly. Jillott was moving over ground that he had seen for the first time only thirty-six hours earlier, and he was finding the way extremely skilfully. It seemed to Emery that things were going well after all. They were on the proper route, and at this rate they would reach Camp IV in little more than an hour. And from Jillott's viewpoint there was no reason why he should worry because Emery was a bit behind. Emery knew the route far better than he did.

Soon they reached the point where the route made a wide detour to the right to avoid the patch of crevassed ground. They could see nothing, but Emery sensed that this was where they were. Here Jillott ignored the detour and went straight on, making a bee-line for Camp IV. Emery shouted after him, but he had got too far behind to make himself heard. Again Emery felt that the best thing to do was to follow.

Soon after leaving the original route Emery found himself descending a very steep slope. He remembered that he had looked at this line with Culbert three days ago, and that at the bottom of this slope was a large crevasse, as one would expect at the change of levels. They had decided against it then and begun on the detour. Now he wondered how Jillott was faring and how he would negotiate the crevasse.

He could just see Jillott's tracks winding on ahead, but half-way down the slope he came to bare ice. Probably Jillott had kicked off the surface as he went down. Almost immediately Emery came off the slope and began falling, down towards the crevasse. Then came oblivion.

He couldn't remember how it had happened, but he was back at base camp now, dreaming, dreaming a nightmare in which he seemed to have fallen into a crevasse. He couldn't understand why he couldn't somehow break out of this dream. Often, in a nightmare, one was able to tear oneself out of it, like coming to the surface out of a deep dive; and he knew he ought to be able to do this now. Yet somehow he couldn't do it, he couldn't thrust the nightmare away from him, it went on and on and he was still in the crevasse. But all the time he had the comforting assurance that after all it was really only a dream, that he was back at base camp having a nightmare. It helped him to relax into oblivion again.

When he awoke again it seemed to be daylight. His mind was working very slowly now and it was an effort to think at all. He began to doubt whether in fact he was really at base camp, whether in fact he had been dreaming. Part of his mind guessed that it wasn't a dream, that the safety of base camp was still remote and unattainable. He was in a crevasse, stuck where the walls had begun to converge and were narrow enough for his body to have jammed between them. The crevasse seemed to go a long way down, and below him it opened out again. It was just narrow enough for him to stick there, one leg twisted out to one side, the other hanging limply down. He was caught and somehow pinned at the pelvis, and suddenly he was conscious of pain.

Gradually he managed to prop himself up and ease his position, and by jamming himself with his crampons against one wall and with his back against the other, he was able to sidle his way along the crevasse. Suddenly the walls seemed to widen, and he half-climbed and half-fell through an opening. He realised that due to a depression in the slope the crevasse must be opening out on to the mountain, at some point lower than the point where he'd fallen in. He could see the surface about twenty feet above him, and he could see that by climbing on what seemed to be frozen snow-debris sticking to the walls of the crevasse he could probably get out. Without an axe he couldn't test the snow to make sure it would hold him, but he trod gingerly on the patches that looked likely to hold and eventually he found his way to the surface. He crawled a little way from the crevasse, and fell asleep again.

When he awoke it seemed to be about mid-morning, possibly noon. The sun was very bright, sparkling on the snow, and the crystal glare struck painfully at his eyes. He squinted into the whiteness, and there about ten feet away were Jillott's tracks, showing up plainly in the snow. Somehow Jillott must have crossed the crevasse safely last night. He got into the tracks and followed them.

His progress now was slow and spasmodic. He would drag himself forward for twenty or thirty yards and then sink down into the snow to rest for a few minutes, and then begin again. Jillott seemed to have avoided the difficulties of the route with great skill. He came to two crevasses where Jillott had traversed along the upper lip in each case before finding a safe crossing; and the whole area was dangerously crevassed and broken. Jillott must have managed all this in the darkness last night.

The tracks came out about half-way up the last snow-slope above Camp IV, the slope they had originally crossed higher up, just below the lip of the crevasse. Looking up to his right he could see the old tracks, still faintly visible; but the tracks ahead of him suddenly stopped.

The snow was deeply disturbed just in front of him, and he could see that Jillott must have slipped and come off as soon as he began across the slope. He could see the broad furrow where Jillott had slithered down; and looking down the slope he could see Jillott's tracks start again at the bottom. Evidently Jillott hadn't hurt himself much in the fall.

Emery knew that he hadn't the strength to climb up to the old track, and he didn't want to follow Jillott down to the base of the slope. The snow across the middle of the slope looked firm, and at the far end of the slope it joined the old track down to Camp IV. He began to traverse across the slope, about half-way between the old track at the top and Jillott's at the bottom. Presently he saw that Jillott's track was climbing slightly to meet the old track at the edge of the ridge above Camp IV, just below the point for which he was aiming himself.

He completed the crossing of the slope, joined the old track, and started down the ridge. This was the ridge on which they had climbed that first day above Camp IV. To his right was the deep crevasse, opening out lower down into the Stak valley, and he kept well back from that side. To his left he could see Jillott's tracks coming up to meet him. Directly below him now he could see the snow-bridge across the crevasse and then the two tents of Camp IV.

He reached the point where Jillott's track joined the track he was on. Here he expected the old track to be very much fresher, as Jillott must have followed it down to Camp IV. But the track ahead was still old and only faintly visible.

Looking down at his feet he saw that Jillott's footmarks went straight across the old track, which he must somehow have missed in the darkness. The footmarks went on for five or six feet until they reached the edge of the ridge, and there they ended. At that point the ground fell away absolutely vertically.

There wasn't even a flurry of snow to indicate that Jillott had realised that he had crossed the old track and reached the point where the ridge fell away. He must have walked straight over.

Emery stood for a moment stupidly, unable to grasp or accept the irrefutable truth that stared back at him from the footprints. He looked in vain for some sign of footmarks leading away from the edge. There was a sheer drop the other side of three hundred feet into the crevasse. At the bottom one would hit ice or possibly rock. Even if the fall only knocked one unconscious, one would be shot out of the crevasse lower down and fall 6,000 feet into the Stak valley. It wasn't a vertical drop, but there was nothing to stop or break one's fall.

When the truth finally penetrated his bemused brain, Emery absorbed it completely, with its terrible implication. Jillott was dead.

Even so, he stepped forward to a point as near the edge as he dared and shouted Jillott's name several times. He did not expect an answer, and none came.

He turned away from the edge of the ridge and began following the old track down to Camp IV, snug in the hollow below. There was a finality about Jillott's end, like a fine road that suddenly disappears in a landslide, that blunted the imagination. That Jillott was dead he knew, but the tragedy of it was too big and terrible to comprehend. In the last few days he had faced death with Jillott, calmly and without regrets or recriminations; and then all four of them had faced death together. Then he and Jillott had escaped from the basin, and their own safety had seemed assured, at least until they went back for the others. Jillott's death now was shocking and unreal. The physical fact of it registered, but his fevered mind boggled at the anguish of it. Jillott, then, was the first to go. He wondered if any one of them would get off the mountain alive.

His first thought when he reached Camp IV was to get something to drink. In the past three days he had sometimes melted snow in his mouth, but one got surprisingly little that way. From handfuls of snow one got no more than a few drops of water. The taste was extremely unpleasant, and the loss of body heat was dangerous. So that for three days at high altitude, when the very act of breathing was desiccating the whole body, he had drunk virtually nothing. But everything at Camp IV would be frozen, and to light a primus would take a long time. He didn't have any matches, and any he could find in camp would certainly be damp. So he rummaged around in the snow outside the tents for the stores, and eventually found a tin of grape-fruit juice. It would be frozen, but it would melt down into fluid in his mouth.

He crawled into the yellow tent and found a small tin opener, and tried to open the tin. Apart from a short period when he had worn a pair of socks on his hands, they had been uncovered ever since the avalanche fall, and they were now completely numb. His fingers closed around the tin-opener, but he felt nothing. In order to get some sort of purchase he had to grip the tin with his free hand, using the sides of his fingers, which seemed to have retained a tiny sense of touch if not of feeling. He put his weight on the tin and began to press on the tin-opener, guiding it with his wrist. As he did so, he saw in a strangely detached way that strips of skin were peeling off his fingers, revealing a sort of red jelly underneath. He hardly realised that it was happening to his own fingers. It didn't hurt at all.

He scooped out about half the frozen juice with the tin-opener, and as it turned to liquid in his mouth and he drank it down he began to feel better. He decided to try to get a primus going. He struggled out to the dump again, found a primus, and crawled back into the tent with it. But when he got inside he collapsed and fell asleep instantly just as he was, still in his overboots and crampons, without even crawling into a sleeping-bag. He slept soundly for some hours.

When he awoke it was late afternoon, and his mind was fairly clear. He remembered that Jillott was dead. There was nothing he could do for him. He remembered that they had left Streather and Culbert in the basin. He didn't really know yet whether he would be able to go back to help them, but he still kept this in his mind as something he had to do, though in his heart he realised it was probably beyond him. He remembered how difficult it had been for Culbert with only one crampon, and he couldn't think how Culbert was going to get out of the basin. About Streather he had absolutely no doubt at all. Streather would get out. They would then go back for Culbert.

He started to work on the primus, but his fingers were numb and torn and the matches were damp. He couldn't seem to get the stove adequately primed. Finally after over an hour he got it going. He had used two boxes of matches in the process. He melted some snow in a dixie and made himself a drink. His mouth was almost unbearably painful, swollen from eating snow and cracked and bleeding where the skin had parted through swelling and desiccation. But again he felt much better for having taken liquid. He began to melt some more snow down with the idea of making soup.

It was almost dark now. He relaxed back on to the sleeping-bag. Suddenly he heard steps outside, followed by a shout. He turned to look out of the tent. He was quite certain it was Streather.

• • •

The next thing Streather was fully conscious of was that he was lying in the bergschrund with Culbert and that it was daylight. He crawled out of the crevasse and Culbert followed. Culbert was very groggy now and his left foot was almost completely useless. They moved across to the foot of the lower slope, but it was bitterly cold and blowing hard, they had been without their eiderdown jackets for two and a half days, and Streather decided that it would be folly to attempt to climb out of the basin before the sun was up. They got back into the crevasse at the point where they'd found shelter two nights before, and huddled together on the ledge, trying to sleep again.

Suddenly Streather, lingering between sleep and consciousness, thought he heard shouting. He told Culbert to stay where he was, and then climbed out of the crevasse again. He had no idea of time now, but everything seemed to have got lighter and whiter since he went back into the crevasse, and the wind had dropped. He thought perhaps he had dreamt that someone was shouting, and then looking along the far side of the crevasse to a point well beyond the lower slope he saw two dark specks which he took to be Jillott and Emery. He couldn't understand how or why they had got over there. They had evidently traversed much too far and gone right on beyond the point where the ice-cliffs petered out, until they had reached a further line of ice-cliffs. They seemed to be standing in a most dangerous place, right underneath these far ice-cliffs, directly in the path of an almost continual avalanche. He shouted up to them, but the distance was too great and they seemed to take no notice.

He started moving across the basin towards them, keeping below the bergschrund. It meant stumbling forward through fresh, knee-deep snow, and he kept on shouting at them as he went. Then a great piece of the overhanging ice-cliff broke off and obliterated them.

He shouted again in horror, and then, as the avalanching snow subsided, he saw that the two specks were still there, exactly as they had been before. It was simply two holes in the slope.

He passed his hand across his eyes despairingly in an attempt to clear his vision. He couldn't remember when he'd lost his snow-goggles, but the mistiness that kept rolling across his eyes and the smarting behind his eyeballs told him that he was suffering from snow blindness. He went back to the crevasse for Culbert. They had better start up the slope.

He tried to do some mental arithmetic, working out how long it must have taken Jillott and Emery to reach Camp IV and how long they would be in getting back. They must have reached Camp IV last night. Then they would cook some food and get some rest. They ought to be back at the point of the avalanche by about midday. He hoped to meet them somewhere on the traverse.

He had no ice-axe now, so there was no point in taking the rope. They left it in the basin. Then they half pushed and half pulled each other across the bergschrund, and started up the lower slope.

Evidently it had snowed in the night, because the old steps were covered in. Streather scooped out the fresh snow until he got down to the hard frozen snow underneath. The slope here was as steep as the steepest roof, and Streather made the steps as large as he could to help Culbert. As he scooped out the snow, revealing the hardened step, he saw that each cavity was stained with bright red. He remembered that he had punched these steps himself with his clenched fists. He looked at his knuckles, and saw that they were blistered and raw.

He still had a woollen glove on his left hand and a canvas overglove or mitt, but his right hand was bare. He tried to pull the sleeve of his pullover down over it, but his left hand was so stiff that the fingers slipped and the hand wouldn't crook. He lifted his wrist to his mouth and pulled the sleeve down with his teeth.

He knew it was about three hundred feet to the platform at the beginning of the traverse, and he knew they were moving very slowly. They might perhaps be half-way there. He hadn't heard anything of Culbert for a minute or so, and he looked round to make sure he was all right. Culbert had gone. Looking almost vertically down he saw that Culbert was in the basin again.

He shouted down to him. "Are you all right, Rae?"

"Yes, I'm all right. I'll try again."

He must have slipped and come off the slope again. He must be terribly weak, and these falls would exhaust him utterly. Yet there was nothing else they could do but keep trying. It was useless to rope up—that only meant that both of them were weakened when one of them fell. He had no axe, and he couldn't pull Culbert out on his own. He was far too weak himself to attempt it.

He saw Culbert start again at the bottom of the slope, and he went on going slowly upwards, cleaning out the steps. He had almost reached the platform and Culbert was catching up quite well, when he looked round again and saw that once more Culbert was at the bottom.

Culbert sat where he fell, looking up the slope at Streather, unable to drag himself to his feet. There was no point in his trying the slope again now. He was clearly all in.

Streather knew how desperately hard it must have been for Culbert ever since he lost the crampon. Bit by bit this tragic misfortune had sapped all his strength. He would never have given in while he could still put one foot before the other.

Streather stood precariously on the slope, motionless, looking over his shoulder at Culbert. The only hope for all of them lay in one or other of them continuing to make progress. He had recognised this ever since the avalanche. Today they had made hardly any progress at all. It must be after midday, they hadn't even reached the traverse yet, and there was still no sign of Jillott and Emery.

"What shall we do?" called Culbert.

"Hang on where you are for a bit," shouted Streather. "I'll go on making the steps. The others are sure to be down soon, and then we'll be able to help you." They would have rested and fed, they would have recovered from the avalanche fall. They would bring food and drink, and perhaps a spare crampon. They would be able to help Culbert climb out.

Streather turned again to the slope. Soon he reached the platform. He looked down again to where Culbert sat, already stirring himself for yet another attempt to climb out. Then he peered despairingly across the upper slope for some sign of the others.

It was no use waiting here for Culbert. He must try to make his way back to Camp IV on his own to see what was delaying Jillott and Emery.

He began along the traverse. Loose snow had blown down into the steps and they were almost completely covered in. He could just see a vague shadow where they were. He started to try to clear the steps, but he found he could not reach the nearest one without losing his balance. The canvas mitt on his left hand was frozen hard, and he took it off and used it as a scoop. This gave him another six or eight inches reach and just enabled him to keep his balance. He scraped the loose snow out of each step, and then put his foot into it. There was no chance to try the step first—he had to put his weight fully forward, holding on as best he could with his right hand against the slope. Every step was a gamble, waiting for the loose snow in the step to pack down under his weight and to know if he had planted his foot in the right place. If he missed a step he would go straight over the ice-cliff again into the basin. Another fall like that would finish him. He would never get out.

What could have happened to the others? They must surely be on their way down. He began to wonder whether perhaps something had gone seriously wrong. They would he certain to come back as soon as they'd rested and fed. Besides, he'd heard Jillott shout down to him when he'd fallen off the traverse into the basin with Culbert. Or had he dreamt it? The memory was clear, but now he was certain of nothing.

If they didn't get down to Culbert soon it would be too late. Neither he nor Culbert had had anything to eat or drink since leaving Camp IV to come down for the others three days ago. Since then they'd had three nights out on the mountain.

He reached the point where Culbert had fallen off the traverse. He kept on trying to scrape out the steps, but it was even more difficult here where the traverse went down. This was the stretch he had been dreading all along. Because of the downward slope he could only reach the beginning of each step with the mitt, and as he put each foot forward he was even less sure if he was stepping in the right place. There was a hundred feet of this downward traverse, and it seemed certain that somewhere in its length he would miss his footing and fall. But at last he got to the end. Then he began up the final slope.

When he reached the point where he had belayed Culbert down the traverse, he saw something sticking out of the slope. It was the ice-axe he had been using then, Culbert's axe, since his own had been lost. He was beyond feeling surprise, or pleasure, or even relief. Instinctively he recovered the axe, and subconsciously he felt renewed strength. Then, moving painfully slowly, he turned again to the slope.

There was nothing in his mind to keep him going, and very little in his body. He knew that somehow he had to get to Camp IV, and that there were powerful reasons why he must succeed, but he had almost forgotten what these were. Culbert was still in the basin, Jillott and Emery were missing, and he had to get back to Camp IV to organise help for Culbert. Otherwise his mind was as numb as his fingers.

He kept on climbing up the slope, hand over hand, never looking to see how near he was to the top, never even trying to guess; like a soul climbing Jacob's ladder. His hands were not capable of cleaning out the steps now, and he jerked his elbows into them, weakly, like a tired, all-in wrestler. At last he found that he had reached the start of the avalanche, and he traversed across to the point where Culbert had belayed him down. He had reached the top.

He saw the rucksack left behind by Jillott and Emery, and he made straight for it, fumbling inside it for the water-bottle, just as the others had done. Like them, he knew for certain that the water would be frozen, but as with them thirst was more powerful than reason. Yet when he saw that the water was frozen he felt a tiny glow of satisfaction which tempered the intensity of the disappointment. Reason had been right.

He found the two packets of glucose tablets, but because of his numbed fingers he couldn't open them. Before him was food and drink, yet he could get at neither. He lodged one of the glucose packets between his fists and brought his hands up towards his mouth. Then he began to chew the paper off. He couldn't grip the packet properly, and suddenly the paper tore in the wrong direction and the tablets scattered into the snow.

He knelt down and began scooping up the snow where the tablets had fallen, shaking it to sift as much snow through his hands as he could before thrusting it into his mouth. The pain of the cold snow on his cracked lips was severe, but he crunched the mixture in his mouth and gulped it down.

He found the break in the cornice, started down the slope on the other side, and then found the strength to hurl himself over the crevasse at the bottom, landing in a heap in the soft snow beyond. He dragged himself to his feet again, and began to follow the track. Soon it seemed to lead over an unfamiliar route, striking off to the left of the original track, which was still just visible. He couldn't understand why Jillott and Emery had taken a different route, but he took the line of least resistance and followed it. In any case it must lead him to them.

It was late evening now but the light was still quite good. He came to a particularly steep pitch, and suddenly the tracks stopped. He looked down the slope and saw the track again at the bottom. Evidently the others had fallen down this slope. He started to edge his way down, but almost at once he slipped and went on sliding down. As he neared the bottom he realised that he was heading straight for a narrow crevasse. This in fact was the crevasse into which Emery had fallen. He pushed hard against the slope as he shot down towards the crevasse and flung himself away from the slope at the last minute. He just cleared the crevasse and landed heavily on the far side.

Here the tracks turned right and ran along the lower lip of the crevasse. Somehow the others must have got over. Now he could see right down to the Haramosh glacier, down to the big basin between the icefall and Camp III, but in his distracted state he couldn't orientate himself. He sensed that the route was taking a dead short-cut, and he wondered how they had managed it in the darkness last night.

Suddenly ahead of him he recognised the familiar steep slope above

Camp IV. Now at last he knew where he was. The tracks seemed to lead across the middle of the slope. He began to follow them, and then suddenly for no apparent reason they divided. One track went on across the middle of the slope, while the other fell away down the slope in a groove and then continued along the bottom. It looked as though one of them had come off the slope here and then made a new track lower down.

He followed the track across the middle of the slope until it joined up with the original track on the ridge above Camp IV. Then he turned and started down the ridge. Deep in the hollow below him, on the far side of the crevasse, he could see the two tents of Camp IV. It was almost dark now.

There was no sign of any movement in camp. He crossed the snowbridge over the crevasse, and as he got near camp he started shouting for Jillott and Emery, expecting them to come out and meet him. Even in his utterly exhausted state, he could feel the joy of having reached his goal.

It wasn't until he was right in the hollow of the camp that he heard a voice from one of the tents. He pulled the entrance to the tent open and there, lying on top of his sleeping-bag, still in all his climbing-clothes and still wearing crampons, was Emery, obviously very shaken and completely exhausted. There was no sign of Jillott.

"Where's Bernard?"

"He's gone, Tony."

"Gone? Gone where?"

"He's gone. He's had it. He's dead."

"What do you mean?"

"He went straight over the crest of the ridge up there and into the crevasse. I saw his footsteps leading up to the edge. He's dead."

"Have you called?"

"Yes." Emery collapsed back on to the air mattress, too overcome for the moment to say more. Then he asked his own question.

"Where's Rae?"

"I don't know. I'm afraid he's still in the basin. He was very weak. He kept slipping off. I doubt if he'll get out by himself. We'll have to go back for him."

"Yes. "

As yet neither Streather nor Emery was fully conscious of the extent of the tragedy. With Jillott dead, Emery severely frostbitten, and Streather himself enfeebled, who was going to go back for Culbert?

"I'm going to call Bernard," said Streather. "It's just possible he might still be alive."

He stumbled back up the slope immediately above Camp IV until he reached the snow-bridge. Then he began shouting down into the crevasse. He knew there was no chance, he knew there would be no answer, but he shouted for several minutes. Then he trudged back to Camp IV.

Jillott's tragic end after reaching safety was a catastrophe too big for either of them to contemplate. Like Emery before him, Streather found that it was something he had to accept and then thrust from his mind. He felt a numb emptiness where thoughts of Jillott had been; but there wasn't the awful sense of personal responsibility that he was feeling for Culbert. Jillott's death was as though some outside force beyond their control had struck at them. It had been a life cut short in full flow; there was nothing for the mind to dwell on except the emptiness of loss.

When Emery arrived at Camp IV, he had got into the yellow tent out of force of habit. But this tent, having been dug out after successive snow-falls, had a steep and icy slope leading down to it which made it very difficult to approach and leave. Inside, the two sleeping-bags fell inwards, the floor of the tent being rounded like the bottom of a boat. The tent Streather and Jillott had brought up with them was much higher and easier to enter, and the two men moved up into it. They began to take their crampons and overboots off, and then their climbing-boots and socks. Emery was unable to manage without help from Streather. Then they examined their feet. Emery's were a bluish colour from the toes to about halfway along the foot. Streather's had a slight blue line just above the toes. Streather found some dry socks, and they put these on. Streather helped Emery into one of the sleeping-bags, and then he put his boots on and went outside to get a primus.

For the next few hours Streather melted snow down almost continually in an effort to satisfy their craving for liquid. He put all kinds of things into it to make it palatable—lemonade crystals, complan, soup, Ovaltine, complan and Ovaltine together, and so on. Sometimes they dozed for a few minutes, but then their thirst would rouse them again and Streather would melt down more snow. And all the time they lay in agony from their frostbitten hands and feet, and from the cracked and broken skin around their mouths and noses, and the burning sand and grit that seemed to lie behind their eyeballs.

They plastered their faces with cream to try to case the soreness; and when at last they felt they had drunk enough, Streather put the primus out and crawled into the other sleeping-bag. He found some sleeping-pills and they each took one. It was the first time either of them had needed one throughout the expedition. They also took antibiotics to prevent their frostbitten hands and feet from becoming infected.

They knew that various people had various theories about what one should do at this stage of frostbite. The only thing one could be fairly certain of was that nothing was likely to work. Intra-arterial injections were discredited. The remedies of the old climbers, like rubbing snow on the affected parts, were quite useless. Emery had discussed the possibility of frostbite with an expert in arterial surgery before he left England. He had been told not to go in for any sort of injection, but simply to take antibiotics and keep the body warm without overheating the affected part. If the hands were affected you could leave them outside the sleeping-bag, and by keeping the body warm you got a reflex opening of the arteries in the extremities. This was what they did.

Now they tried to sleep. Exhaustion and the effects of the sleeping-pills eased their pain, but their thoughts would not leave the basin where Culbert was spending his last hours. There was no pill they could take that would case their agony of mind.

• • •

Next morning they melted more snow down and drank large quantities of liquid, but all they were able to eat was glucose. They took antibiotics, and also some vitamin pills. For a time they kept up the pretence, at least to themselves, that they were preparing to go back for Culbert; but neither really believed in it. Emery was almost helpless; he couldn't even stand up, and Streather doubted whether he would ever get him off the mountain. To attempt to go above Camp IV again with him was unthinkable. He himself was hardly able to crawl out of the tent. Everything he tried to do exhausted him and he knew there was nothing he could do for Culbert. He hadn't been able to help him yesterday and still less would he be able to help him today.

They had all survived three nights in the open above 20,000 feet, under the worst possible conditions, and this in itself had been a near miracle. He thought he would not have survived a fourth night himself, and Culbert had been much weaker than him. Besides, last night Culbert had been alone. He had not only been without the warmth of another body to lie against, but without the immense moral sustenance of a companion. However strong one's character might be, that made a tremendous difference.

The truth that stared them in the face, but which they still refused to accept, was that Culbert had very probably died last night. Even if he were still alive now, he would be dead before they could get to him. And what of Emery? Culbert had risked his life, had lost his life, in an attempt to save Jillott and Emery. Would it not make his sacrifice pointless and empty if one at least of these two lives were not saved?

These were the thoughts that ran through Streather's mind, in an order that was only partly coherent. The decision could not be delayed. He had to make it now, before the last of his strength finally deserted him. And he knew there was only one decision to make.

To leave a man to his fate on a mountain was something that no mountaineer ever contemplated. The tradition was as old as mountaineering, and it embraced the primitive peoples of the hills as well as the climbers themselves. The Sherpas would never leave anyone to die. They would stay with them and die with them rather than leave them. For a man like Streather, indeed for any man, it was a terrible decision to have to make. It was a decision the necessity of which would haunt him all his life. Yet fundamentally it wasn't a decision at all. There was no choice.

If they could reach Camp III, he might succeed with Hamilton's help in getting Emery off the mountain. But he was now quite incapable even of the climb up to the northeast ridge, let alone of negotiating that treacherous avalanche slope and the traverse across the top of the icecliffs and the final slope down into the basin.

Ever since the moment of the avalanche, Streather had not spared himself in his efforts to bring the whole party safely off the mountain. He had found a way down into the basin. He had led the way out. It had been his strength and skill on which all their lives had depended. He had belayed Culbert along the last piece of the traverse, knowing that if Culbert slipped the rope might steady him but that if he fell the belay would be difficult to hold. From this point on he had pinned his faith in the promised return of Jillott and Emery, only to find on reaching Camp IV that Jillott was dead and Emery exhausted and frostbitten. This situation, shocking enough in itself, held fatal repercussions for Culbert. Streather had reached his goal full of hope, only to be presented with the loss of Jillott and the abandonment of Culbert as a *fait accompli*.

There was no tragic dilemma, no question of weighing the chances of one man's life against another's. To set off up towards the ridge would be a prodigal and pointless gesture, certain to add two and possibly three lives to those already lost. He must do what he could to save Emery. He must turn his back on Culbert.

Streather knew all this instinctively. His mind was too bludgeoned by travail and tragedy to be capable of conscious reasoning. Yet he shrank from that final act of abandonment.

He would be leaving the one man among all men for whom he would willingly have given his life. His admiration and affection for Culbert had grown throughout the expedition, until now he felt about him as he had felt about Charles Houston, the American leader of the K2 expedition. He loved him as a man loves a brother.

from Adrift On an Ice-Pan
by Sir Wilfred Grenfell

Sir Wilfred Grenfell (1865-1940) set up a mission along the Labrador coast in 1892, providing medical and educational services to fishermen and Native people. Danger was part of daily life in this land where a single mistake could be fatal. One day Grenfell and his dog team cut across an ice-covered bay on an emergency run from his station to a village to the south. The shortcut didn't work out.

I t was Easter Sunday at St. Anthony in the year 1908, but with us in northern Newfoundland still winter. Everything was covered with snow and ice. I was walking back after morning service, when a boy came running over from the hospital with the news that a large team of dogs had come from sixty miles to the southward, to get a doctor on a very urgent case. It was that of a young man on whom we had operated about a fortnight before for an acute bone disease in the thigh. The people had allowed the wound to close, the poisoned matter had accumulated, and we thought we should have to remove the leg. There was obviously, therefore, no time to be lost. So, having packed up the necessary instruments, dressings, and drugs, and having fitted out the dog-sleigh with my best dogs, I started at once, the messengers following me with their team.

My team was an especially good one. On many a long journey they had stood by me and pulled me out of difficulties by their sagacity and endurance. To a lover of his dogs, as every Christian man must be, each one had become almost as precious as a child to its mother. They were beautiful beasts: "Brin," the cleverest leader on the coast; "Doc," a large, gentle beast, the backbone of the team for power; "Spy", a wiry, powerful black and white dog; "Moody," a lop-eared black-and-tan, in his third season, a plodder that never looked behind him; "Watch," the youngster of the team, long-legged and speedy, with great liquid eyes and a Gordon-setter coat; "Sue," a large, dark Eskimo, the image of a great black wolf, with her sharp-pointed and perpendicular ears, for she "harked back" to her wild ancestry; "Jerry," a large roan-colored slut, the quickest of all my dogs on her feet, and so affectionate that her overtures of joy had often sent me sprawling on my back; "Jack," a jet-black, gentle-natured dog, more like a retriever, that always ran next the sledge, and never looked back but everlastingly pulled straight ahead, running always with his nose to the ground.

It was late in April, when there is always the risk of getting wet through the ice, so that I was carefully prepared with spare outfit, which included a change of garments, snowshoes, rifle, compass, axe, and oil-skin overclothes. The messengers were anxious that their team should travel back with mine, for they were slow at best and needed a lead. My dogs, however, being a powerful team, could not be held back, and though I managed to wait twice for their sleigh, I had reached a village about twenty miles on the journey before nightfall, and had fed the dogs, and was gathering a few people for prayers when they caught me up.

During the night the wind shifted to the northeast, which brought in fog and rain, softened the snow, and made travelling very bad, besides heaving a heavy sea into the bay. Our drive next morning would be somewhat over forty miles, the first ten miles on an arm of the sea, on salt-water ice.

In order not to be separated too long from my friends, I sent them ahead two hours before me, appointing a rendezvous in a log tilt that we have built in the woods as a halfway house. There is no one living on all that long coast-line, and to provide against accidents—which have happened more than once—we built this hut to keep dry clothing, food, and drugs in.

The first rain of the year was falling when I started, and I was obliged to keep on what we call the "ballicaters," or ice barricades, much farther up the bay than I had expected. The sea of the night before had smashed the ponderous covering of ice right to the landwash. There were great gaping chasms between the enormous blocks, which we call pans, and half a mile out it was all clear water.

An island three miles out had preserved a bridge of ice, however, and by crossing a few cracks I managed to reach it. From the island it was four miles across to a rocky promontory—a course that would be several miles shorter than going round the shore. Here as far as the eye could reach the ice seemed good, though it was very rough. Obviously, it had been smashed up by the sea and then packed in again by the strong wind from the northeast; and I thought it had frozen together solid.

All went well till I was about a quarter of a mile from the landing point. Then the wind suddenly fell, and I noticed that I was travelling over loose "sish," which was like porridge and probably many feet deep. By stabbing down, I could drive my whip-handle through the thin coating of young ice that was floating on it. The sish ice consists of the tiny fragments where the large pans have been pounding together on the heaving sea, like the stones of Freya's grinding mill.

So quickly did the wind now come off shore, and so quickly did the packed "slob," relieved of the wind pressure, "run abroad," that already I could not see one pan larger than ten feet square; moreover, the ice was loosening so rapidly that I saw that retreat was absolutely impossible. Neither was there any way to get off the little pan I was surveying from.

There was not a moment to lose. I tore off my oilskins, threw myself on my hands and knees by the side of the komatik to give a larger base to hold, and shouted to my team to go ahead for the shore. Before we had gone twenty yards, the dogs got frightened, hesitated for a moment, and the komatik instantly sank into the slob. It was necessary then for the dogs to pull much harder, so that they now began to sink in also.

Earlier in the season the father of the very boy I was going to operate on had been drowned in this same way, his dogs tangling their traces around him in the slob. This flashed into my mind, and I managed to loosen my sheath-knife, scramble forward, find the traces in the water, and cut them, holding on to the leader's trace wound round my wrist.

Being in the water I could see no piece of ice that would bear anything up. But there was as it happened a piece of snow, frozen together like a large snowball, about twenty-five yards away, near where my leading dog, "Brin," was wallowing in the slob. Upon this he very shortly climbed, his long trace of ten fathoms almost reaching there before he went into the water.

This dog has weird black markings on his face, giving him the appearance of wearing a perpetual grin. After climbing out on the snow, as if it were the most natural position in the world, he deliberately shook the ice and water from his long coat, and then turned round to look for me. As he sat perched up there out of the water, he seemed to be grinning with satisfaction. The other dogs were hopelessly bogged. Indeed, we were like flies in treacle.

Gradually, I hauled myself along the line that was still tied to my wrist, till without any warning the dog turned round and slipped out of his harness, and then once more turned his grinning face to where I was struggling.

It was impossible to make any progress through the sish ice by swimming, so I lay there and thought all would soon be over, only wondering if any one would ever know how it happened. There was no particular horror attached to it, and in fact I began to feel drowsy, as if I could easily go to sleep, when suddenly I saw the trace of another big dog that had himself gone through before he reached the pan, and though he was close to it was quite unable to force his way out. Along this I hauled myself, using him as a bow anchor, but much bothered by the other dogs as I passed them, one of which got on my shoulder, pushing me farther down into the ice. There was only a yard or so more when I had passed my living anchor, and soon I lay with my dogs around me on the little piece of slob ice. I had to help them on to it, working them through the lane that I had made.

The piece of ice we were on was so small, it was obvious we must soon all be drowned, if we remained upon it as it drifted seaward into more open water. If we were to save our lives, no time was to be lost. When I stood up, I could see about twenty yards away a larger pan floating amidst the sish, like a great flat raft, and if we could get on to it we should postpone at least for a time the death that already seemed almost inevitable. It was impossible to reach it without a life line, as I had already learned to my cost, and the next problem was how to get one there. Marvellous to relate, when I had first fallen through, after I had cut the dogs adrift without any hope left of saving myself, I had not let my knife sink, but had fastened it by two half hitches to the back of one of the dogs. To my great joy there it was still, and shortly I was at work cutting all the sealskin traces still hanging from the dogs' harnesses, and splicing them together into one long line. These I divided and fastened to the backs of my two leaders, tying the near ends round my two wrists. I then pointed out to "Brin" the pan I wanted to reach and tried my best to make them go ahead, giving them the full length of my lines from two coils. My long sealskin moccasins, reaching to my thigh, were full of ice and water. These I took off and tied separately on the dogs' backs. My coat, hat, gloves, and overalls I had already lost. At first, nothing would induce the two dogs to move, and though I threw them off the pan two or three times, they struggled back upon it, which perhaps was only natural, because as soon as they fell through they could see nowhere else to make for. To me, however, this seemed to spell "the end." Fortunately, I had with me a small black spaniel, almost a featherweight, with large furry paws, called "Jack," who acts as my mascot and incidentally as my retriever. This at once flashed into my mind, and I felt I had still one more chance for life. So I spoke to him and showed him the direction, and then threw a piece of ice toward the desired goal. Without a moment's hesitation he made a dash for it, and to my great joy got there safely, the tough scale of sea ice carrying his weight bravely. At once I shouted to him to "lie down," and this, too, he immediately did, looking like a little black fuzz ball on the white setting. My leaders could now see him seated there on the new piece of floe, and when once more I threw them off they understood what I wanted, and fought their way to where they saw the spaniel, carrying with them the line that gave me the one chance for my life. The other dogs followed them, and after painful struggling, all got out again except one. Taking all the run that I could get on my little pan, I made a dive, slithering with the impetus along the surface till once more I sank through. After a long fight, however, I was able to haul myself by the long traces on to this new pan, having taken care beforehand to tie the harnesses to which I was holding under the dogs' bellies, so that they could not slip them off. But alas! The pan I was now on was not large enough to bear us and was already beginning to sink, so this process had to be repeated immediately.

I now realized that, though we had been working toward the shore, we had been losing ground all the time, for the off-shore wind had already driven us a hundred yards farther out. But the widening gap kept full of the pounded ice, through which no man could possibly go.

I had decided I would rather stake my chances on a long swim even than perish by inches on the floe, as there was no likelihood whatever of being seen and rescued. But, keenly though I watched, not a streak even of clear water appeared, the interminable sish rising from below and filling every gap as it appeared. We were now resting on a piece of ice about ten by twelve feet, which, as I found when I came to examine it, was not ice at all, but simply snow-covered slob frozen into a mass, and I feared it would very soon break up in the general turmoil of the heavy sea, which was increasing as the ice drove off shore before the wind.

At first we drifted in the direction of a rocky point on which a heavy surf was breaking. Here I thought once again to swim ashore. But suddenly we struck a rock. A large piece broke off the already small pan, and what was left swung round in the backwash, and started right out to sea.

There was nothing for it now but to hope for a rescue. Alas! there was little possibility of being seen. As I have already mentioned, no one lives around this big bay. My only hope was that the other komatik, knowing I was alone and had failed to keep my tryst, would perhaps come back to look for me. This, however, as it proved, they did not do.

The westerly wind was rising all the time, our coldest wind at this time of the year, coming as it does over the Gulf ice. It was tantalizing, as I stood with next to nothing on, the wind going through me and every stitch soaked in ice-water, to see my well-stocked komatik some fifty yards away. It was still above water, with food, hot tea in a thermos bottle, dry clothing, matches, wood, and everything on it for making a fire to attract attention.

It is easy to see a dark object on the ice in the daytime, for the gorgeous whiteness shows off the least thing. But the tops of bushes and large pieces of kelp have often deceived those looking out. Moreover, within our memory no man has been thus adrift on the bay ice. The chances were about one in a thousand that I should be seen at all, and if I were seen, I should probably be mistaken for some piece of refuse.

To keep from freezing, I cut off my long moccasins down to the feet, strung out some line, split the legs, and made a kind of jacket, which protected my back from the wind down as far as the waist. I have this jacket still, and my friends assure me it would make a good Sunday garment.

I had not drifted more than half a mile before I saw my poor komatik disappear through the ice, which was every minute loosening up into the small pans that it consisted of, and it seemed like a friend gone and one more tie with home and safety lost. To the northward, about a mile distant, lay the mainland along which I had passed so merrily in the morning—only, it seemed, a few moments before.

By mid-day I had passed the island to which I had crossed on the ice bridge. I could see that the bridge was gone now. If I could reach the island I should only be marooned and destined to die of starvation. But there was little chance of that, for I was rapidly driving into the ever widening bay.

It was scarcely safe to move on my small ice raft, for fear of breaking it. Yet I saw I must have the skins of some of my dogs—of which I had eight on the pan—if I was to live the night out. There was now some three to five miles between me and the north side of the bay. There, immense pans of Arctic ice, surging to and fro on the heavy ground seas, were thundering into the cliffs like medieval battering-rams. It was evident that, even if seen, I could hope for no help from that quarter before night. No boat could live through the surf.

Unwinding the sealskin traces from my waist, round which I had wound them to keep the dogs from eating them, I made a slip-knot, passed it over the first dog's head, tied it round my foot close to his neck, threw him on his back, and stabbed him in the heart. Poor beast! I loved him like a friend—a beautiful dog—but we could not all hope to live. In fact, I had no hope any of us would, at that time, but it seemed better to die fighting.

In spite of my care the struggling dog bit me rather badly in the leg. I suppose my numb hands prevented my holding his throat as I could ordinarily do. Moreover, I must hold the knife in the wound to the end, as blood on the fur would freeze solid and make the skin useless. In this way I sacrificed two more large dogs, receiving only one more bite, though I fully expected that the pan I was on would break up in the struggle. The other dogs, who were licking their coats and trying to get dry, apparently took no notice of the fate of their comrades—but I was very careful to prevent the dying dogs crying out, for the noise of fighting would probably have been followed by the rest attacking the down dog, and that was too close to me to be pleasant. A short shrift seemed to me better than a long one, and I envied the dead dogs whose troubles were over so quickly. Indeed, I came to balance in my mind whether, if once I passed into the open sea, it would not be better by far to use my faithful knife on myself than to die by inches. There seemed no hardship in the thought. I seemed fully to sympathize with the Japanese view of hara-kiri.

Working, however, saved me from philosophizing. By the time I had skinned these dogs, and with my knife and some of the harness had strung the skins together, I was ten miles on my way, and it was getting dark.

Away to the northward I could see a single light in the little village where I had slept the night before, where I had received the kindly hospitality of the simple fishermen in whose comfortable homes I have spent many a night. I could not help but think of them sitting down to tea, with no idea that there was any one watching them, for I had told them not to expect me back for three days.

Meanwhile I had frayed out a small piece of rope into oakum, and mixed it with fat from the intestines of my dogs. Alas, my match-box, which was always chained to me, had leaked, and my matches were in pulp. Had I been able to make a light, it would have looked so unearthly out there on the sea that I felt sure they would see me. But that chance was now cut off. However, I kept the matches, hoping that I might dry them if I lived through the night. While working at the dogs, about every five minutes I would stand up and wave my hands toward the land. I had no flag, and I could not spare my shirt, for, wet as it was, it was better than nothing in that freezing wind, and, anyhow, it was already nearly dark.

Unfortunately, the coves in among the cliffs are so placed that only for a very narrow space can the people in any house see the sea. Indeed, most of them cannot see it at all, so that I could not in the least expect any one to see me, even supposing it had been daylight.

Not daring to take any snow from the surface of my pan to break the wind with, I piled up the carcasses of my dogs. With my skin rug I could now sit down without getting soaked. During these hours I had continually taken off all my clothes, wrung them out, swung them one by one in the wind, and put on first one and then the other inside, hoping that what heat there was in my body would thus serve to dry them. In this I had been fairly successful.

My feet gave me most trouble, for they immediately got wet again because my thin moccasins were easily soaked through on the snow. I suddenly thought of the way in which the Lapps who tend our reindeer manage for dry socks. They carry grass with them, which they ravel up and pad into their shoes. Into this they put their feet, and then pack the rest with more grass, tying up the top with a binder. The ropes of the harness for our dogs are carefully sewed all over with two layers of flannel in order to make them soft against the dogs' sides. So, as soon as I could sit down, I started with my trusty knife to rip up the flannel. Though my fingers were more or less frozen, I was able also to ravel out the rope, put it into my shoes, and use my wet socks inside my knickerbockers, where, though damp, they served to break the wind. Then, tying the narrow strips of flannel together, I bound up the top of the moccasins, Lapp-fashion, and carried the bandage on up over my knee, making a ragged though most excellent puttee.

As to the garments I wore, I had opened recently a box of football clothes I had not seen for twenty years. I had found my old Oxford University football running shorts and a pair of Richmond Football Club red, yellow, and black stockings, exactly as I wore them twenty years ago. These with a flannel shirt and sweater vest were now all I had left. Coat, hat, gloves, oilskins, everything else, were gone, and I stood there in that odd costume, exactly as I stood twenty years ago on a football field reminding me, of the little girl of a friend, who when told she was dying, asked to be dressed in her Sunday frock to go to heaven in. My costume, being very light, dried all the quicker, until afternoon. Then nothing would dry any more, everything freezing stiff. It had been an ideal costume to struggle through the slob ice. I really believe the conventional garments missionaries are supposed to affect would have been fatal.

My occupation till what seemed like midnight was unravelling rope, and with this I padded out my knickers inside, and my shirt as well, though it was a clumsy job, for I could not see what I was doing. Now, getting my largest dog, Doc, as big a wolf and weighing ninety-two pounds, I made him lie down, so that I could cuddle round him. I then wrapped the three skins around me, arranging them so that I could lie on one edge, while the other came just over my shoulders and head.

My own breath collecting inside the newly flayed skin must have had a soporific effect, for I was soon fast asleep. One hand I had kept warm against the curled up dog, but the other, being gloveless, had frozen, and I suddenly awoke, shivering enough, I thought, to break my fragile pan. What I took at first to be the sun was just rising, but I soon found it was the moon, and then I knew it was about half-past twelve. The dog was having an excellent time. He hadn't been cuddled so warm all winter, and he resented my moving with low growls till he found it wasn't another dog.

The wind was steadily driving me now toward the open sea, and I could expect, short of a miracle, nothing but death out there. Somehow, one scarcely felt justified in praying for a miracle. But we have learned down here to pray for things we want, and, anyhow, just at that moment the miracle occurred. The wind fell off suddenly, and came with a light air from the southward, and then dropped stark calm. The ice was now "all abroad," which I was sorry for, for there was a big safe pan not twenty yards away from me If I could have got on that, I might have killed my other dogs when the time came, and with their coats I could hope to hold out for two or three days more, and with the food and drink their bodies would offer me need not at least die of hunger or thirst. To tell the truth, they were so big and strong I was half afraid to tackle them with only a sheath-knife on my small and unstable raft.

But it was now freezing hard. I knew the calm water between us would form into cakes, and I had to recognize that the chance of getting near enough to escape on to it was gone. If, on the other hand, the whole bay froze solid again I had yet another possible chance. For my pan would hold together longer and I should be opposite another village, called Goose Cove, at daylight, and might possibly be seen from there. I knew that the komatiks there would be starting at daybreak over the hills for a parade of Orangemen about twenty miles away. Possibly, therefore, I might be seen as they climbed the hills. So I lay down, and went to sleep again.

It seems impossible to say how long one sleeps, but I woke with a sudden thought in my mind that I must have a flag; but again I had no pole and no flag. However, I set to work in the dark to disarticulate the legs of my dead dogs, which were now frozen stiff, and which were all that offered a chance of carrying anything like a distress signal. Cold as it was, I determined to sacrifice my shirt for that purpose with the first streak of daylight.

It took a long time in the dark to get the legs off, and when I had patiently marled them together with old harness rope and the remains of the skin traces, it was the heaviest and crookedest flag-pole it has ever been my lot to see. I had had no food from six o'clock the morning before, when I had eaten porridge and bread and butter. I had, however, a rubber band which I had been wearing instead of one of my garters, and I chewed that for twenty-four hours. It saved me from thirst and hunger, oddly enough. It was not possible to get a drink from my pan, for it was far too salty. But anyhow that thought did not distress me much, for as from time to time I heard the cracking and grinding of the newly formed slob, it seemed that my devoted boat must inevitably soon go to pieces.

At last the sun rose, and the time came for the sacrifice of my shirt. So I stripped, and, much to my surprise, found it not half so cold as I had anticipated. I now re-formed my dogskins with the raw side out, so that they made a kind of coat quite rivalling Joseph's. But, with the rising of the sun, the frost came out of the joints of my dogs' legs, and the friction caused by waving it made my flag-pole almost tie itself in knots. Still, I could raise it three or four feet above my head, which was very important.

Now, however, I found that instead of being as far out at sea as I had reckoned, I had drifted back in a northwesterly direction, and was off some cliffs known as Ireland Head. Near these there was a little village looking seaward, whence I should certainly have been seen. But, as I had myself, earlier in the winter, been night-bound at this place, I had learnt there was not a single soul living there at all this winter. The people had all, as usual, migrated to the winter houses up the bay, where they get together for schooling and social purposes.

I soon found it was impossible to keep waving so heavy a flag all the time, and yet I dared not sit down, for that might be the exact moment some one would be in a position to see me from the hills. The only thing in my mind was how long I could stand up and how long go on waving that pole at the cliffs. Once or twice I thought I saw men against their snowy faces, which, I judged, were about five and a half miles

from me, but they were only trees. Once, also, I thought I saw a boat
approaching. A glittering object kept appearing and disappearing on
the water, but it was only a small piece of ice sparkling in the sun as it
rose on the surface. I think that the rocking of my cradle up and down
on the waves had helped me to sleep, for I felt as well as ever I did in
my life; and with the hope of a long sunny day, I felt sure I was good
to last another twenty-four hours—if my boat would hold out and not
rot under the sun's rays.

Each time I sat down to rest, my big dog "Doc" came and kissed my
face and then walked to the edge of the ice-pan, returning again to
where I was huddled up, as if to say, "Why don't you come along?
Surely it is time to start." The other dogs also were now moving about
very restlessly, occasionally trying to satisfy their hunger by gnawing at
the dead bodies of their brothers.

I determined, at mid-day, to kill a big Eskimo dog and drink his
blood, as I had read only a few days before in "Farthest North" of Dr.
Nansen's doing—that is, if I survived the battle with him. I could not
help feeling, even then, my ludicrous position, and I thought, if ever I
got ashore again, I should have to laugh at myself standing hour after
hour waving my shirt at those lofty cliffs, which seemed to assume a
kind of sardonic grin, so that I could almost imagine they were laughing at me. At times I could not help thinking of the good breakfast that
my colleagues were enjoying at the back of those same cliffs, and of the
snug fire and the comfortable room which we call our study.

I can honestly say that from first to last not a single sensation of fear
entered my mind, even when I was struggling in the slob ice. Somehow
it did not seem unnatural; I had been through the ice half a dozen
times before. For the most part I felt very sleepy, and the idea was then
very strong in my mind that I should soon reach the solution of the
mysteries that I had been preaching about for so many years.

Only the previous night (Easter Sunday) at prayers in the cottage, we
had been discussing the fact that the soul was entirely separate from
the body, that Christ's idea of the body as the temple in which the soul
dwells is so amply borne out by modern science. We had talked of

thoughts from that admirable book, *Brain and Personality*, by Dr. Thompson of New York, and also of the same subject in the light of a recent operation performed at the Johns Hopkins Hospital by Dr. Harvey Cushing. The doctor had removed from a man's brain two large cystic tumors without giving the man an anesthetic, and the patient had kept up a running conversation with him all the while the doctor's fingers were working in his brain. It had seemed such a striking proof that ourselves and our bodies are two absolutely different things.

Our eternal life has always been with me a matter of faith. It seems to me one of those problems that must always be a mystery to knowledge. But my own faith in this matter had been so untroubled that it seemed now almost natural to be leaving through this portal of death from an ice-pan. In many ways, also, I could see how a death of this kind might be of value to the particular work that I am engaged in. Except for my friends, I had nothing I could think of to regret whatever. Certainly, I should like to have told them the story. But then one does not carry folios of paper in running shorts which have no pockets, and all my writing gear had gone by the board with the komatik.

I could still see a testimonial to myself some distance away in my khaki overalls, which I had left on another pan in the struggle of the night before. They seemed a kind of company, and would possibly be picked up and suggest the true story. Running through my head all the time, quite unbidden, were the words of the old hymn:

> "My God, my Father, while I stray
> Far from my home on life's dark way,
> Oh, teach me from my heart to say,
>   Thy will be done!"

It is a hymn we hardly ever sing out here, and it was an unconscious memory of my boyhood days.

It was a perfect morning—a cobalt sky, an ultramarine sea, a golden sun, an almost wasteful extravagance of crimson over hills of purest snow, which caught a reflected glow from rock and crag. Between me and the hills lay miles of rough ice and long veins of thin black slob that had formed during the night. For the foreground there was my poor, gruesome pan, bobbing up and down on the edge of the open sea, stained with blood, and littered with carcasses and debris. It was smaller than last night, and I noticed also that the new ice from the water melted under the dogs' bodies had been formed at the expense of its thickness. Five dogs, myself in colored football costume, and a bloody dogskin cloak, with a gay flannel shirt on a pole of frozen dogs' legs, completed the picture. The sun was almost hot by now, and I was conscious of a surplus of heat in my skin coat. I began to look longingly at one of my remaining dogs, for an appetite will rise even on an ice-pan, and that made me think of fire. So once again I inspected my matches. Alas! the heads were in paste, all but three or four blue-top wax ones.

These I now laid out to dry, while I searched about on my snow-pan to see if I could get a piece of transparent ice to make a burning-glass. For I was pretty sure that with all the unravelled tow I had stuffed into my leggings, and with the fat of my dogs, I could make smoke enough to be seen if only I could get a light. I had found a piece which I thought would do, and had gone back to wave my flag, which I did every two minutes, when I suddenly thought I saw again the glitter of an oar. It did not seem possible, however, for it must be remembered it was not water which lay between me and the land, but slob ice, which a mile or two inside me was very heavy. Even if people had seen me, I did not think they could get through, though I knew that the whole shore would then be trying. Moreover, there, was no smoke rising on the land to give me hope that I had been seen. There had been no gun-flashes in the night, and I felt sure that, had any one seen me, there would have been a bonfire on every hill to encourage me to keep going.

So I gave it up, and went on with my work. But the next time I went back to my flag, the glitter seemed very distinct, and though it kept disappearing as it rose and fell on the surface, I kept my eyes strained upon it, for my dark spectacles had been lost, and I was partly snowblind.

I waved my flag as high as I could raise it, broadside on. At last, beside the glint of the white oar, I made out the black streak of the hull. I knew that, if the pan held on for another hour, I should be all right.

With that strange perversity of the human intellect, the first thing I thought of was what trophies I could carry with my luggage from the pan, and I pictured the dog-bone flagstaff adorning my study. (The dogs actually ate it afterwards.) I thought of preserving my ragged puttees with our collection of curiosities. I lost no time now at the burning-glass. My whole mind was devoted to making sure I should be seen, and I moved about as much as I dared on the raft, waving my sorry token aloft.

At last there could be no doubt about it: the boat was getting nearer and nearer. I could see that my rescuers were frantically waving, and, when they came within shouting distance, I heard some one cry out, "Don't get excited. Keep on the pan where you are." They were infinitely more excited than I. Already to me it seemed just as natural now to be saved as, half an hour before, it had seemed inevitable I should be lost, and had my rescuers only known, as I did, the sensation of a bath in that ice when you could not dry yourself afterwards, they need not have expected me to follow the example of the apostle Peter and throw myself into the water.

As the man in the bow leaped from the boat on to my ice raft and grasped both my hands in his, not a word was uttered. I could see in his face the strong emotions he was trying hard to force back, though in spite of himself tears trickled down his cheeks. It was the same with each of the others of my rescuers, nor was there any reason to be ashamed of them. These were not the emblems of weak sentimentality, but the evidences of the realization of the deepest and noblest emotion of which the human heart is capable, the vision that God has use for us his creatures, the sense of that supreme joy of the Christ—the joy of unselfish service. After the hand-shake and swallowing a cup of warm tea that had been thoughtfully packed in a bottle, we hoisted in my remaining dogs and started for home. To drive the boat home there were not only five Newfoundland fishermen at the oars, but five men with Newfoundland muscles in their backs, and five as brave hearts as ever beat in the bodies of human beings.

So, slowly but steadily, we forged through to the shore, now jumping out on to larger pans and forcing them apart with the oars, now hauling the boat out and dragging her over, when the jam of ice packed tightly in by the rising wind was impossible to get through otherwise.

My first question, when at last we found our tongues, was, "How ever did you happen to be out in the boat in this ice?" To my astonishment they told me that the previous night four men had been away on a long headland cutting out some dead harp seals that they had killed in the fall and left to freeze up in a rough wooden store they had built there, and that as they were leaving for home, my pan of ice had drifted out clear of Hare Island, and one of them, with his keen fisherman's eyes, had seen something unusual. They at once returned to their village, saying there was something alive drifting out to sea on the floe ice. But their report bad been discredited, for the people thought that it could be only the top of some tree.

All the time I had been driving along I knew that there was one man on that coast who had a good spy-glass. He tells me he instantly got up in the midst of his supper, on hearing the news, and hurried over the cliffs to the lookout, carrying his trusty spy-glass with him. Immediately, dark as it was, he saw that without any doubt there was a man out on the ice. Indeed, he saw me wave my hands every now and again towards the shore. By a very easy process of reasoning on so uninhabited a shore, he at once knew who it was, though some of the men argued that it must be some one else. Little had I thought, as night was closing in, that away on that snowy hilltop lay a man with a telescope patiently searching those miles of ice for *me*. Hastily they rushed back to the village and at once went down to try to launch a boat, but that proved to be impossible. Miles of ice lay between them and me, the heavy sea was hurling great blocks on the landwash, and night was already falling, the wind blowing hard on shore.

The whole village was aroused, and messengers were dispatched at once along the coast, and lookouts told off to all the favorable points, so that while I considered myself a laughing-stock, bowing with my flag to those unresponsive cliffs, there were really many eyes watching me. One man told me that with his glass he distinctly saw me waving the shirt flag. There was little slumber that night in the villages, and even the men told me there were few dry eyes, as they thought of the impossibility of saving me from perishing. We are not given to weeping overmuch on this shore, but there are tears that do a man honor.

Before daybreak this fine volunteer crew had been gotten together. The boat, with such a force behind it of will power, would, I believe, have gone through anything. And, after seeing the heavy breakers through which we were guided, loaded with their heavy ice battering-rams, when at last we ran through the harbor-mouth with the boat on our return, I knew well what wives and children had been thinking of when they saw their loved ones put out. Only two years ago I remember a fisherman's wife watching her husband and three sons take out a boat to bring in a stranger that was showing flags for a pilot. But the boat and its occupants have not yet come back.

Every soul in the village was on the beach as we neared the shore. Every soul was waiting to shake hands when I landed. Even with the grip that one after another gave me, some no longer trying to keep back the tears, I did not find out my hands were frost-burnt—a fact I have not been slow to appreciate since, however. I must have been a weird sight as I stepped ashore, tied up in rags, stuffed out with oakum, wrapped in the bloody skins of dogs, with no hat, coat, or gloves besides, and only a pair of short knickers. It must have seemed to some as if it were the old man of the sea coming ashore.

But no time was wasted before a pot of tea was exactly where I wanted it to be, and some hot stew was locating itself where I had intended an hour before the blood of one of my remaining dogs should have gone.

Rigged out in the warm garments that fishermen wear, I started with a large team as hard as I could race for the hospital, for I had learnt that the news had gone over that I was lost. It was soon painfully impressed upon me that I could not much enjoy the ride, for I had to be hauled like a log up the hills, my feet being frostburnt so that I could not walk.

Had I guessed this before going into the house, I might have avoided much trouble.

It is time to bring this egotistic narrative to an end. "Jack" lies curled up by my feet while I write this short account. "Brin" is once again leading and lording it over his fellows. "Doc" and the other survivors are not forgotten, now that we have again returned to the less romantic episodes of a mission hospital life. There stands in our hallway a bronze tablet to the memory of three noble dogs, Moody, Watch, and Spy, whose lives were given for mine on the ice.

In my home in England my brother has placed a duplicate tablet, and has added these words, "Not one of them is forgotten before your Father which is in heaven." And this I most fully believe to be true. The boy whose life I was intent on saving was brought to the hospital a day or two later in a boat, the ice having cleared off the coast not to return for that season. He was operated on successfully, and is even now on the high road to recovery. We all love life. I was glad to be back once more with possibly a new lease of it before me. I had learned on the pan many things, but chiefly that the one cause for regret, when we look back on a life which we think is closed forever, will be the fact that we have wasted its opportunities. As I went to sleep that first night there still rang in my ears the same verse of the old hymn which had been my companion on the ice, "Thy will, not mine, Lord."

The Flesh Eaters

by Geoffrey Childs

Geoffrey Childs (born 1946) sketches this fic-

tional scene: When a pair of climbers does not

return, two sets of rescuers set out—one for the

"experience" and the other to save their

friends. In the aftermath of the event, motives

and feelings are just as divided.

The Monk sits on a pink high stool of granite, his legs spread
apart and his arms hanging down at his side, palms up.
Spindrift is gathering like dust on his thighs and in the folds of
his jacket. His large head is back and up, his eyes open sight-
lessly, no longer even blinking away the flakes that land between the
grey lids. The oval of his face is colourless. There are several long lines
of ice dangling in broken chains from his moustache. Only his bottom
lip is visible beneath it, a black scrawl drawn back into his mouth like
rubber. Vomit glistens on his chin until it is absorbed by his beard. In
back where his helmet is propped against the rock, his brains are seeping out of his broken skull and collecting in a wet sack in the hood of
his cagoule. Lafferty has pulled the hood tight to the back of the
Monk's head and wrapped it with an elastic bandage. It is as close to
medicine as his wooden fingers would allow him to get.

Lafferty had invented the climb. It was his confidence that had
brought the Monk here and placed him beneath the rock. But there is

no blame, only coincidence; only the providence that saves one and sacrifices another. They had been standing side by side, Lafferty had heard the rock first and screamed but the Monk had moved in the wrong direction. The small boulder struck the back of his helmet and dumped him unconscious down on the ledge. Lafferty could tell by the sound of the impact—like a softball, hitting a mattress—that there would be little he could do, but he had not understood the worst of it until he had placed his hand on back of his friend's head to give him water. He had felt the splintered edges of the hole with his fingers then and his hand had come away wet. His stomach had shrunk and turned over with horror and yet something, whether curiosity or concern, he did not know which, had made him slip a finger inside the Monk's balacava and pull it away from the side of his head. Brain mixed with bits of blue wool, black hair and pieces of white shining skull had slithered around the Monk's neck towards his ear. Lafferty had then pressed the cap back against his friend's head and bandaged it. As he worked it occurred to him that they would both die on the ledge: The Monk very soon, possibly not until early morning for him. He accepted this calmly and finished his business, then coiled up the rope and made a seat out of it. Now that the excitement is over the cold is beginning to settle on him. He no longer looks over at his friend's crushed head but pulls in close to him, drawing his feet up underneath his coat, leaning against him to absorb the heat. They tilt together like children away from the void.

By dawn the suspicion in the valley that they are in trouble has been confirmed. The excitement is almost tangible. Young men walk through the fog to Grant's shop where they stand around the stove in knickers and patched wind jackets, wearing boots half tied and talking quietly, intently. There is a rumour of a rescue attempt going around and they are volunteering by their presence. Not that they will all be able to go on the operation, what is important is that they will be close enough to it to later say they had been *there*. Coffee cups form them into small huddles and outside there is the smell of early morning marijuana. Jarold Grant, who runs the climbing school, is on the phone with Tasker who runs the park. "Fish and Game," Jarold is telling him, "is just not up to something like this." The heads in the room nod and smile knowingly. But Tasker is unmoveable. He has the bills, he replies, for having had his men trained by Jarold to be up to it. It is a hard line to argue and Grant is quiet as Tasker establishes his paper proof. Jarold's unusual silence spreads disappointment in the room behind him. It has been a slow winter and everyone wants very much to be in on this one. When he has his chance again, Jarold explains to Tasker in his most amicable voice that the weather is the unforeseen factor for which "experience is the only preparation." Tasker agrees to this that, yes, his men need this rescue for the experience. A *sotto voce* slur from the back of the shop mentions that lives are more important than the rangers getting "experience." Jarold is already pursuing the same point, only with greater subtlety, and eventually Tasker gives in to the possibility of bad press if something goes wrong. He agrees to two teams: four rangers and four local climbers, one group being lowered to the ledge and the other approaching by the ice fall. Arrangements are quickly made for the airlift, team leaders (Jarold, of course, and an ex-Yellowstone ranger named Ferthe), food, equipment and camera teams. The local television station has asked permission to send along a crew and Tasker has attached them to the rangers. Jarold is too anxious to care about that now and quickly closes the conversation. He turns smiling to the climbers filling the room. No one claps but there is applause in the air. Anticipation spreads like fervour as his face again turns serious. Almost as a single body the climbers seem to lean forward towards him.

"Fine tune, goddammit!" Lafferty mumbles, his head jerking slightly. "I can't see a bloody thing for chrissakes! Got to tune this damn thing in!" He searches the rock around him for the dials with his bare hands. His mittens have fallen off unnoticed and lie in the snow at the base of the ledge. He is not aware of any discomfort; his arms are dead now to above his elbows. He searches over the Monk who is dead, too, and frozen hard. Lafferty does not know this. He no longer has any accurate memory of the Monk or the climb. He has entered the limbus, gone crazy with the cold and the slow work of dying, shrinking like plastic wrapping in a fire from the torment on the surface and drawing down to what little of the process there is left. Timeless grey light is on him. He sees images lurking in shadows, sees them moving, even recognises a few, he thinks, and calls out to them, but they shrink back into the mist the closer he comes. "Fine tune, goddammit," he grunts again.

The rescuers are flown to the top of the mountain and lowered to the dead on a winch. Lines are attached to the bodies and they are lifted up the face like freight. An arm is lost. At the summit Lafferty and the Monk are packed in bags and taken away, nothing very dramatic. The team crossing the glacier is called back before they have even reached the base. Later, Jarold refuses Tasker's offer to come to the press conference and instead goes to Collin's tavern with the others and gets very drunk. They drink 'boiler-makers' in silence as more people enter and gather a respectful distance to form a ring of small whispering groups. The four climbers do not talk between themselves or to anyone else. They do not need to. The knowledge has already spread that they were the four who reached the bodies, the four who touched the dead. To discuss the event now would be to limit its proportions. At 6.15 the end comes when they all turn to watch Tasker on the news. He is dressed in his climbing clothes, he is very sombre, he chooses his words carefully, almost wearily, seeming to think out the tangents before answering. It gives his statements a philosophical, climberly effect. He closes with a postscript on safety, his arms folded on the table and his mouth very near the microphones. When the television is snapped off Jarold leans back into single view from the table and shakes his head ironically. "What the hell does that son-of-a-bitch know?" he asks no one and everyone. "Hell, he wasn't there. He didn't know them. He didn't have to stuff them in bags for godsakes." Respect flows towards him like a river.

• • •

Time has passed. On the mountain it is a year now and snow has piled up in the Monk's corner until all that is left of his ever having been there is a red smudge on the rock where his helmet had scraped against it. The two pitons planted by Lafferty still remain. They are referred to in Jarold's updated guidebook of the region as the 'death belay'. No one needs to ask why. Everyone has read his story of the rescue, watched him on television and seen the prize-winning photograph of him, his face grim and drawn, his hands in his pockets, his head down and the two bodies wrapped in black plastic shrouds lying in the snow behind him. The same photo that now hangs in a wooden frame over the ice-axe display in his shop. The photographer had given him a copy at Tasker's request. Perhaps to avoid any unkindness, Tasker's name had been left out of the article, but his television appearance had done him all the good he needed, anyway. In the spring he was transferred to Washington, DC, and placed in charge of a study formulating policy on climbing safety in the national parks. Tasker wears climbing boots to work these days and is known to have seen the dead. For this he is greatly respected in the nation's capital.

from The Breath of Angels
by John Beattie

Sailing in the Caribbean hundreds of miles from land, John Beattie (born 1951) woke up one morning to find a raft bobbing close to his 35-foot yacht, the Warrior Queen. The raft carried a man who was close to death. Suddenly Beattie's trip changed—from an aborted cruise around the world to a voyage with a deeper meaning.

We sailed from Carenero on Saturday, 24 April 1993 at 4.33 p.m. I was on my way home. For the last eight months the compass had always been showing south and west, but from now on it would show north and east. We motored out of the anchorage, before swinging her on to a north-easterly course. I turned to Hamish, smiled and said, 'This is it, Hamish—the turning point. It's a really big moment for me.'

'I'm sure it is, John—but you do have Laura to go home to,' Hamish replied. The bow of the boat was pointing directly to where she was, thousands of miles away—over the horizon of the empty Caribbean Sea and beyond across the Atlantic Ocean, she was waiting for me. Panama was west, and if my original plans had worked out, I would have been halfway across the Pacific by now. But then I would have missed the carnival in Trinidad and the trip up the river. I felt I had done as well as could be expected, given all the mechanical problems at the outset, and was happy to be going home. There had been enough high drama for a lifetime, and I was hoping that the home-ward passage would be easy and uneventful—little did I realise what lay in store.

The first leg of the journey was to Antigua—about 650 miles across the open Caribbean. Antigua race week, which had already started, was due to finish next Friday. There was an outside chance we could be there before it was all over. It was, by all accounts, a big splurge—if it hadn't been for the pump we could have got there in plenty of time. The main problem with the passage was the wind direction. It was likely that it would be against us all the way. When I talked to friends in Trinidad about making this trip, they all thought I had no chance and would be lucky to make a northerly course and hit the Mona Passage between Hispaniola and Puerto Rico. But Hamish was prepared to give it a go. If we continually tacked this way and that, taking advantage of each wind shift, we might just do it.

The coastline of Venezuela was already distant by nightfall; by midnight the lights had sunk below the horizon. There was no shipping—we were well clear of commercial shipping lanes. No other sailboats would be about—anyone sailing west to Panama would clear into Venezuela at the island of Margarita before sailing along the coast. The course was altered about six times on the first night, but we were not able to make what was needed and were already much further to the west than we wanted to be. On the second day, the wind dropped a bit, so I started the engine and we motored due east to try to make good the loss. We both kept a close eye on the water pump but decided after a few hours to close the engine down and sail, even though we couldn't make the course. The wind usually drops off before it begins to blow hard, and by late afternoon of the second day it was blasting in from the east. We sailed close-hauled on the wind, struggling to make a northeasterly course. As the wind picked up even more, we were forced to reduce canvas and bear away to the north. The seas were building all the time. Our second night at sea was a tough one. Waves came over the bow, flooding the cockpit. With the wind a good force seven, we were knocked about a bit. I had never seen the Caribbean so rough and thought it strange that there was no rain. I was thankful for the fact. It hadn't rained for a long time.

On the third day the wind eased somewhat and we managed to sail closer to it, altering course from north to north-east. Two aboard is sometimes more tiring than one, because you feel compelled to keep a 24-hour watch, only getting snatches of three hours' sleep at a time. When you are on your own, it's impossible to stay awake all the time, so once you know you are in open, clear water, you can have a good sleep. I was tired from the lack of sleep and hard sailing. On the third night I explained to Hamish that we could both go to sleep if we wanted to. He wasn't happy about the idea of the boat being left unattended but I assured him that she could sail herself better than we could and that tiredness was a real danger at sea. We were more than 200 miles from the nearest land. There was no possibility of a collision. At midnight on the third night, when it was my turn to relieve Hamish, I told him I was going to bed and that he should do likewise. Before turning in, I had a little nightcap of rum. I poked Hamish in the shoulder in a friendly way, saying, 'Don't worry. There's nothing out here, we are all alone.'

The boat sailed on its own through the night—no helmsman was at the wheel, no navigator plotted a course, no lookout scanned the horizon. Guided by the wind, it weaved its way across the dark, empty sea. Tired from hard work and fresh air, I slept the sleep that only sailors and babies are privileged to—a deep, dreamless, contented sleep. Hamish also slept.

It was a new dawn when I heard banging on the hatch of the aft cabin. Hamish was shouting. I was disorientated and asked him bad-temperedly what he wanted—he knew I didn't like getting out of my bunk without being given a cup of tea first. He rattled the hatch and snapped, 'You'd better get up, John, quick. There's a boat here. It's in trouble.' I didn't know what he was talking about. Half-thinking that there must be a large fishing or cargo boat a mile or two off, I pulled on a pair of shorts, rubbed the sleep from my eyes, slid the hatch back and stuck my head out. When I looked over the port side, I couldn't believe what I saw. There was a small, open boat less than 20 yards away. It was rolling and pitching. There was a man in the boat. He was trying to stand up, holding on to the side with one hand and waving with the other. His eyes were white and wide open. They looked straight into mine. I had never seen eyes like his before. I was transfixed. They were the eyes of a man haunted by a spectre and they spoke a thousand words—words of pain and suffering and fear and hope. They held on to me, imploring me to help him.

A boat like this had no business being so far from land, and the sight of it made me realise just how much a small boat is tossed about by the waves. Hamish and I knew that the situation was as serious as it can get. We quickly started the engine and began to lower the sails. We muttered all kinds of grim things to each other as the work was being done. At one point Hamish turned to me, saying under his breath, as if he was reluctant to express the words, 'I hope there are no dead bodies on board.' I didn't reply.

Hamish made his way to the bow to talk to the man. The engine was thump-thumping, and I couldn't hear what the man said above the din but Hamish relayed his words to me. 'He buried his partner at sea two days ago. He's been adrift for 11 days without food or water.'

I felt the muscles in my face tense as a sense of disbelief and personal inadequacy overwhelmed me. Then I heard myself call out to him. It was almost as if someone else was speaking. I couldn't believe I was saying the words. They came from somewhere deep down and were beyond my control. It was a bit like the primordial scream I screamed in the Bay of Biscay, but this time the words were directed to another human being instead of the elements. At the top of my voice, I called out, 'May God be with you.'

By the time we had lowered all sails, we were already a couple of hundred yards away from the open boat. Hamish returned to the cockpit. We started to motor back. With the sails down, my boat was wallowing from side to side and the engine seemed deafening in the silence of the dawn. The small boat almost disappeared from view in the rolling swell, and the man in it kept looking at us all the time. Hamish asked whether he should get his camera—I said it was OK but urged him to be quick about it. He was rummaging around his things, unable to find it. I told him to forget about it and to write down the time and position instead. He found a pencil but nothing to write on. I shouted at him to write it in the back of the book lying on the chart table. It was Tuesday, 27 April, and in the inside cover of Slocum's *Sailing Alone Around the World*, he wrote:

6.0 a.m.
13°54′ . 1N
64°44′ . 7W

I asked Hamish to take the wheel, before going aft to prepare a line. All the time, the man's eyes were fixed on me like hooks. I wanted to reassure him that whatever happened we wouldn't leave him. I called out, 'Don't worry, don't worry, we're not going to leave you, we're not going to leave you, we'll get you aboard, I promise you, we'll get you aboard.' I threw him the line. It missed. He then threw me his line, which I caught. Now that we had a line on him, I was going to try to pull him up close. It was only as he came close for the first time that I realised the danger involved. With the heavy sea running from the winds of the previous few days, my stern was pitching up and down in the swell. His pointed bow was pitching even more. The danger was confirmed when the stern took a hit, catapulting the navigation light 20 feet in the air. His bow smashed down on the teak toerail, shattering it. Then it caught under the swimming ladder, buckling it out of shape. If a limb got in the way it would be snapped like matchwood.

The man was now close enough to talk to me. His first words, as we stood less than four feet apart in a heavy dawn sea, were the epitome of politeness—a politeness that I found almost impossible to believe in the circumstances but which was to last until we parted company. He simply said, 'I don't want to damage your boat.'

I thought of a reply, which had something to do with not worrying about the bloody boat, but didn't bother saying it. I eased the line a bit for him to back off, before hauling him up close again when the sea state permitted. I had no idea what to do but felt an urgent need to keep him close to us. As he came close for the second time, he said he could jump and had already positioned himself on the bow of his boat. Hamish called out, 'He's going to be very weak.'

I hauled him up as close as I dared and told him to wait until I gave him the signal to jump. He never stopped looking straight at me. When there was a momentary lull in the swell, I pulled him right up tight and yelled, 'JUMP.' He leaned forward with his arms outstretched and made it halfway over the back-rail. I caught hold of the upper part of his body. His arms went over my shoulders. I could feel his bones close to the surface of his jet-black skin. We seemed to be frozen in this position, but somehow his legs came over the rail. I fell backwards on the deck. He came down on top of me.

We helped him into the cockpit and sat him down. Hamish had now found his camera, which was sitting on the seat beside the chart table all the time. It was a cheap, disposable affair with two or three pictures left in it. He took one photograph of the man aboard the *Warrior Queen* before we helped him down below, where we sat him in the most comfortable place. His eyes were still wide open—two piercing white balls in a black, sunken face—but now it was with utter disbelief and an unspoken, heart-rending gratitude. He had been delivered from death, and his eyes told us that he knew it. They drilled into Hamish and me. I passed him a bottle of mineral water and poured myself a large rum. He thanked me for the water and asked, 'Do you have any ice?'

For the second or third time in less than half an hour, I couldn't believe my ears. I told him that the *Warrior Queen* was a simple cruising boat and that we didn't have any ice, but we had plenty more water and loads of food. Hamish and I watched him drink the water. The parrot had climbed along the side of the cabin cushions and was now sitting on his shoulder. 'It's very friendly,' he said, with an expression that was deadly sombre.

'We all are,' I replied, pouring myself another large rum. I offered Hamish one but it was 6.30 a.m. and he said it was a bit too early in the day for him.

There we sat, the four of us. A black man from God knows where, but without doubt the luckiest man in the world at that moment; Hamish, my crewmate and a fine one, too; Hamish the Parrot, perched on the black man's shoulder — its head cocked to one side looking straight at him; and myself demolishing a bottle of rum. He began to tell us his story. We listened silently.

His name was Martin Simon. He came from the island of Grenada. He was 29 years old. The outboard engine on his open boat had broken down a mile or so off the coast of Grenada, and the west-setting Antilles current had swept the boat out to sea. When the engine broke down it was just after nightfall, and he and his partner were heading back to the capital of St Georges after having dropped some people off at a small island at the north end of Grenada. They put the anchor down but it didn't touch bottom. They thought about trying to swim for shore but decided against it and remained in the boat. At dawn next day Grenada was gone. They found themselves drifting in a lonely sea with no food and not a drop of water. He had drunk some seawater but not as much as his partner did. His partner had died some days earlier, and he kept the body for two days before burying it at sea. He realised how lucky he was but was very distressed about the death of his friend.

We knew he would tell us more in time, but after eating a little bread he wanted to rest. Hamish and I left him to sleep and went out to the cockpit to talk. It was my first chance to think about what had happened in the last hour, and I wanted to know how Hamish had found him. I had difficulty taking in all that had occurred but what Hamish was about to tell me would be even harder to accept. When Hamish woke me, unknown to me at the time, he, like me, had been asleep below decks just a few minutes before banging on my cabin hatch. In his sleep he heard a man's voice. He thought he was dreaming and went back to sleep. He heard another noise in his sleep—this time he thought it was a seabird. Then he heard a noise for a third time, and he decided to come on deck to have a look. When he came out to the cockpit, he saw the boat upwind of us. The man in it was shouting and whistling and waving.

Had it been night, we would not even have seen him, though we might have heard him. Had he been downwind, his voice would not have carried. Had we been 10 or 20 yards further from him, he would have been out of hailing range. Had the engine been running, it would have drowned out his voice. Had I been on my own, I would have slept through the whole thing and sailed straight past him. Had he been asleep or unconscious, the two boats would have passed within 50 feet of each other, and nobody would have known anything about it. Had any of these things happened, the man's heart and spirit and body would have broken and he would certainly have died that day.

The thought that we could so easily have missed him made me feel ill. The idea of a man on the verge of death seeing a boat sail by within hailing range and not coming to his aid was too much to contemplate. As was the thought of him lying in the bottom of the boat asleep or delirious with thirst, while another boat glided past with two men tucked up in their bunks—waking up later in the day none the wiser. I had been trained as a professional mathematician, and my specialism is probability theory. I knew that the chances of us even coming within five miles of each other were minimal. We were already way behind schedule, and it was only because the water pump delayed us that we were there when we were. Apart from that, it was a crazy passage to try to make in the first place. We had been altering course 10 or 12 times a day since leaving. Even ignoring all these factors, the likelihood that the two boats should come within feet of each other in an area as big as France and Spain put together was beyond comprehension.

Hamish and I sat and talked about these things but the conversation wasn't very coherent. There was lots of, 'I can't believe it' and, 'I can't either.' Hamish then rested his head in his hands. He looked down, as if he was staring into some deep pool of emotion, and said very quietly and with true humility, 'It's a good feeling to save a man's life.'

I thought for a long time before replying and tried to say, 'It's a rare privilege,' but I wasn't able to get the last word out.

I was deeply moved by Martin. Everything about him conveyed strength and stoicism—there wasn't a trace of self-pity or self-importance. In his circumstances any man could be forgiven any amount of these vanities but he displayed none of them. I resolved to do all I could to help him. Now that he was safely aboard, the next priority was to take care of his boat. It was only attached by a thin line. Hamish went over the side to swim to it in order to secure a strong rope. He was a little worried about sharks, but I did my best to reassure him before he took the plunge. He was aboard in less than a minute and attached a heavy line. When he swam back and I helped him up the buckled swimming ladder, he told me that there was a terrible smell aboard.

The boat that we were towing was a heavy, fibreglass, general purpose open boat—the kind that you see all over the Caribbean and the type used by the boatboys who come out to meet you at sea to offer to escort you into an anchorage. We were worried that it would come racing down the side of a wave, crashing into the stern of the *Warrior Queen*. I was next over the side and was climbing aboard in even less time than it took Hamish. I felt very uncomfortable in this boat, knowing that a man had recently died a terrible death in it. It was like being in an open grave. I didn't linger. Hamish threw me the end of my longest and heaviest rope, which I tied to the stern and trailed out the back. This acted like a shock absorber and helped prevent it careering into the stern of our own boat. It still didn't tow right because the prop from the outboard was in the water, offset to one side. Hamish went over the side again and managed to lift the outboard engine up to get the prop out of the water. We now had it under control—she stayed a long way back and towed straight.

The best place to head for was Grenada. We swung the boat on to the new course but the wind was against us and the current that had set him and his friend 210 miles out was now keeping us from getting there. After a few hours of going nowhere, I explained to Martin that we couldn't make Grenada but would try to sail to Antigua. That was still 255 miles away in a straight line, but more like 350 by the time we had put in a few tacks. One way or the other, it was going to take three or four days. The fact that his boat was 25 feet long and mine was only 35 feet slowed us down even more.

When Martin woke from another sleep later that morning he asked me if he could bathe. We helped him into the head, where I showed him how to use the shower. I got him a fresh towel, gave him a clean white shirt, a pair of trousers and underpants, and told him to use as much water as he wanted. When he came out half an hour later he was wearing my clothes and looked a bit better. I asked if he minded me examining him. He was in a dreadful state: his hands and feet were swollen out of shape; the dark-brown skin on his body was burned anthracite black by the sun and covered in ulcers; and the tongue in his mouth was a piece of leather that nearly choked him. I asked him if he was in pain. He acknowledged that all his joints were sore but made no fuss about it. He went back to sleep with a bottle of water by his side.

I had never believed in being sentimental about boats—my own had nearly broken my heart at the start of the trip. It was nothing special, just a mass-production plastic boat. But she did have a long, heavy keel, which made her a fine sea boat, and she sailed well. While Hamish and I slept, she sailed *on her own* through the night and came straight to Martin. Now she had, as Hamish said, a spirit.

On his first night aboard my boat, Martin did not sleep well. That night, at about three o'clock in the morning, I was sitting at the chart table playing chess with my computerised board. I found it hard to concentrate on the game and the pieces were sliding about the board a little. The only light burning was the small chart-reading lamp, which cast shadows all over the confines of the cabin. The parrot was out for the count, perched on one leg with its head tucked over its shoulder. Hamish was even deeper in sleep, tucked up in the forepeak. Not more than three feet away from me, this other man from another country, another culture and another race was sleeping fitfully—on the bunk that my brother had collapsed on to after our party in Scotland; which Keenan had snored in when he joined me in Ireland; which I had made up into a little cot when I crossed the Atlantic; and which I had recently made up into a double berth when Laura visited in Venezuela. This little space, which was more intimate to me than any bed, now had someone I never expected sleeping in it.

His presence was all-pervasive: I couldn't take my mind off him. The yacht was sailing through the night—alone again on an empty sea, save for the boat of death towed astern. I could hear Hamish's snores from the forepeak, and every now and then Martin made disturbed sounds as if he was gasping for breath. The water lapped against the side of the hull, and the bow made regular soft pounding noises as it cut through the seas. The ropes squeaked in the sheaths, and I could feel the gentle vibrations of the propeller feathering in the water beneath the boat. Out of the corner of my eye, I saw Martin toss and turn. I knew that by every rule in the book of chance, he should be a dead man. These thoughts flooded my mind and I found it hard to believe that this emaciated man was lying next to me. All Hamish and I had done was pick him up at sea—anyone would have done that—but somehow there seemed to be more to it than this. Up until now I had been playing a game—the game of the sailor in his yacht. It's a good game to play and it has high stakes but ultimately it is only a game and it was as meaningless as the chess pieces in front of me. I wasn't earning my living from the sea, and I didn't need to be there. But now, for the first time, the entire voyage, and even my life itself, seemed to have what it never had before—a vague sort of purpose.

Martin suddenly awoke from his restless sleep, his eyes wild with fear. 'There's someone talking,' he exclaimed.

'No, there's no one talking, Martin. Go back to sleep. It's alright.'

'I can hear it. Can't you hear it? It's coming from there.' he said, pointing to below the galley.

'Do you mean that gurgling noise?'

'Yes.'

'That's just the sound of the water rushing past the seacocks. That's all it is. It's nothing to worry about,' I explained. After a while Martin settled down and realised the noise wasn't made by his dead friend trying to talk up through the pipes. He then asked to go outside to relieve himself. I sat where I was but kept a close eye on him—I didn't want him falling overboard. When he came back down below and was unable to sleep, he asked me to teach him how to play chess. We had a few games.

It was nice for me to win for a change. After the chess, he got his wallet out and showed me pictures of his beautiful baby daughters, which he had looked at every hour while he was adrift. He wasn't married and the kids all had different mothers, but he loved them dearly and the thought of seeing them again had kept him going. At one point, his eye passed over the bookcase and fell upon a classic sea tale—*Survive the Savage Sea*—and he said that maybe one day he would write a book.

As the days and nights passed, Martin's condition improved and he told us more details of his ordeal. At first, he was disoriented in relation to time and couldn't remember the precise sequence of events. It emerged that he had been adrift for nine days—not 11—and that his partner, a man called Rodney Cord but known as Rastaman, had died after six days and was buried at sea the day before we picked Martin up. While his friend was alive, they talked about what they would do when they reached land (they would never have reached land alive) or were rescued. They both agreed that they would get a bucket of ice, fill it with water and drink the lot. That's why Martin asked for ice when I gave him the first bottle of water. His friend died in his arms. The last thing he asked for was a strong mint. After his friend died, he still found the body company. During the night of the force 7, when we had been knocked about and I was thankful that there was no rain, Martin had been alone aboard his boat with the body of his dead friend beside him and was being swamped with large waves—the sheer horror of that was impossible to imagine. He thought the boat was lost and had decided to use his outboard fuel tank as a buoyancy aid should it sink. Somehow he managed to keep the boat afloat to survive that night. He wanted to keep the body of his friend, so that he could return it to his relatives, but decided that it was unwise to do so after two days. It only rained once while he was adrift and only for a short while. He had no way of catching rainwater, but he was able to lick up the droplets from the inside of his boat. The night after he buried the body, he imagined hearing his friend call out to him all through the dark hours and was 'surrounded by evil spirits'. Then a sailboat with two sleeping sailors and a comatose parrot aboard came over the horizon with the rising sun and was, as he told me, guided straight to him by an Angel of Mercy in answer to the prayers which he had said all night long.

Throughout the time he was aboard the boat, he never complained once despite his swollen feet and skin ulcers. When he was ready for solid food, I prepared some lasagne. I took great care over its preparation and set the dining table in the cabin with Laura's dinner set of parrot plates. Hamish the Parrot sat on my shoulder the whole time I worked at the galley and stayed there over dinner. Martin seemed to enjoy it and ate it very slowly. Italian food is not widely available in the Caribbean, and he had never had the dish before. When he finished he said, 'You are a good cook, John. I want you to give me the recipe for this.' Hamish and I drank beer with dinner, but all Martin would have to drink was water. 'You need water, man, you need water. You can't live without it,' he said. Everyone knows that water is essential for life, but as he spoke these words, while looking at the glass of water in his hand, Hamish and I knew we were hearing a fundamental truth.

The thing that troubled him most was the death of his friend. I knew he was thinking about this all the time. He sometimes had a distant expression on his face and would sit on his own for hours without saying anything. At other times, he talked about his friend and the suffering he endured and how he died peacefully in the end. His decision to bury his friend's body at sea had been the hardest of his life, and he needed reassurance that he had done the right thing. There was no doubt that he had. I told him that if his friend's body had been aboard when we picked him up, I would have buried the body at sea, even against his will. This reassured him.

We eventually picked up the outline of the coast of Antigua at dawn on the last day of race week and spotted the first shipping we had seen since leaving Venezuela. While sailing between the islands of Nevis and Montserrat, an open boat, similar to the one we were towing, approached us to find out what was going on. I was asleep in the aft cabin at the time but I was wakened by the sound of their voices and came on deck to have a look. Martin and Hamish were explaining to them what had happened. I could see that they were surprised to encounter a yacht that had been towing a boat like theirs for 300 miles. They gave us all a clenched-fist distant handshake—more like a salute—and I remembered the men who had saved my boat when it nearly went ashore on the island of Canouan. We were all brothers at sea. My debt had been repaid in full.

Antigua was coming up fast. On the way in, two miles from English Harbour, the ever-vigilant Hamish looked over the stern and saw that the line on Martin's boat had parted. His boat was gone. Amid loud cries of swearwords, we scanned the horizon and could just spot it. A quick turn round and we were alongside it in less than half an hour. We were not going to tow it all these miles only to lose it in broad daylight in the last two.

I boarded Martin's boat at sea for the last time and secured the lines. When it was safely under tow, I hitched a short ride on the high, pointed bow. It was a glorious sunny day, with only a few puffy, white clouds hanging in the sky over the islands. We were now in relatively shallow water. The deep blue of the open Caribbean had changed into mint green, and the sunlight from a thousand aqueous fleeting mirrors danced over the small ripples of the sea. In front of me I could see Martin and Hamish in the cockpit of the *Warrior Queen* doing a little sail-trimming. To the west I could see over 100 sailboats round Johnson Point on the last leg of the big race. I glanced over my shoulder to look at Martin's boat. I could see the half-dismantled engine that they had tried desperately to fix, rusted tools scattered all over the deck, and two pairs of shoes.

from Arctic Adventure
by Peter Freuchen

338

At the age of 19, Peter Freuchen (1886-1957)

set out with the Danmark Expedition to explore

Greenland. He and two companions were

returning from an overland trip when they found

that a bear had ravaged their food cache.

Freuchen finally secured food—and was then

forced to grapple with moral questions that he

had never considered before.

I had been in the harness all day and now that no traces held me back, it was easy just to walk, just to put one foot ahead of the other. Acute hunger seems to sharpen the other senses and, while my movements were automatic and I was too tired to sit down and rest, my brain was unnaturally alert.

It was my first spring in Greenland, 1907. Three of us, Gundahl, Jarner and I, had left the base of the Danmark Expedition to northeast Greenland, to familiarize ourselves with the landscape and collect such stray geological specimens as we could find. We had chosen to pull the sledges ourselves. You get to know the land much better that way than by sitting on the sledge, occupying yourself with the dogs and looking straight ahead.

Food and kerosene had been cached for us along the way, but when we reached the cache we found that a bear had been there before us. Even the canned goods were gone—the animal had chewed open the tins and eaten everything. He had examined the kerosene tank and, finding that it was of no use to him, given it a slap with his big paw, crashing it open. We knew that we could expect to find neither musk oxen, rabbits nor ptarmigans. The bear who had visited the spot some days before had not bothered to wait for us.

There was another cache for us to return to at the Koldewey Islands, enough food to last us several days while we studied geological formations. But even if we could, by hurrying, cover twice as much ground as we had anticipated, it would still take us three days to reach the Islands. We set out. There was nothing else to do.

We made slow progress. It was our fifth day now without anything to eat. We were weak and when we camped that night we cut some pieces of wood from the sledge and built a fire in order to melt ice for drinking water. After the tent was up there seemed nothing to say. It was useless to try to forget our present situation; we were too far sunk to try to think of anything else. We were so wretched that we were irritated at the sight of each other's faces.

In desperation I took my gun and walked away. I saw traces of rabbits, a few foxes and ptarmigans, but nothing living. I trudged uphill and downhill—there was no use going back to look into the haggard eyes of those two poor fellows.

At length I saw a rabbit. Unless I had been terribly hungry, I doubt very much that I would have spotted him. A cute, white little thing among the boulders. Unfamiliar with men, he paid me slight heed and allowed me to come near. When he decided to run I fired, and he disappeared over the top of the hill. When I finally reached the spot where I had last seen him, the rabbit lay dead only a few paces distant.

I felt as if I had been hauled suddenly out of the sea after all hope of rescue was gone! I took the dead rabbit in my hands, hefted it—rabbits often weigh eight pounds up north—and realized what it would mean to us—a fine stew for three men and a chance, after what seemed months, of feeling that heavenly filled-up sensation.

I was so weak after the excitement subsided that I sat down on a stone to rest. I thought about eating the rabbit. Should we eat it all today, or keep some for tomorrow? Better eat all of it at once, and then walk as fast as possible for the cache. Chances were that we would find something else on the way. I sat and made plan after plan, each born of the fact that I had a rabbit and an hour ago I had had none.

At last I got up, and started back toward camp. The rabbit was heavy and, hanging on a string over my shoulder, interfered with my progress. I thought, "If I cut it open and take out the guts it will be much lighter." But back of that was the idea of eating the raw liver and heart, and not sharing it with the other two men who lay starving in the tent. I was ashamed of my treason, and hurried on, but soon I had to sit down again and rest, and temptation returned doubly strong.

Since I had killed the rabbit, and walked so far to get it, wasn't I entitled to half of it? If I ate it, wouldn't I be much stronger and able to do a greater share of the work? Yet if I ate a mouthful of the rabbit I might not be able to stop until I had devoured the whole of it. Suppose I did eat it all?—I would never have to tell Jarner and Gundahl that I had killed a rabbit.

It was not possible for me to resist as long as I sat still. I jumped up again.

I remember the voices that talked within me. With eight pounds of meat dangling from my shoulder, all the gnawing pangs of hunger returned tenfold. I commenced to sing in order to drown out any thoughts prompted by my stomach. Half singing, half crying, fighting the temptation to steal the food from the two men in camp, I walked on, hardly able to put one foot before the other. Whenever I sank to the ground from exhaustion I could think of nothing but my stomach.

I told myself that I could at least take the legs and chew on them. And surely nobody would want the ears—I could eat them. Finally I decided to eat it all, and then confess to myself that I was not fit for Arctic exploration, and give it all up. Then I felt calmer. I said to myself: "No, I'll wait until I reach the next hilltop." But when I reached the next hilltop something made me decide that this was not the place to eat—I would try to make the next.

And so, playing this trick upon my stomach time after time, I reached a hill from which I could see our tent in the valley below, a tiny white spot against the rocks. There my two friends waited patiently and trustingly for my return. I felt as if I had been rescued, but I was more ashamed than I had ever been in my life. I am sure that if I had not seen the tent at that moment nothing could have prevented my selfish betrayal of my comrades. And I could never have felt any pride in myself after that.

It was like reaching a friendly shore after the hazards of an uncharted sea, and my strength returned. Jarner and Gundahl saw me coming and greeted me with weak, but excited yells. I was close to tears, but I tried to conceal them while my two friends prepared the meal. We had camped in a patch of cassiope, that fine fuel which the Arctic produces—a small plant which covers the ground like a carpet and can be burned, either wet or dry, and will hold a fire for twenty-four hours in its ashes.

Jarner and Gundahl acted as though they were celebrating Christmas. I lay inside the tent, tired and faint, and every time I heard them exclaim over the quality of the meat and the excellent hindquarters, and say, "Freuchen gets the best piece because he found the rabbit and killed it," I felt that I was having my ears boxed. Even as we were eating, I could not feel as jubilant as they.

In the Arctic one's job is accomplished against a backdrop of continual struggle—continual struggle for existence. A great deal depends on the individual. If he gives less than his best he is finished, and his failure may be fatal to the men of his outfit as well as to himself.

I have heard it said that Arctic explorers are inferior men who would be lost in the civilized world. This may be true of some of them, but character and an iron will are frequently demanded of a man in the North. I have seen bravery there among explorers and more generally among the natives, a quiet bravery seldom found or required in civilization. It is taken for granted. And I learned that no man should go into the Arctic before he is sure of himself. As for me, I was lucky. I saw my tent in time.

from In the Zone
by Peter Potterfield

When Peter Potterfield (1949) fell during a rock climb in the Northern Cascades, he figured he would catch some air time—no big deal. But something went very wrong with his belay. Potterfield plummeted more than 100 feet, sustaining severe injuries. He huddled on a tiny ledge while his climbing partner went for assistance. When a helicopter flew by that evening, Potterfield knew that help was on the way. He did not know whether it would come in time to save him.

n the course of the night I was startled by a small, furious movement on top of me. One or two small rodents scurried across my body. I suddenly jerked upright. That scared me, as a sudden reflex move like that could throw me off my perch. The audacious animals skittered away, but they had given me an idea, or what seemed like an idea. Reaching for my knife, I opened the blade with my teeth, and laid it down beside me. If the creatures came again, I thought, I'll try to catch one, kill it if I can, and drink its blood. I was ready to do it, but I never got the chance. The rock rodents, as Doug and I called them, did not come again.

Late that night, I was surprised by a familiar discomfort: the need to urinate. Surely, the state of extreme dehydration I was in would preclude taking a leak, or so I thought. But it was a fact. I considered for a moment how this might be accomplished in my permanent sitting position. No problem. I simply got one of the empty water bottles, struggled with the fly of my wind pants and layers of shorts and long underwear, and slowly produced about an inch or two of bloody urine. In the moonlight it was as dark as wine.

What occurred to me next is perhaps obvious. There, suddenly, was liquid, right in the water bottle. I knew you could not drink seawater without becoming sick, but, I wondered, what about urine? Didn't that politician, Desai, do it in India? Had I heard stories about people stranded in the desert surviving by drinking urine? Or was it radiator water? Well, I was a guy already chewing on plants and quite prepared to drink the blood of small mammals, so I seriously considered it. I held the bottle to my lips. It was nauseating. I let a little liquid touch my lips. It stung. The thirst I felt was overwhelming, but I could not bring myself to swallow the evil-smelling, highly concentrated, bloody urine. I gagged and gagged. I put the lid back on. Maybe later.

Impatiently, I awaited the graying of the sky, the fading of stars that would come before dawn. But the moon still shone brightly down and the wooded valley remained a dark void. The glacier below, by contrast, was so brightly lit by moonlight that I could have seen people walking on it even at that distance. There was nothing. After peering all day and all night into the void of sky and valley, this scene, I thought, will remain permanently burned into my cortex, like words on a computer screen left on too long.

But now as I looked beyond the glacier into the void of that valley, where the trees were impenetrably black even under the moon, I saw movement. And light.

Actually rubbing my eyes with disbelief, I focused on a small point of light moving slowly deep within the forest of the valley bottom. Could it be rescuers approaching on foot, using headlamps like coal miners? No, it was too far. As I watched, I realized the light was part of a pair. It was a car or truck. And there were others behind it. The vehicles were a long way off, maybe ten miles. I put them somewhere just north of Cooper Lake. But they were real. I watched the slow movement of the lights without euphoria, but with the relief of the certainty that my rescue effort was truly underway.

I thought I knew precisely what was going on. No motorized vehicles could negotiate the trails Doug and I had come in on, but just to the east of that trail from Cooper Lake, and paralleling it for several miles, was a logging road that had formerly been open to hikers and climbers. The forest service had closed that road several years back, adding two or three miles to the hike into Pete Lake and the back-country around it. Loggers don't work at three o'clock in the morning, so it seemed logical that the road had been opened to provide access for the rescue operation. Even from my distance I could make out the bouncing of the headlights as they moved slowly along the rough road. Incredible. From my perch high on the mountain, I could see hun-dreds of square miles. I was heartened to see the lights move slowly through the trees. I knew, though, that my position was still at least eight to twelve hours of hard hiking and climbing from where that road ended. If these guys were just getting to the road end, it would be afternoon before climbers could get up to me. That was disheartening. I wasn't sure I could last another six or seven hours under the sun. I was so thirsty. I looked everywhere in that big, dark valley, trying to pick out other lights, perhaps those of people on foot, closer to me. But I saw nothing except the lights on the logging road. They moved slowly.

The night grew colder, my hands and feet became chilled and clammy. I tried to warm them by rubbing the extremities with my right hand. I was glad for the wool hat to ward off hypothermia. Bare heads lose more heat than any other part of the body. Warmth—and dawn—was not far off now. But that would also bring the relentless sun, and I was no longer so sure of what else it might bring. In fact, I felt a new and escalating anxiety about the morning.

I was getting weaker. I was weary of darkness, thirst, and pain. I longed for a drink, for the light of day. Scanning the horizon, I noticed a faint but definite orange glow. Could that be sunrise at last? But wait—it was not yet four o'clock. And that was the wrong direc-tion. I stared at the bright patch of color against the black sky—too far south of east to be sunrise this time of year. What was that? I had no way of knowing that the orange glow marked the site of a major forest fire burning out of control near Snoqualmie Pass. At the time it mystified me, made me doubt my ability to reason.

I began to shiver against the cold. It wasn't the exhausting, killing shiver of being wet in winter, but it worried me. I knew the dangers of hypothermia, I knew I couldn't take too much of this. I was suffering from exposure. I tried to make myself small, to keep as much heat in my body as possible. My legs, hands, and feet became very cold, particularly my left arm and hand. If only I could move around, get some blood flowing. There was no clothing left to put on, nothing else I could do. The mysterious warm glow low in the southern sky continued to perplex me as, teeth chattering, I sat on the ledge. Now I feared my weakened condition might make me careless. I tried to be ever more vigilant.

I had been watching for this event for hours, yet oddly, when it finally came, it seemed to be well along before I recognized it. The black of night had faded to gray. I welcomed the first colorless light, then the band of orange to the east. Ah, and there was the familiar scene of forest, lakes, and mountains. The valley revealed, a tinge of blue appeared in the eastern sky. The rising sun was blocked by the mountain behind me, but I was relieved that it appeared on time and in the right place. The glow to the south was gone. In the valley, the trees were suddenly green. Morning had come, swiftly. As I gazed out over my world, not a soul stirred on the glacier below, nor could I see any activity farther down below. What was taking so long? I said it out loud. "Come on." The helicopter at sunset, the headlights in the night had not been hallucinations. "So where *is* everybody?"

My apprehensions turned to black despair. Thirst raged. My thinking seemed clouded and slow. I felt physically weaker. I tried to calm myself, to muster patience, to wait without anxiety, but I was overcome. I reached down for the watch—the time was near 6:00 A.M. As high as I was, day had fully arrived. Another perfect summer morning was getting on—good flying weather. But soon the sun would emerge from behind the main peak of Chimney and once again roast me. I couldn't believe I was going to have to deal with it again. I felt the sick, overpowering rise of panic. I could not withstand another day under that sun without water. Cold and shivering, I was terrified by the rising sun. *Where is everybody?*

I had no way of knowing that I wasn't the only impatient person on the mountain that morning. At the dusty end of the logging road a man named Bob McBride, sheriff of Kittitas County, was organizing a large and technically difficult rescue involving twenty-five climbers and rescue professionals from four cities, ham radio operators, the Red Cross, the U.S. Forest Service, and two military bases. Six people had been climbing toward my position since half past ten the previous night, many more were waiting to be airlifted to the mountain, others were standing by at various locations. The problem was a lack of air support. The county helicopter—the one I had seen last night—was out of commission. The military would eventually come through, but in the meantime McBride and the growing collection of rescuers were becoming alarmed at the passing hours.

When the sun finally did reach me, its first warming rays brought relief from the cold. This early in the day, the warming was gentle. I felt myself regain body heat. The shivering stopped. But I could feel the sun begin to burn the skin on my face, which had taken a blasting the day before. My lips were cracked and split. I swapped my wool hat for my baseball hat. I wasn't sure I had the strength to rig my shade again. I was disconsolate. I had managed to hang onto my tiny ledge for a full day and night, I had survived the fall and kept myself going, and yet help had not arrived. After mere minutes in the sun, I overheated to the point where I had to struggle out of my windbreaker, and open the zipper on my fleece jacket. I did not have sufficient strength to get out of my wind pants.

I took one last look at the watch—8:30. It seemed remarkable that it had survived on the ledge all day and night. Since it had, I felt I ought to take better care of it, so I put it in my pack. I gagged almost constantly. The raw, parched tissues in my throat tormented me.

With the first puny light of dawn, I had become intently watchful. Leaning out over the edge of my ledge, I constantly scanned the glacier below for activity. I searched the sky each time I heard a distant jet, but saw one only infrequently. I tried to pick out the spot where the lights had stopped last night, but could see only trees. I could discern no detail in the forest at that distance.

I leaned back against the face in despair. I could hear the meltwater stream below begin to gurgle audibly as the sun came upon it. The sun was building back up to its ferocity of the day before, yet I couldn't muster the effort to replace the ice ax in the rock above me to rig a sun shelter. Instead, I simply draped the jacket over my head. Soon I was stifled by the heat but was, at least, protected from the direct rays. My thirst was impossible. Hearing another aircraft, I looked out from under the jacket. I saw nothing in the sky. But something caught my eye down on the far edge of the glacier, perhaps 1,500 feet below me and a mile or two away. I stared more intently. There was movement. There were people.

Two tiny figures appeared at the edge of the glacier, so far away I had to squint to make sure it wasn't glacial debris. They moved. Definitely, then, people. Then a third figure, lagging behind, came into view. They looked like climbers—helmeted, small packs, ice axes. They moved incredibly slowly. I could relate. Chugging up that slope was a grunt. I could only hope they were part of a rescue effort. I would not admit the possibility that here were three guys out to do Chimney mid-week. But even if they were part of a rescue, it would be afternoon before they could reach me.

I watched them trudge up the ice slope. God, it was going to take forever. I calculated: three hours to the top of the snow chute, then another couple of hours up to Doug's and my previous high point, then somehow down to me, if only a water bottle on the end of a rope. That meant a drink no earlier than 2:00 p.m., almost twenty-four hours since my last drink, and four or five more hours without water in this wilting heat. I put the jacket back over my head.

But immediately I jerked it away. Suddenly there was that sound, the sound I had been listening for since sunrise: the heavy, percussive beat of a big helicopter. I looked around but couldn't see it. There was a huge red dust cloud, however, building in a clearing way down in the valley, maybe eight or ten miles away. I realized that must be somewhere near the terminus of the logging road. It was a spectacularly big cloud of dust, spreading and rising, easily visible from my perch. Out of it emerged a big green helicopter. It hovered, rotated and then headed my way. The whop and slap of its rotors grew rapidly to a deafening racket as it flew toward me with impressive speed. With none of the maneuvering of last night's light helicopter, this one fairly screamed up out of the valley toward my position. I recognized it immediately as a Huey, the classic Vietnam-era army helicopter. It was big and loud and to me, in my demoralized state, a beautiful sight.

The Huey flew right at me. As it approached, I could see the red cross painted against a white field. Otherwise it was all drab military green. The noise became deafening as the Huey flew nearer the face, then hovered just as last night's helicopter had. It pointed right at me, wobbling slightly. I could see the pilots in their flight helmets, visors down against the glare of sun. It looked as if there were a lot of people on board, maybe four or five besides the guys in front. I waved my jacket. The pilots acknowledged my wave and looked me over for a good, long while, my clothes flapping in the rotor wash. The helicopter then flew higher and hovered again as the pilots examined the face above me. Then, the Huey ascended higher still, and finally disappeared from view altogether. I heard it fly way off to the left someplace, but could not see it. The noise of the helicopter reverberated off the mountain walls of that high cirque and became Wagnerian: loud and spooky, booming beyond belief. After ten minutes or more, I saw it reemerge by the North Peak of Chimney and fly back down the valley. It landed in the clearing, throwing up another big dust cloud.

I watched it disappear into the dust. At that distance it was almost impossible to see, but the moving rotors gave it away. After a few minutes another dust storm arose as the Huey took off once more. This time, it flew not toward me, but off to my left. It soon moved out of sight, booming away invisibly in the cirque as it had before. This was puzzling. Surely they had seen me. What were they doing way over by the North Peak?

I watched the Huey make another round-trip identical to the last, finally settling back into its dust cloud down in the valley. It remained there only briefly, then ascended. This time it flew away—south down the valley. I wondered what these guys were up to. From the two-year stint I had spent in association with a mountain rescue team in Santa Fe, I knew how troublesome technical cliff rescues could be, and my situation was even worse than most. It would be nearly impossible to climb up the face from the glacier to reach my ledge. It was surely impractical—requiring a day at least. The face was covered with loose rock, and two or even four climbers struggling to put up a first ascent could carry no rescue gear. Help would not come from that direction.

Sending climbers down from up above me made more sense. But I didn't see how anyone could come from above without dropping a bunch of rocks on me. Even if climbers were able to reach me, the ledge wasn't big enough for people to gather and work. I could not imagine how these people would go about trying to get me down. The activity I had observed so far from my front-row seat gave me no clue. Putting climbers on top seemed the most likely course of action, but I did not believe that had happened.

I slumped back against the rock. Nothing to watch now but the three climbers moving slowly up the glacier, one continually lagging behind the others. They climbed carefully, deliberately. Climbing up the slope looked like hot work.

I needed to let these guys know where I was—from their perspective, I would be lost in the vastness of the face. Fearing that my voice might fail me, I dug around in my pack until I found the little blue stuff sack that held my lighter, emergency matches, compass, C-rat can opener, and other miscellaneous gear. I pulled out the small plastic whistle and looped the lanyard around my neck. When they got within range I'd blast them with the whistle—which, like my first-aid handbook, I had been carrying around for years without ever having used.

The sun increased in intensity as it rose. My mouth and throat felt like dried-out leather; I could muster no moisture at all. I watched the climbers approach, watched them occasionally drink from their water bottles. I got a great idea.

In my pack was a small ditty bag of various repair items—an extra crampon strap, some ripstop nylon tape, parachute cord, needle and thread, and boot laces. I estimated the guys coming up the glacier would reach the meltwater stream below my perch in about an hour. I would rig up a way to lower a water bottle down to them. Those guys could fill it for me, I could pull it back up and have a drink hours before they could get to me.

The prospect of water filled me with a sense of mission. Frantically, I pulled out every possible piece of cordage I carried, and begin tying them together, an exceedingly difficult task with one hand. I couldn't let the climbers reach the stream before I was ready. I worked like a man dying of thirst, desperately tying together slings, shoelaces, short lengths of parachute cord I used for hanging the packs from trees in bear country. I was using simple overhand knots, but with only one hand and my teeth, it took a long time.

As I worked I began to hear the climbers. At times it sounded as if they were shouting to other people on the mountain, although I could see no one else. But the three I could see were making measurable progress, better than I had thought possible. But so far, no one had acknowledged me. Had the chopper pilots told them where I was? How else would they know? It was time to make sure.

The theory is that the sound of a whistle carries much farther than a human voice, and you're not supposed to shout when you're in trouble, anyway, as it causes panic. I put the whistle in my mouth and gave three shrill blasts, the signal for trouble. To me the whistle sounded incredibly loud, rude almost, ringing out among the peaks and glaciers. To my surprise, one of the figures down below stopped and shouted up at me. I thought I could hear my name, but he was too far away for me to be certain. At that distance, I didn't attempt to yell back. When they got no response they continued their deliberate movement up the glacier.

At last I finished my feverish tying of knots. My lowering system was ready. Everything I could find was tied together into one line. As the climbers moved up the slope, I gave a few more blasts on my whistle. I could see them look up at me. They definitely knew where I was now. I tied the end of a spare red shoelace into a loop on the water bottle just as I heard a faint but distinct, "Hello!" I waved back. They climbed nearer, talking in low voices. I realized there must be another group directly under the face. Suddenly climbers appeared on the glacier immediately below me, 600 or 700 feet straight down. I leaned over. Where had they come from? They were so close to the rock face I could have dropped stones on this new group.

"Are you OK?" someone shouted.

"I need water badly," I croaked. "Come quickly."

"We're coming. We're paramedics. Hang on."

I waved the water bottle tied to my makeshift rope. "Can you get me some water?"

There was no reply. I counted seven or eight people total standing on the glacier. The bigger group, hidden from me before by the steep face, was maybe 20 or 30 yards from the first three. People in both groups were talking to each other. Everyone was looking up at me.

"Are you anchored in?" one of them shouted to me.

"Yes," I lied. I held up my empty water bottle by the shoelace. "Can you fill the bottle for me?" There was another awkward pause.

"Sit still," the spokesman replied. "It won't reach from there. Hang on. We have a shitload of water. We're coming." Four or five of them started up the couloir toward the U Gap.

I was abashed. Jesus Christ, I thought, I must be losing it. In my experience there was no such thing as a thousand-foot climbing rope, much less a thousand-foot shoelace. My water bottle would have dangled down maybe thirty feet off the ledge, and there I was asking those guys, hundreds of feet below, to fill it for me. They must have thought I was crazy. I sat there holding my pitiful homemade rope and felt foolish.

I wondered where the other people had come from. The helicopter must have carried them high on the mountain, depositing them on the flat stretch of upper glacier over by the North Peak. They had not had to sweat their way up from the valley bottom and were moving fast. I figured I might have a drink in two or three hours. I reckoned the time to be around 11:00 a.m., maybe noon.

Meanwhile, I roasted in the sun. My thirst tortured me, my left arm, hip, and leg roared with pain. I felt stunned. Help was almost here, help was coming. My solitary ordeal was ending, and I began to prepare for the arrival of people. I poured out my urine lest my rescuers think me some sort of degenerate drinker of body fluids. I tidied up the little pile of rubble—the alcohol wipe wrappers, some debris from my splint-making. I stuffed my extra clothes back into my pack, stowed away the shoe laces and parachute cord, put my knife back in my pocket, zipped up my pack.

A small group of people had remained on the glacier. I could see them sitting on their packs out on the expanse of ice. They looked up at me. I felt embarrassed to have caused all this trouble. I had never been rescued before. I felt ignoble.

I made no move to protect myself from the sun. What the hell, I reasoned, I can make it a few more hours. I felt a detached curiosity about how the rescue would be implemented, as if someone else were being saved. This ought to be interesting, I thought. My despair was banished.

Occasionally, I heard shouts and scrapes from the couloir, off to my right. The noises gradually moved higher as the rescuers progressed, until they came from above me. Serious rockfall began to roar off the face to my right, but harmlessly, missing me by 20 or 30 feet. More noises came from above and the falling rocks began to edge closer to me. I could now hear warning shouts of "Rock!" when the missiles whistled past. The sound of a hammer driving in a piton rang out. People on the glacier were gesticulating and talking on radios; they seemed to be directing the people higher on the mountain. Every now and then I'd let fly with a few blasts from my whistle.

Suddenly, from surprisingly close range, I heard a voice from above: "We hear you. Can you show us exactly where you are?"

I took off my bright yellow baseball cap and put it on the end of my ice ax. With my arm fully extended, I waved it around over the edge of the ledge.

"OK! I see you!"

"Come quickly," I said.

More hammering ensued. More rocks sailed past, closer now, a scant 10 or 15 feet off to my right. I heard the electronic squawking of radios.

"Wave the hat again!"

I did so.

"OK. We're coming. Cover your head."

My crack hat had come off in the fall and I had nothing else to protect my head. A pack always makes good makeshift headgear, but there was no way I could manage that. I pulled Doug's jacket from under my butt, placed it on my head, ducked, and turned my head against the rock wall. I got as close to the face as I could. With my good right arm I covered my head and face. A shower of rocks, some mere pebbles, some the size of grapefruit, rained down, but most fell off to the side. All I got was a little gravel and dust.

The end of a doubled rope sailed out and hung in space about 15 feet to my right. The face was so steeply overhanging there that the rope hung free from the lip above until it came back in contact with the rock a little below my ledge. The rope was far from reach. As I watched, it danced around as someone above waved and shook it to get out the kinks. I knew that motion well—someone was getting ready to rappel down the rope. And down he came, in a shower of rocks and stones, an undamaged human being. I could hardly believe my eyes.

I thought, so that's how they avoided killing me with rockfall: by descending to my position off to the side of my ledge. But that tactic created problems as well. Sliding slowly down the rope, dangling in midair too far from the face to make contact with his feet, was a stocky young guy in shorts, a T-shirt, and a purple helmet. His rappel was slow and controlled. He descended until he was precisely at the level of my ledge. Still, he was a good 10 to 15 feet away, and he was in a fix. There was no place for him to go. I didn't see how he could get over to me, and there was no ledge or other stopping place for him to alight.

He hung there from his rope, looking over his options. I left him alone to figure out his next move. He finally spoke. "I don't think I can get to you," he said casually. "I'm going to have to go down and climb back up."

I looked over the ledge.

"Boy, that looks pretty hard," I rasped. I had been looking at that cliff for more than a day. It was high fifth class, a tough go. He didn't argue with me. I was dying for a drink. "Do you have any water?" I asked.

"I do," he said, looking around. I wanted water so badly I would have done anything to get it.

"Look," I said. "Throw me the end of the rope. I'll pull you over."

He was skeptical. "Can you do that?"

"I think so. Give it a try."

"OK," he said. But it was awkward. Hanging in midair, he had to hold his rappel with one hand, then gather up the rope below him and try to throw the end of it over to where I sat planted on the ledge. He missed the first two times. On the third try, both strands of the doubled rope came within reach of my good hand and I gathered it in.

My rescuer was a kid of about twenty. He looked strong, but was sweating profusely in the heat. He watched me carefully. I knew that the right side of my ledge had a good lip on it. Putting the rope in my teeth so I wouldn't drop it, I shifted my position slightly so that my good right leg pointed at him, knee bent, the heel locked on the lip. I reached way out, grabbing as far down the rope as I could, and wrapped it around my right hand.

"Wrap it a couple of times," he suggested.

"Ready?" I asked.

"Do it."

If my foot slipped from the lip, or if the lip gave way, I'd sail right off the ledge. There would be nothing to stop me. I couldn't extend my leg, but the big muscles took the force comfortably. I pulled out the slack and felt his weight push my boot heel against the small lip. *Here goes.* With a heave I hauled this stranger toward my perch. The maneuver went fairly well, but it was not quite enough to bring him all the way to the ledge. I tried to lock the rope in my teeth again so I could reach down for another armful of rope, but with his weight on the rope I was afraid I'd lose him, send him penduluming back in the opposite direction, bouncing off the face. He saw what was happening. With me still holding him fairly close, he grabbed the rope between us, pulling himself over the last few feet. He put a foot on the ledge, reached around, found a hold, and pulled himself up. He was here, standing virtually on top of me, his feet on either side of me.

I heard him bang in a pin and clip into it. He adjusted his stance until he was standing on the extreme right side of the ledge, the toes of his boots touching my right thigh. He removed his pack, reached in, and handed me a plastic quart water bottle with a blue top and piece of blue tape wrapped around its middle.

I'll never forget that water bottle, the look of it, the magic weight of it. I heard the rescue guy talk to his buddies above on a small radio as I unscrewed the lid and began drinking. Never has anything tasted so sweet, been so quenching, provided so much relief as that water. I drank in long gulps, stopping halfway through to breathe before finishing it off in another series of gulps.

" . . . he's drinking water now," I heard him say into radio. Right you are, I thought.

"Got any more?" I asked. He handed me another bottle wrapped from top to bottom in, of all things, adhesive tape. I drank it all in one chugalug, leaving a few swallows in the bottle to pour over my over-heated head. God, I felt like a new man.

"Nice to meet you. Thanks for the water," I said. "My name's Peter."

"I know. I'm Mike. No problem."

Mike, struggling to stand on his tiny footholds, got back on the radio to warn his companions of the hot rappel. It was an impossible arrange-ment on the ledge with both of us there. Mike banged in some more pins and clipped his pack, himself, my pack, and me into his anchors. He took off his hard hat and put it on me, fastening the buckle. He then climbed up above the ledge into the slight depression that creased the face above and to the left of my ledge, and found some footholds. He immediately started hammering in more pitons. The rope started to flap and shake as a second rescuer rappelled down.

Mike and I both hugged the wall as more rocks came zinging past the ledge. I was better protected now with the helmet. As the new guy came into view over the lip, Mike directed him—"OK, a little farther. Stop." He had tied off the end of the rope, so the second guy had a much easier time getting on the ledge. With help from Mike, the new guy scrambled up, putting one foot on either side of me, as Mike had done.

"How's it going?" I asked. "My name's Peter."

"I'm Bruce. You doing OK?"

"Now I am. Got any water?"

He stood there a minute while he clipped into Mike's anchors, then he, too, managed to climb above me and find a some footholds on which to stand. Soon he was handing me another water bottle. I drank it right down. Bruce dug around in his pack some more, and to my surprise, pulled out my blue Ultimate helmet. It was totally roached, with big scrapes and gouges in it, the black trim band gone. But it was in one piece.

"We found it down on the glacier," he said, smiling, looking around in disbelief at the ledge. "Thought you might want it." Mike gladly accepted his own helmet back and helped me put mine on.

The two rescue guys climbed around and above me, into the narrow chute near the ledge, and began placing anchors. They carried a lot of hardware, virtual big-wall racks, and they were driving pins in all over the place. After my solitary vigil, all this was sensory overload in more ways than one. Both had radios, and the entire rescue establishment was on the same channel talking to everybody else. I immediately became very well informed. I could hear my two guys talk to their comrades higher on the mountain, and could hear the people at base camp—down where the chopper kicked up all that dust—talking to people all over the mountain. There was another team waiting at the U

Gap, plus the team down on the glacier. Outstanding, I thought, these guys know what they're doing.

A small rock slide announced the arrival of someone new down the dangling rope. Here came a vaguely familiar, helmeted figure carrying a pack with several long, skinny cardboard tubes sticking out of it. He wasn't quite as comfortable with the overhanging rappel as the other guys had been and had a little more trouble scrambling onto the ledge.

"We saw you here last night," he said, smiling. "How are you holding up?"

It was Red Shirt himself. He introduced himself as Steve, a paramedic. Hanging from the anchors Mike and Bruce had placed on my left side, Steve got into the little chute beside me, below the others, and managed to lean down and work on me. The tubes sticking out of his pack were medical gear, and he set about putting needles in my right arm to rig an IV.

"Here. Hold this." He gave me a plastic IV bag of clear fluid.

My formerly solitary ledge had become a beehive of activity. While Steve administered first aid, and resplinted my left arm after praising my amateur efforts, the other guys worked at their anchors. It wasn't easy. I frequently heard the dull thud of pitons being hammered into rotten rock (they ring out when driven into good placements), and the men's vocal frustration at the lack of solid rock. They could work in the vertical environment of the shallow depression above my ledge by standing on holds, protected by the anchors.

Still another person was descending the rope, in the usual shower of rocks and stones. I thought I saw a radio sail by in the rock slide.

Suddenly, in a sickening moment, the latest rescuer came into view in a horizontal position. He was carrying a metal litter broken down into two sections, plus his other gear. The weight of the load had almost turned him upside down during the free rappel, a situation that can lead to a person's falling out of his rappel. Somehow, this guy managed to keep his act together. With considerable help from Mike, he arrived on the ledge exclaiming the excitement of his descent, admitting to losing a radio on his scary ride down. He introduced himself to me as Denny, and I learned he was one of the original three climbers I had seen hours before on the glacier. He had climbed all night to get here while the others had been airlifted up in a matter of minutes by the Huey. Denny was excited. He told me that he was known as the Angel of Death, because so many of the accident victims he reaches are dead when he gets there. He said he expected me to be dead, too.

I introduced myself and told him I was glad to break his string. I asked him if he had any water. He handed me a quart bottle, which I drank right down, saving those last few swallows to pour on my head.

I was feeling better. I had just consumed a gallon of water (a trauma physician later told me that the volume of water had saved my kidneys, barely) in the past half hour. Steve finished wrapping me up and sticking me with needles, and turned on the morphine. For the first time in thirty hours I stopped hurting. I didn't feel high or giddy, just free of pain. But I was still thirsty. I had drunk all the water on the ledge except for Steve's. Having seen me drink everyone's bottle bone dry, he wouldn't trust me with his. Instead, he doled out a few gulps to me, then passed the bottle around. More rocks began to rain down. Somebody else was coming. We all huddled against the face.

Like the others, the new guy glided down the rope, clambered aboard, straddled me, then climbed the face above me to find a spot. Fred Stanley didn't have much to say. Even older than my thirty-eight years, he arrived quietly. He carefully went about checking the anchors and discussing with the others how best to set up the lowering system. He worked calmly, but with obvious urgency.

The guys on the ledge said the best way to get me down was to assemble the litter, put me in it, and in a series of lowering operations, move down the face ledge by ledge until we reached the glacier. There were problems: the litter's support system had not been attached to it, so one had to be improvised out of the sling material on hand. No one was happy about the anchors, either. With all the hammering and sling-tying going on around me, I offered up my own hardware for use. Somebody dug it out of my pack, and my stoppers and hexes went to the cause.

My rescuers were a friendly lot, and brushed aside my apologies for causing them so much trouble. I was still thirsty, but as far as I knew I would be thirsty for the rest of my life. At least I was no longer in emergency need of water. And I was no longer in agonizing pain.

Steve's big syringe of morphine was plugged into my IV; he shot me up at regular intervals. When he forgot, I reminded him. He was humorous and easygoing, and somehow expressed genuine concern for my physical well-being while he worked in perilous circumstances. He had cut away my shirt to resplint my arm and check out my shoulder, given me two bags of some kind of IV fluid, and was almost finished with his ministrations.

The climbers cautiously moved around in the vertical environment of the ledge, connecting the anchors with slings and ropes. These strangers who had roped down to me were outwardly calm—casual to me and to each other. But they were busy, and I detected a certain amount of masked anxiety about the passing time and technical difficulties of the rescue. Two of them, one above the other, were assembling the metal stretcher Denny had brought down. I was a little anxious about how they were going to get me into it. Otherwise, I was calm and curious. I was doped up, but lucid. I watched with detached interest the activity of this group of people working furiously, high in the middle of the huge face. The radios squawked and hissed, carrying conversations between the mountain and base. Concern was expressed about getting another helicopter. Base camp wanted to know when we would be down on the glacier, so one could be waiting for us. It was a question no one could answer. But the day was getting on, around 3:00 p.m., and the time had come to strap me into the litter.

The litter was supported by four nylon slings, one at each corner, which met about three feet up at a big locking carabiner. Into that 'biner was tied one end of a 300-foot rescue rope, twice the length of a standard climbing rope. The rope went from the litter to several belay devices attached to the anchors, so the rescue guys could control the speed of descent by applying friction as required. The system was not a thing of beauty. There were a dozen or more points of attachment to the rock. But it definitely appeared bombproof. Stanley manned the lowering devices while the other guys, hanging from their anchors, maneuvered the litter alongside the ledge. Steve had begun to roll me into the stretcher when Stanley suddenly said, "Wait a minute. Is all the load coming on that green sling?"

Everybody turned to look, including me. I could see how one particular piece of nylon carried much of the weight. It was one of my slings they had incorporated into the system, and I told them that it was sort of old and probably shouldn't be completely trusted.

It took a minute or two to rearrange the supporting slings. But soon the system passed everyone's critical examination. Hanging from their anchors, Mike and Steve did most of the work of manhandling me into the basket-style litter, an awkward and scary maneuver. The jostling caused my injuries to reach up out of the morphine and get me again. But after a minute of awkward struggle, I was lying in the litter. Steve packed some of my clothes and Doug's blue jacket in around me. He then pulled a down jacket out of his pack and covered my upper body where he had cut away my shirt. He gave me a big shot of morphine, then began to cinch down the smaller nylon straps that held me in the litter. At one point I had to stifle a reflexive cry of pain as he pulled on a strap that ran across my shoulder. After a little adjustment, I was totally strapped in, quite snug, staring up at the sky and the sheer upper face of Chimney.

Steve clipped a Jumar ascender—a rope clamp that slides up but not down—onto to the rope above the point where the litter was affixed to it via the big 'biner. That way he could adjust his position relative to the litter. I gathered he was going to make the entire descent at my side, hanging off the same rope that supported me and the litter. Right there next to the ledge, the system worked well: I was lying in the metal litter, Steve hung comfortably at my side from his Jumar, with his legs protruding under the litter so he could hold it off the rock face with his feet. He could more or less walk down the face as the litter was lowered.

A safety line was added to the system: a belay rope tied into my seat harness, then to Steve's, was attached via belay devices to a different set of anchors up on the ledge. If the rope supporting the litter should fail, Steve and I would be suspended from the belay rope by our seat harnesses. I didn't want to seriously consider the reality of a fall from the litter—Steve, me, and the litter bouncing around at the end of the belay rope. But I was glad there was, at least, some sort of backup. Stanley announced that the lower was ready to begin. I asked him some uptight questions about the security of the anchors and the 300-foot rope ("Where'd you get that thing, anyway?"). He looked at me with a crooked grin.

"Don't worry. We've done this before."

After three hours of preparation we were finally off. There was a quick, sickening drop of a few feet, and we dangled around at the end of the rope, bumping into the face just below the ledge. But then things smoothed out. As the guys on the ledge paid rope into the belay devices, Steve and I gradually moved downward. Lying flat on my back, I got my first view of all those people working like spiders on a wall. Ropes zigzagged through the anchors, and people and hardware and packs hung all around my little ledge. Steve's radio squawked. I heard the people on the ledge report that we were on our way. I heard the guys down on the glacier report that they could see the litter descending.

When we were 20 or 30 feet down, I stared up at that huge face and the tiny ledge where I had spent the past two days alone. I was amazed by the whole affair, not least by the fact that I was inching my way down this vast vertical cliff, completely reliant on a pencil-thin rope in the hands of total strangers.

Strapped into the metal basket, I registered a subtle change in the proceedings. Since Mike's arrival at my lonesome perch, I had been part of the goings-on and preparations. Through the introductions and water drinking and first aid and conversations about strategy, I had been a participant. Now I was something else—Spam in a can, a sack of potatoes, cargo. I didn't mind. As we descended, I looked up at the cliff and the sky and that thin red rope stretching up to the ledge, and I was glad to be making progress at last. I should have been scared out of mind but I wasn't and presumed the morphine had blunted my sensibilities.

As we descended the cliff Steve occasionally asked me how I was feeling. He injected me with morphine every now and then, but mostly he was concerned about driving the stretcher. At times it was quite controlled: as the stretcher descended, Steve merely guided us down the face with his feet. In those places where the face was too steep, however, we hung free in space, at times twisting an uncontrolled 360 degrees. We bumped into things, got hung up on protrusions and little ledges, and rocked from side to side as we descended. At times the rope inexplicably slipped a few feet, and a brief, scary drop ensued. I never got used to it, nor, I think, did Steve. Rocks occasionally whizzed past, but none hit us.

Steve stayed in radio contact with the team on the ledge. Most of the time we were forewarned of any unusual movement or delay. Once or twice I heard Stanley tell Steve, "Hang on now, we've got to pass a knot through the 'biner." Steve and I hung motionless for a couple of minutes while the system was torqued around to let the knot pass, and down we would go again. From virtual midface, my view was spectacular: the sculptured rock rose hundreds of feet up to my ledge, where tiny figures worked the ropes. The vast upper part of the face loomed above them to the blue sky, the cable-straight lowering rope and the slack belay rope flowing gracefully upward.

After literally hours of our slow ride down, we approached another ledge in the face. This one, about 300 feet below our starting point, was much more commodious than mine had been. It was big and flat, with room for all of us. I hadn't noticed at the time, but Denny had rappelled down to this ledge before the litter lowering had begun and he was waiting for us. He guided the litter down to the middle of the ledge, tying us into the anchors he had already established.

When Steve and I were secured, the climbers from above dismantled the lowering system and rappelled down the face one at a time to the new ledge. Then, with more hammering of pitons and placing of hardware, new anchors were placed. Soon, the lowering was resumed. The beginning was the hardest part of each stage of the descent and this new ledge had an even more awkward launch than the first. The litter actually had to be pushed off the ledge, and Steve and I suddenly dropped several feet. But from then on, the ride was as smooth as before, with the occasional pause as the guys working the system made adjustments.

During this second lower, radio conversations increased significantly. The rescuers at base camp indicated they were having trouble securing another helicopter. It was getting late. There was talk about moving faster so nightfall would not catch us on the mountain. One helicopter from the Yakima Firing Range, a military installation east of the Cascades, had been dispatched but had turned back because we would not be on the glacier in time, and the helicopter could not wait. Another was being sought from Fort Lewis, near Tacoma.

It was strange being so well informed since I was a nonplayer, being lowered like a handbag down the face. The news made me start to feel a little anxious. I thought I could detect, too, a rising anxiety among the rescuers with me. It was actually getting dark, approaching the end of the second full day of my ordeal. If we didn't reach the glacier soon I'd have to spend another night out, a prospect I did not want to contemplate. I didn't think I could survive another night.

It was getting cold. Steve and I dangled at the end of the long rescue rope. The strain was beginning to show in his face. We had been at this for six or seven hours. I began to get chilled where he had cut away my shirt, and where the down jacket had come loose. He injected me with more morphine. The rescue people worked away out of sight on the ledge above. To us they were just voices on the radio, but they sounded focused, in control. I developed a real liking for these guys.

The lowering went faster as we neared the bottom of the face. It wasn't so steep there as above, and Steve had better control of the litter. The cliff seemed impossibly huge from my perspective, the plumb-line straight lowering rope disappearing into its vastness.

Suddenly, I heard voices that did not come over the radio. People were climbing up the moderate slabs of the lower face, the same people

I had seen waiting down on the glacier. The light of day was failing. I felt as if I had been dangling from ropes most of the day. I had. From about noon, when Mike reached my ledge, until now, eight hours had passed.

The guys who had come up from below were talking to Steve about pulling the stretcher over to the east about 50 feet, where the glacier met the rock face at a higher altitude. Otherwise, they said, another lowering system would have to be set up—and there wasn't time for that. There was a flurry of conversation between Steve and these guys, and, by radio, the team on the ledge. I lay in the litter and listened. I was cold and now I was worried.

Near the glacier the face leaned back considerably. One of the guys began pulling the stretcher out of the fall line, hauling it off toward the east, with Steve helping as much as he could from his position at the side of the litter. I was uneasy about this development. We were still suspended by the rope, and if the stretcher got away from these guys it would pendulum way over very fast, careening out of control. Steve unclipped from his Jumar and began pulling from the end of the litter with the other two guys. More people showed up to help move the litter sideways toward the glacier. They leaned into their work, pulling the heavy litter at the end of the long rope. We had literally turned the corner, so far out of the fall line that the rope curved out of sight around a corner of the face. Soon the litter was completely resting on low-angled slabs. Instead of dangling from the rope, we scraped along the rock. Then I could hear the stretcher bottom scrape on ice. We had reached the upper glacier, which sloped steeply downhill from where it met the rock face.

Besides Steve, I recognized none of the others who were around the litter. Here was a whole new group of people. Their radios were alive with reports that a chopper was on the way, and that the "victim"— me—had to be moved to the glacier landing zone some distance away. The guys pulling the litter reported that there wasn't time. "Ask the helicopter pilot if he can land higher on the glacier," the rescuers near me said into the radio. "He will try," came the reply, "but it's getting dark, and windy, too." "It doesn't look good," they said.

Now resting completely on the ice, the litter was unclipped from the lowering rope. Steve unclipped us both from the belay rope. Seven or eight people attached short slings about two feet long to the rails of the litter, and began to drag it sideways to the slope, across the glacier. It was hard work. The rescuers grunted and panted in the thin air, trying to move fast but having to stop for short rests. From my reclining position I watched them lean on their knees and pant. There was genuine urgency in their work. We moved 100 or 200 yards in this manner until the slope relented, but it was still far from level. The light was almost gone. It was past eight o'clock, and we were deep in shadow. I could feel the cold breath of a freshening wind as it blew across the ice. I heard a helicopter.

From my horizontal position in the stretcher, I could see little save the brilliant orange-red sky of sunset. But the sound of the chopper increased in volume quickly. Someone shouted to pop smoke. Someone else said, "He's coming in." With that, the people who had carried me across the ice all turned and knelt beside the litter, surrounding it, leaning over to protect me from the blowing bits of ice churned up by the rotor wash. I stared up into the faces of seven or eight strangers. I was moved by this gesture. Everybody looked alike in their helmets and parkas. Beards and glasses were the only identifying features.

I heard the chopper come in, the sound of it growing as it had on the ledge. It remained at that crescendo level. It was here. Then, to my disbelief, I heard it back off and fly back down the valley. The rescue guys all stood up and watched it go.

I don't remember any radio conversations at this point. I think that, like me, everyone knew that it would be hard to get a big helicopter to land at 6,500 feet on a sloping glacier in the near dark with a wind kicking up. If the helicopter couldn't get in it would take two days to carry me off this mountain, assuming it could even be done. I didn't think I could last that long. I lay listening. I heard the helicopter return.

The people in the rescue team once again knelt beside the stretcher.

The chopper sounded even louder this time, kicking up ice like crazy, the noise growing until it sounded as if it were right on top of us. The rotor wash blew like a hurricane, flapping the clothes of those around me. Over the din someone shouted, "Now!"

The stretcher was jerked off the ice, and I looked up to see the open door of the helicopter, two green-helmeted crew members reaching out to take the litter. I was fairly tossed on board, sliding across the floor. The door slammed shut. Immediately we lifted off. But rather than climb upward, I felt the helicopter fall away down the valley in a radical maneuver. It was warm inside the Huey. I lay sideways, head toward one door, feet toward the other. I could see the backs of the pilots' helmets. One crew member sat against the bulkhead looking right down into my face. Another guy sat down by my feet. They were strapping themselves in. I asked the guy above me if he had anything to drink.

It was loud in there, and the guy leaned down and said, "What?"

"Do you have anything to drink?" I rasped. For some reason I thought he might have a soda or something.

He thought for a minute and rooted around in his medical bag. He produced an IV bag and held it up.

"No thanks," I said. "I've already had one of those."

We rode for a while in silence. I looked out the windows at the sunset sky, all I could see from the floor. I was getting tired of looking up at sky. The guy above me pulled out a notepad and asked me my name, address, those kinds of questions. He wrote down my answers.

"Where're we going?" I asked.

"Harborview."

I knew Seattle's famous trauma center by reputation only, but that institution and I were to become intimately acquainted. But on the floor of that helicopter it was enough to know I was on my way. A minute or two before, I had been lying on a glacier not sure I'd survive. Now, I lay there in the vibrating machine, on the wings of an angel, flying full speed toward salvation. I was amazed and exhausted, but I felt very alert. My mood was excellent. I was alive, with good prospects for staying that way. My last morphine shot had been some time before, and the pain was getting bad again. But I could handle it. Wouldn't be long now.

"Can I sit up and look out?" He shook his head. No.

"Where are we?" I asked.

"Three more ridgelines to go." I thought that was a strange answer.

I felt the machine make some turns. I was disappointed to have missed a sunset ride through the heart of the Cascades, but I didn't really mind. I felt more turns. In the chopper window, the top few floors of the Columbia Center, the highest building in Seattle, went by. We're here, I thought.

The helicopter made a series of tight turns, hovered, then hit the ground with a slight bump. The door shot open. My litter began to slide out. Two guys in white shirts with "Shepard Ambulance" embroidered on them were holding the front end of the litter. I was carried across the helipad. It was a warm summer evening. The sky to the west, beyond Puget Sound, still had some color. The ambulance guy looked down at me.

"Get ready for the shortest ambulance ride of your life," he said, and gave a little laugh. He seemed to be in a hurry. As I slid onto the floor of one of those truck-like ambulances, I noticed that the army guys had carried the back end of the litter and were coming along. The doors closed.

We drove perhaps a hundred yards, fast, with sharp turns, then stopped. The ambulance drivers and the army crew members carried me through the trauma center doors into the white-walled, fluorescent-lit realm of the hospital. The army guys down at the foot of my stretcher looked strange in their big green helmets. I was placed on a rolling cart and moved through a doorway. A heavyset man with horn-rimmed glasses came into my field of vision, a normal guy in a shirt and tie, the first I had seen in some time.

"Who should we call?"

"Anne," I said, "call Anne."

I was wheeled beneath a big fixture with a bright light. A man with

Asian features leaned over close and looked into my eyes. "I'm Doctor Chen. You're at Harborview Medical Center." Then he was gone.

I could feel myself being unstrapped and rolled out of the litter onto an operating table. Many people seemed to be working on me without saying anything, or, at least, not to me. Someone was removing my helmet, which I had forgotten I still wore. Someone else was cutting off my clothes. Someone else was undoing the laces on my heavy mountaineering boots. I heard the clang of stainless steel bowls and felt needle pricks and blood pressure cuffs. Out of this chaos of activity came a voice that cut through the pain and loneliness of the past few days to speak to my soul. Doctor, nurse, I don't know, but it was a woman's voice, strong and clear:

"We've been *waiting* for you."

With that, I let go. It was over.

acknowledgments

Many people contributed to this anthology and I thank them all.

At Thunder's Mouth Press and Avalon Publishing Group:
Neil Ortenberg, Susan Reich, Dan O'Connor and Ghadah Alrawi offered indispensable help.

At Balliett & Fitzgerald Inc.:
Will Balliett offered assistance at every stage of the project and helped the book come together under a very tight deadline. Designer Sue Canavan has done a masterful job. Production editor Maria Fernandez oversaw production with patience, competence, and aplomb. Proofreader Theresa Kimm and assistant editor Meghan Murphy did meticulous and skillful work.

At the Writing Company:
Series editor Clint Willis gave me direction and support while allowing me to pull together my own idea of this book. Shawneric Hachey helped with permissions, scanned and proofread copy, did stellar work as photo editor, and was generous with advice.

At the Maine State Library in Augusta, Maine:
The staff cheerfully located and borrowed books from across the country, helped me track down obscure information, and gave me every assistance.

Among friends and family:
Friends graciously proposed authors and ideas. My husband Ben Townsend steered me toward authors, read many of the selections, provided thoughtful observations, and negotiated on my behalf. As important, he whisked me away on climbing and paddling trips so I wouldn't get book-bound.

Finally, I am grateful to the writers whose work appears on these pages.

We gratefully acknowledge all those who gave permission for written material to appear in this book. We have made every effort to trace and contact copyright holders. If an error or omission is brought to our notice we will be pleased to remedy the situation in future editions of this book. For further information, please contact the publisher.

Excerpt from *We Aspired: The Last Innocent Americans* by Pete Sinclair. Copyright © 1993 by Pete Sinclair. Reprinted by permission of the author. ✤ Excerpt from *Working on the Edge* by Spike Walker. Copyright © 1991 by Spike Walker. Reprinted by permission of St. Martin's Press, LLC. ✤ Excerpt from *Wind, Sand and Stars*, copyright 1939 by Antoine de Saint-Exupéry and renewed 1967 by Lewis Galantière, reprinted by permission of Harcourt, Inc. ✤ Excerpt from *The Perfect Storm* by Sebastian Junger. Copyright © 1997 by Sebastian Junger. Used by permission of W.W. Norton & Co., Inc. ✤ Excerpt from *The Everest Years: A Climber's Life* by Chris Bonington. Copyright 1987 by Chris Bonington. Published by Weidenfeld and Nicolson. Reprinted by permission of The Orion Publishing Group Ltd., London. ✤ Excerpts from *To Timbuktu* by Mark Jenkins. Copyright © 1997 by Mark Jenkins. Reprinted by permission of HarperCollins Publishers, Inc. ✤ Excerpt from *Threading the Currents* by Alan Kesselheim. Copyright © 1998 by Island Press. Reprinted by permission of Island Press, Washington, DC. ✤ "Consequences: Part II" by Dorcas S. Miller. Copyright © 1997 by Dorcas S. Miller. Reprinted by permission of the author. ✤ Excerpt from *The Climb Up to Hell* by Jack Olsen. Copyright 1962, 1998 by John Edward Olsen. Reprinted by permission of Scovil, Chichak and Galen Literary Agency. ✤ Excerpt from *Raft of Despair* by Ensio Tiira, copyright 1954 by E.P. Dutton & Co., Inc., renewed © 1982 by Ensio Tiira. Used by permission of Dutton, a division of Penguin Putnam Inc. ✤ Excerpt from *West With the Night* by Beryl Markham. Copyright © 1942, 1983 by Beryl Markham. Reprinted by permission of North Point Press, a division of Farrar, Straus and Giroux, LLC. ✤ Excerpt from *The Last Blue Mountain* by Ralph Barker. Copyright 1959 by Ralph Barker. Reprinted by permission of the author. ✤ "The Flesh Eaters" by Geoffrey Childs. Copyright © 1975 by Geoffrey Childs. Reprinted from *Climbing* magazine by permission of the author. ✤ Excerpt from *The Breath of Angels* by John Beattie. Copyright John Beattie 1995. Reprinted by permission of the pub-

b i b l i o g r a p h y

The selections used in this anthology were taken from the editions listed below. In some cases, other editions may be easier to find. Hard to find or out-of-print titles often can be acquired through inter-library loan services. Internet sources also may be able to locate these books.

Barker, Ralph. *The Last Blue Mountain.* New York: Doubleday, 1960. London: Chatto & Windus, 1959.

Beattie, John. *The Breath of Angels: A True Story of Life and Death at Sea.* Dobbs Ferry, New York: Sheridan House, 1997.

Bonington, Chris. *The Everest Years: A Climber's Life.* London: Hodder & Stoughton, 1986. New York: Viking, 1986.

Childs, Geoffrey. "The Flesh Eaters." *Climbing*, November 1975.

Freuchen, Peter. *Arctic Adventure: My Life in the Frozen North.* New York: Farrar & Rinehart, 1935.

Grahame, Kenneth. *The Wind in the Willows.* New York: Scribner's Sons, 1961.

Grenfell, Sir Wilfred T. *Adrift On an Ice-Pan.* Boston: Houghton Mifflin Company, 1909.

James, Thomas. *Three Years Among the Indians and Mexicans.* New York: J.B. Lippincott Company, 1962.

Jenkins, Mark. *To Timbuktu: A Journey Down the Niger.* New York: Quill/William Morrow, 1997.

Junger, Sebastian. *The Perfect Storm.* New York: W.W. Norton, 1997.

Kesselheim, Alan. *Threading the Currents: A Paddler's Passion for Water.* Washington D.C.: Island Press, 1998.

Markham, Beryl. *West With the Night.* San Francisco: North Point Press, 1983.

Miller, Dorcas S. "Trial by Water." *Sports Afield*, September, 1997.

Olsen, Jack. *The Climb Up to Hell.* New York: St. Martin's Griffin, 1998.

Potterfield, Peter. *In the Zone*. Seattle: The Mountaineers, 1998.

Saint-Exupèry, Antoine de. *Wind, Sand and Stars*. Translated by Lewis Galantière. New York: Harcourt, Brace & World, Inc., 1940.

Sinclair, Pete. 1993. *We Aspired: The Last Innocent Americans*. Logan, Utah: Utah State University Press, 1993.

Tiira, Ensio. *Raft of Despair*. New York: E.P. Dutton & Co., 1955.

Walker, Spike. *Working on the Edge*. New York: St. Martin's Press, 1991.